# Mustard Seeds in the Public Square

Between and Beyond Theology, Philosophy, and Society

Edited by
Sotiris Mitralexis
City University of Istanbul & University of Cambridge

Authors

Jonathan Cole
Charles Sturt University (CSU), Canberra, Australia

Marc W. Cole
University of Leeds

Chris Durante
Manhattan College

Angelos Gounopoulos
Aristotle University of Thessaloniki

Raffaele Guerra
University of Salerno (Italy) & Institut Catholique de Paris (France)

Daniel Isai
Alexandru Ioan Cuza University of Iasi

Sotiris Mitralexis
City University of Istanbul & University of Cambridge

Dylan Pahman
Acton Institute

Dionysios Skliris
University of Paris (Sorbonne-Paris IV)

Chrysostom Gr. Tympas
University of Essex

Vernon Series in Philosophy
VERNON PRESS

Copyright © 2017 Vernon Press, an imprint of Vernon Art and Science Inc, on behalf of the author.

All rights reserved. No part of this publication may be reproduced, stored in a retrieval system, or transmitted in any form or by any means, electronic, mechanical, photocopying, recording, or otherwise, without the prior permission of Vernon Art and Science Inc.

www.vernonpress.com

In the Americas:
Vernon Press
1000 N West Street,
Suite 1200, Wilmington,
Delaware 19801
United States

In the rest of the world:
Vernon Press
C/Sancti Espiritu 17,
Malaga, 29006
Spain

Vernon Series in Philosophy

Library of Congress Control Number: 2017934968

ISBN: 978-1-62273-246-3

Product and company names mentioned in this work are the trademarks of their respective owners. While every care has been taken in preparing this work, neither the authors nor Vernon Art and Science Inc. may be held responsible for any loss or damage caused or alleged to be caused directly or indirectly by the information contained in it.

# Table of Contents

*Introduction*   9

*List of Contributors*   15

Chapter 1   Understanding the "Real" through consciousness and history: Maximus the Confessor's vision of the One Logos in many logoi and Hegel's progressive consciousness   17

Chrysostom Gr. Tympas

Chapter 2   The ontology of mode in the thought of Maximus the Confessor and its consequences for a theory of gender   39

Dionysios Skliris

Chapter 3   The communo-centric political theology of Christos Yannaras in conversation with Oliver O'Donovan   61

Jonathan Cole

Chapter 4   An ontology of the historico-social: Christos Yannaras' reading of European history   93

Sotiris Mitralexis

Chapter 5   Symphonia as a social ethic: toward an Orthodox Christian multiculturalism   113

Chris Durante

Chapter 6   Asceticism and creative destruction: on ontology and economic history   139

Dylan Pahman

| | | |
|---|---|---|
| Chapter 7 | The common path of ontology and history: Orthodoxy and theology of liberation in dialogue | 165 |
| | Angelos Gounopoulos | |
| Chapter 8 | Mustard seeds and the *Eschaton*: how an Aristotelian metaphysics solves the paradox between history and Eschatology | 191 |
| | Marc W. Cole | |
| Chapter 9 | The Incarnation as a saturated phenomenon: Between ontology, phenomenology and theology | 223 |
| | Daniel Isai | |
| Chapter 10 | Potency of God: hypostaticity and living being in Gregory Palamas | 241 |
| | Raffaele Guerra | |
| *Index* | | *261* |

# Introduction

This volume seeks to initiate an exploration of the "gap" between ontology and political theology, initially by bringing them side by side.

In investigating how theology relates to politics, society, economics and history, political theology (i.e. *theologically informed political thinking* in general—rather than merely a furthering of particular trajectories of thought) often focuses on what *behaviors*, individual and collective alike, are dictated by or follow from the teachings of the Christian church(es)[1] or Scripture; as such, it is not uncommon to encounter morality-centered versions thereof. Rather than that, what is here suggested is that the question of how political community, society and state emerge and function or *could* and *should* function directly relates to the inquiry concerning the nature of beings themselves, i.e. what, or rather *how*, humanity, the world and God *are*—their ontology.

At times directly and at times indirectly, the studies included here touch upon this convergence of political theology and ontology—at the very least, by setting the debate, i.e. by studying these two thematic areas side by side. The volume explores the intersection of theology, philosophy and the public sphere not by referring the social and political to ethics and deontology as is often the case, but rather to ontology itself. The meaning of history and historicity is most pertinent to this inquiry and is approached here both from the perspective of social reality and from the perspective of ontology. Joining together contributions focusing on theory of the public sphere and metaphysics, chapters explore subjects as diverse as the political implications of the Incarnation, the paradox between ontology and history, politically left and right appropriations of Christianity, the fecundity of Maximus the Confessor's (c. 580-662) insights for a contemporary political philosophy, modern Orthodox political theology focusing on Christos Yannaras and numerous other areas that together form

---

[1] This volume focuses mainly, but not exclusively, on Orthodox Christianity.

the mosaic of the inquiry in question. The aim of the volume is signaled in its very structure: we begin with a study on theological ontology, comparing Hegel to Maximus the Confessor; we then proceed to essays in diverse aspects of political theology, in order to eventually return to non-political theological ontology, underscoring the pertinence of the main ontological questions for any such inquiry.

The volume begins with Chrysostom Gr. Tympas' *"Understanding the "Real" through consciousness and history: Maximus' vision of the one Logos in many logoi and Hegel's progressive consciousness."* Tympas notes that Maximus the Confessor speaks of an eschatological reality, the not-yet-revealed eternal well-being, by theorizing the uncreated foundations of beings, namely their ontological principles/*logoi*. In Maximus' ontological system, however, historical incarnations and modern constructs find difficulty to be convincingly explained. On the other hand, Hegelian progressive consciousness towards the Absolute can provide interpretations of history by embracing human acts in complex schemes (science, the arts, religion). This chapter endeavors to tackle this question and suggests critical points in which Maximus' theory of the ontological *logoi* could address modern constructs by introducing aspects of the Hegelian synthesis.

With chapter two we enter into the narthex of the domain of political theology à propos ontology, and into the gender discussion within it in particular. Dionysios Skliris presents the consequences of the ontology of mode (*tropos*) as it was developed by Maximus the Confessor for a political philosophy which would actualize his thought in a post-modern context. The author examines how Maximus' *logos-tropos* distinction could be applied in a fecund way to a political theory of gender. Gender could thus be considered as not pertaining to the *logos* of human nature, but to a historical modality, which is however important for the actualization (ἐνέργεια) of humankind.

In chapter three, Jonathan Cole attempts a juxtaposition of Christos Yannaras' political theology with Oliver O'Donovan's. Here, Yannaras is explicitly approached as the author of an original political theology, and all the distinctive elements of that contribution are present, recapitulating it as "communo-centric politics": (a) Yannaras' communal epistemology, (b) his relational ontology of the social, (c) his critique of rights due to (d) the conception of agency as personhood, (e) his dialectics of freedom and alienation, (f) his focus on direct democracy, as well as (g) the distinctly ontological nature that is ascribed to politics, i.e. politics as authentic existence rather than simply co-existence, and so on. Bringing Yannaras in discussion with O'Donovan is a contribution of its own, as contemporary Orthodox political theology seldom becomes part of the relevant discussions that unfold in the West. The next chapter is in many ways a long footnote to Jonathan Cole's, for it explores Christos Yannaras' reading of European history as a foundation of his political theology and discusses some of the criticism that has been directed against this reading.

Following this, Chris Durante formulates an Orthodox Christian approach to multiculturalism. How might the Orthodox Christian tradition make sense of its place within the current pluralistic era? Durante proposes that the Byzantine religio-political ideal of *symphonia* might be able to speak to such issues and examines the applicability of the historical concept of symphonia in our contemporary context, exploring ways in which it might be capable of serving as the foundation of a social ethic for Orthodox Christianity.

The next two chapters offer two very different approaches to what a political reflection and appropriation of Christianity could be, situated as it were in opposite corners of the political spectrum. In chapter six, Dylan Pahman develops an exposition of asceticism and explores parallel responses to that ontology in economic history and public policy in two parts: firstly, drawing upon the Church fathers, Vladimir Solovyov, Fr. Pavel Florensky, and Christos Yannaras, et al., Pahman outlines the ontological foundations of Christian asceticism, such as the pluriformity and mutability of the world and personal identity, human mortality, and the potential for growth as well as decay, i.e. for resurrection unto life or to second death, not only at the *parousia* but daily. And secondly, Pahman bring this ascetic perspective to bear on the question of economic history, examining Joseph Schumpeter and "creative destruction" in particular, as well as Nassim Nicholas Taleb, to develop from that history non-predictive policy, analogous to the memento mori and other ascetic practices, adapted to the reality of creative destruction and what Taleb calls Black Swans—random, unforeseen shocks that so often cripple fragile systems. In chapter seven, Angelos Gounopoulos brings Orthodoxy and the theology of liberation in dialogue: he argues that Christian theological thought understands the relationship between ontology and history as similar to the relationship between secularization and the Eschaton. In the Orthodox tradition, and in the Latin American Theology of Liberation, there is a deep connection and unity between secularization and the Eschaton in the history of incarnation. The history of incarnation is the history of salvation that focuses on the person and presence of Jesus Christ. The history of the world's and the human person's creation is the history of Logos incarnation; the Theology of Liberation named this history the "great history of God." Therefore the history of man is not separated from the "great history of God," leading to theologically informed politics focusing on the poor as the epicenter of such an outlook.

After these chapters, we return to studies focusing more on theological ontology and its relationship to history, eventually leading to the Eschaton, rather than on political theology. In chapter eight, Marc W. Cole attempts to solve the paradox between history and eschatology through an Aristotelian metaphysics. He notes that Catholic Church teaching tells us that the Eschaton was fully inaugurated by the life, death, and resurrection of Jesus Christ. But Church teaching also affirms the reality of history, complete with evil and free will. Held together, these teachings seem to contradict. Cole sets to make progress on this paradox by employing a neo-Aristotelian hylomorphism. This is followed by Daniel Isai's exposition of the Incarnation as a *saturated phenomenon,* following Jean-Luc Marion's phenomenological method. After this, Raffaele Guerra studies theological anthropology *via* ontological notions in Gregory Palamas, bringing this volume's circular motion, from ontology to political theology and then back to theological ontology, to a conclusion.

The initial inspiration for this volume emerged during the international conference *Ontology and History: A Challenging and Auspicious Dialogue for Philosophy and Theology* at the European Cultural Centre of Delphi, Greece (May 29-31, 2015), which was organized by Dr. Andrew Kaethler and myself. This is one of the publications inspired from the discussions in that conference, and claims ontology and political theology as its epicenter; another volume, focusing on different thematic areas, is forthcoming as well. This volume is published here in the hope that it may prove to be a contribution, however small, to the widening of the scope and horizons of political theology.

*Sotiris Mitralexis*

# List of Contributors

Jonathan Cole is a research member of the Centre for Public and Contextual Theology at Charles Sturt University, Canberra, Australia. His publications include "Personhood in the Digital Age: the Ethical Use of New Information Technologies," St Mark's Review 233:3 (2015).

Marc W. Cole is a doctoral candidate at the University of Leeds. He is working on hylomorphic solutions to mind/body problems.

Chris Durante is Visiting Assistant Professor at the Department of Religious Studies, Manhattan College. He holds a doctorate from the Faculty of Religious Studies of McGill University

Angelos Gounopoulos is a PhD candidate at the School of Political Science of the Aristotle University of Thessaloniki specializing in Political Theory and Philosophy. His PhD research focuses on political theology, and more specifically the historical experience of the Latin-American Liberation Theology.

Raffaele Guerra is a doctoral candidate at the University of Salerno (Italy) and at the Institut Catholique de Paris (France). His research deals with the concept of hypostasis in the doctrine of Gregory Palamas in the three domains of Triadology, Anthropology and Economy. His publications include book reviews on *Byzantinoslavica* and *Byzantinische Zeitschrift* and the Italian translation of John Panteleimon Manoussakis' *For the Unity of All* (Bose: Qiqajon 2016).

Fr. Daniel Isai holds a doctorate from the Faculty of Theology of the "Alexandru Ioan Cuza" University of Iasi. His research focuses on the dialogue between theology and phenomenology, with a focus on the theological dimension of Jean Luc Marion's phenomenology.

Sotiris Mitralexis is Assistant Professor of Philosophy at the City University of Istanbul and Visiting Fellow at the University of Cambridge, as well as Visiting Senior Research Associate at Peterhouse, Cambridge (January–April 2017). He received his doctorate in Philosophy from the Freie Universität Berlin (2014) and his degree in Classics from the University of Athens. His publications include *Ludwig Wittgenstein Between Analytic Philosophy and Apophaticism* (2015) and *Ever-Moving Repose* (2017).

**Dylan Pahman** is a research fellow at the Acton Institute for the Study of Religion & Liberty, where he serves as managing editor of the *Journal of Markets & Morality*. He is also a fellow of the Sophia Institute: International Center for Orthodox Thought and Culture.

**Dionysios Skliris** received a doctorate from the Faculté des Lettres et Sciences Humaines of the University of Paris (Sorbonne-Paris IV). He studied Classics and Theology at the University of Athens and completed a Master's degree in Late Antique Philosophy at the University of London (King's College) and a Master's degree in Byzantine Literature at the University of Paris (Sorbonne—Paris IV).

**Fr Chrysostom Gr. Tympas** has degrees in medicine and theology from the Aristotle University of Thessaloniki and a PhD from the University of Essex Centre for Psychoanalytic Studies. Recent publication: Carl Jung and Maximus the Confessor on Psychic Development, Routledge 2014.

Chapter 1

# Understanding the "Real" through consciousness and history: Maximus the Confessor's vision of the One Logos in many logoi and Hegel's progressive consciousness

Chrysostom Gr. Tympas

Philosophical ideas that investigate the depths of human nature and the cosmos always were deeply related to the exploration of the divine realm and God(s). In ancient Greek philosophy there was no specific ontological distinction between God(s) and the cosmos existed, in either Platonic or Neo-platonic philosophy. The nature of God was indefinite and rather unapproachable, so was the human nature with regard to its very *ontological* quality (reality). As a result, human nature was almost indistinguishable from the nature and qualities of the divine, whereas human and divine realms were understood as a *continuum*, especially in Greek philosophy. A further step was taken by Neo-Platonic traditions that developed the idea of a *void* between the two great principles that comprise reality, the *Pleroma* and the *Demiurge*, which also adopted by the Gnostics. It was with the advent of Christianity that these ideas did find a rival from the then progressively advanced theology. Christian theologians clearly established a hitherto unprecedented distinction between God and the cosmos, by introducing the principle of a God-creator *ex nihilo*. Subsequently, for the theologians, "*it was necessary to find an ontology that avoided the monistic Greek philosophy as much as the "gulf" between God and the world taught by the gnostic systems."*[1] Theology was about to openly rival philosophy, which later on, in modernity, appears to gradually emancipate from its preferences for ontological inquiries and thus to give place to phenomenological approaches.

Nowadays, it is widely accepted that modernity witnessed a paradigm shift from antiquated "ontological" to modern "phenomenological" considerations, namely from the question "what is real?" to "what can be experienced?" This significant turn, in essence, has little to do with the theoretical and at once "unapproachable reality," i.e. the ontological question regarding the real nature of beings; rather, it introduces a different epistemology of "know-how," through the experience of the self-consciousness, which perceives things as *they appear* "here and now" (and not as *they are* in their unknown reality). Phenomenology in fact is based on the capacity of human "consciousness" to recall inner experience, which can advance towards the ultimate reality that the consciousness can perceive via various constructs. Aligned with this approach, Hegel basically articulates an understanding of "consciousness" as a progressive knowledge-experience towards the *Absolute*, which incorporates, amongst other constructs, arts and history—namely the ultimate sum of human experience and activity. In this paper, I will discuss the discourse between ontology and phenomenology through the concepts of two great representatives of ontological and phenomenological approaches, that is, respectively, through Maximus the Confessor and G.W.F. Hegel.

We live an interdisciplinary era and allegedly welcome the encounter of theology with philosophy, sociology or other disciplines. From a theological point of view, Maximus the Confessor's ontological system, based on the dynamics of the *one Logos-Christ in many logoi/ontological principles* (as both the foundations and the telos of all beings) sounds a rather complete structure-system. In addition, Maximus does not introduce an ontological system alone, but also clearly suggests that humans can

---

[1] John Zizioulas, *Being as Communion. Studies in Personhood and the Church* (Crestwood, New York: St Vladimir's Seminary Press, 1985), 16.

openly experience these *ontological logoi* as the divine qualities/virtues—and thus he affirms a strong experiential/phenomenological aspect that is incorporated in his ontology. However, I will argue that Maximus' system could still be benefited from other systems of thought, which stress the inner experience that gradually reflects on, and incorporates in, an understanding of things through science, history, arts etc.—as precisely Hegel's system does. For this purpose, I will refer to some of the key aspects of Maximus the Confessor's worldview of "the real," that is the communion of the *one Logos in many logoi*, in juxtaposition to Hegel's theory of *progressive consciousness* towards the *Absolute*. This is an endeavor to address both the ontological and experiential dynamics of Maximus' theory along with the spatiotemporal and socio-cultural elements of Hegel's phenomenology. Let us begin with Maximus.

## Maximus' vision of *the one Logos in many logoi* as the defining principle of reality

Maximus the Confessor was one of the greatest theologians and philosophers of early Christian times (580–662 AD) whose importance, in contrast with many other Christian writers, has thoroughly been acknowledged in both the East and the West. He was honored as *"one of the outstanding thinkers of all time,"*[2] with his work drawing a considerable body of modern academic theological research. In a prefigurative way, the fact that Maximus sought and found support for his ideas from the West is more evident nowadays, since his work is becoming increasingly influential in western contexts. Therefore, it appears that his life paradoxically reconciles all the tensions, old and contemporary, between "eastern" and "western" strands of theological thinking. The dynamics of his thinking is a result of a rich legacy by great theologians (in particular Origen, Evagrius, Gregory of Nazianzus, Gregory of Nyssa, and Dionysius the Areopagite, all of them exerted a significant influence on Maximus), as well of such

---

[2] Lars Thunberg, *Man and Cosmos: The Vision of St Maximus the Confessor* (New York, Crestwood: St Vladimir's Seminary Press, 1985), 7.

vigorous at the time philosophical currents as Neo-Platonism. Maximus the Confessor, following his predecessor theologians, introduces the ontology of the uncreated God and of a created cosmos both united in Logos the Christ:

> *"For the union between Creator and creation, rest and motion ... has been manifested in Logos the Christ ... and in itself brings God's foreknowledge to fulfillment, in order that naturally mobile creatures might secure themselves around God's total and essential immobility ... so that they might also acquire an active knowledge of him."*[3]

Maximus needed a concept that could bridge that gap between the uncreated God and the created world and this was the λόγοι τῶν ὄντων/*logoi of beings* (perhaps a loan from Philo of Alexandria). The *logoi* define not only the foundations and the beginning of the beings, but also their development as well as their *telos*. Each being (either unanimated or animated) is endowed with, and defined by, one specific *logos*. Maximus makes a special reference to man's fundamental *"logos of the nature"* (λόγος τῆς φύσεως), which is a *logos* that defines his constitution (κρᾶσις), and also to distinct *logoi* that describe man's power, functions, or other characteristics of beings, such as quantity, quality, relation, place, time, position, motion, stability.[4] Similarly, other numerous *logoi* correspond to multiple qualities-virtues of God. It is apparent that to the same human person correspond not only his/her unique/particular *logos*, but also a multitude of *logoi* that are united to the universal *logoi*, the divine qualities-virtues.[5]

---

[3] Maximus the Confessor, *Quaestiones ad Thalassium* 60 (Corpus Christianorum Series Graeca (CCSG), Turnhout: Brepols 1953ff, Vol. 22), 79.

[4] Maximus the Confessor, *Ambigua ad Ioannem* (J.P. Migne, ed., *Patrologiae cursus completes (PG). Series Craeca*, Paris, 1857ff., Vol. 91), 1217AB; 1228A-29A.

[5] Maximus clearly suggests that the *logoi* of the particular (beings) are united within the *logoi* of the universal, that is the *logoi* of prudence, judgment, peace and love, namely the catholic virtues (see *Ambigua* PG 91, 1248Aff). Ultimately, it is the uncreated Logos the Christ that unites all the *logoi*; in essence, all the *logoi* proceed from the Logos, the centre of life and reality.

In Maximus, the highest and all-included *logos* is the Logos' "love" for mankind, the sacrificial and unconditional mode of love. "Love" should not be seen as merely a spiritual quality or *virtue*, but as primarily the intrinsic attribute that the beings must acquire to establish a "loving" relationship amongst them and between them and God: this is the ultimate purpose of all beings. In Maximus' definition love is *"the inward universal relationship to the first good (the Logos) connected with the universal purpose of our natural kind."*[6] Accordingly, it is the universal principle of love that unites all the beings with the Logos, and, as a consequence, all the *logoi* of beings are gathered in Logos. This union between Logos and *logoi* is described by Maximus through the multifaceted concept *"one Logos in many logoi."*[7]

The outstanding potential of nature to reach love through the relationship with the Logos is described precisely by Maximus in the case of the archetypal man, the Christ, whose body and soul are the "reservoirs" of the totality of the *logoi*: *"logoi of sensible things are to be comprehended the flesh of Christ, logoi of intelligible [things] his blood... while the bones [are] the logoi of deity above any comprehension."*[8] In this respect, Christ's flesh, body and soul, *"functions as the "bridge" between the intelligible and the sensible spheres."*[9] As a result, the very limbs/body of Christ acquire an extraordinary value, thus being the means of perfection. Maximus considers these limbs as the recapitulation of the *logoi-as*-virtues; when a man attains a virtue, at the same time partakes of the correspondent to this virtue-Christ's limb:

> *"[One will partake Christ's] legs and feet, if he keeps unwavering and steadfast the soul's underpinnings on the ground of faith, virtue and knowledge...; hands if he... maintains the practical psychic aspect alert and robust*

---

[6] Maximus the Confessor, *Epistulae* 2, PG 91, 401D.

[7] Maximus, *Ambigua* 21, PG 91, 1248A-49C.

[8] Maximus, Quaestiones ad Thalassium, Ibid., 35: 239; also Capita theologica et oeconomica II.10, PG 90, 1129A.

[9] Adam G. Cooper, *The Body in St Maximus the Confessor: Holy Flesh, Wholly Deified* (Oxford: Oxford University Press, 2005), 38.

> *for the fulfillment of the divine commandments;... eyes, he, who appreciates the creation in a spiritual manner...; breast, if he fills his heart with notions of theological contemplation...."*[10]

The participation to Christ's limbs-as-virtues is the first path towards the communion of the *logoi*, namely the path through the sacraments. Maximus suggests a different, not less important though, path, the ascetic struggle, which engages the whole spectrum of the soul's functions. He actually speaks of a well-structured psychic model with three main functions, which he names "motions." According to him, the sagacious,

> *"illuminated by grace [teach that] the soul/psyche has three modes of motion that converge into one: that of the nous [mind/intellect], that of the logos [rational function/reason] and that of the aesthesis [sense/perception]. By the first [motion], which is inconceivable, the soul ineffably approaching God, knows him in a transcendent way... by the second, which distinguishes according to the causes of the unknown, the soul physically applies its knowledge to all the natural principles of those things, which are known with regard to causality... [whereas the motion] of the aesthesis is a synthetic one and, through symbols of the sensible things, gains some impression of their innate logoi... Within these motions... the aesthesis, by perceiving the logoi of the creatures in the visible world,*

---

[10] Maximus, *Ambigua* 48, PG 91, 1364C-65C. It is clear that the Logos in many *logoi* becomes the ultimate purpose of man, and within man of all creation, in a communion beyond time and space in a relationship that unites the ontological with the experiential element of reality. Loudovikos has extensively commented on this passage as the foundation of Maximus' Eucharistic ontology (the term from Nikolaos Loudovikos, *A Eucharistic Ontology. Maximus the Confessor's Eschatological Ontology of Being as Dialogical Reciprocity.* trans. Elizabeth Theokritoff (Brookline, Massachusetts: Holy Cross Orthodox Press, 2010), 33ff), whereas Zizioulas speaks of a "relational ontology"; see also Christos Yannaras, *Relational Ontology* (Brookline MA: HC Press, 2011).

*is ascended up to the nous through the logos; the logos conceiving the logoi of the intelligible creatures unify them with the nous in a simple inseparable prudence; in this way the nous, freed and pure of any motion around any creature... is raised up to God."*[11]

In Maximus' view, the functions-motions of the soul are in a constant dialogue and exchange with the *logoi of beings* designated to these specific functions, of which the highest, the intellect-nous, is meant to offer as a sacrifice to God the totality of the *logoi*. It is apparently another vision of Maximus' *Mystagogy*, in which all three parts of the building of the church (nave, sanctuary, altar) stand for the three main psychic motions.[12] These passages clearly indicate man's potential towards communion with *Logos in many logoi* both via the sacramental and the ascetic path. However, due to man's free will, which Maximus further distinguishes between the *will of nature* and the *will of gnome* (the natural and the gnomic will)[13] such a potential is not always achieved. Man often fails to reach his/her *logos*-potential to unite with the Logos-Christ. To cover all possibilities of human nature and of all beings, Maximus

---

[11] Maximus, *Ambigua* 10, PG 91, 1112D-13A.

[12] See Maximus, *Mystagogia* 4, PG 90, 672BC: "...man [may stand for] a mystical church, because through the nave, which is his body, he brightens by virtues the ascetic psychic aspect [aesthesis], via the observance of the commandments in moral philosophy. Through the sanctuary ... he conveys to God by the logical function in natural contemplation the logoi of the aesthesis purely and in a spirit cut off from matter. Finally, through the altar of the nous [intellect] he summons the silence abounding in hymns in the innermost recesses of the invisible and unknown utterance of divinity...[where] he dwells intimately in mystical theology."

[13] Maximus' analysis is based on the model of the Christ's two wills, the human and the divine, according to his double nature comprising one hypostasis (*Opuscula theologica et polemica* 3, PG 90, 48CD); he also applies the distinction between man's ability-will to act that belongs to nature and *"disposed by nature"* (natural will) and the way one acts-will, since *"how you speak belongs to the hypostasis"* (γνώμη or gnomic will) (48A). In this way, *"the Incarnate Word [Christ] possesses as a human being the natural disposition to will, and this is moved and shaped by the divine will"* (Ibid.), but without it being subject to the differentiation of the natural and gnomic will which applies to humans. This is because *"it was only this difference of our gnomic will that introduced into our lives sin and our separation from God"* (Ibid. 56B); and because Christ is unsinful, he cannot have a gnomic will opposing the will of his divine nature.

further articulates the theory of *final restoration* to show that God's ultimate purpose is to "unify by right faith and spiritual charity [love] those whom vice has sundered in various ways."[14] Therefore, it is extremely interesting to see how Maximus thinks of God's ultimate treatment of those who have failed to fulfill their specific *logos of virtue*. Attaching greater importance to one's potential-*logos* and lesser to one's transgressions, he writes:

> *"The church acknowledges three restorations. The first is that of each one according to the logos of virtue, in which one is restored having fulfilled his/her intrinsic logos of virtue. The second is that of the restoration of the whole creation into incorruptibility and immortality through the resurrection. The third, which actually Gregory of Nyssa misused in his own works, is that of the restoration of the psychic functions fallen in transgressions into their natural condition before the fall. Just as the whole nature will receive in resurrection the incorruptibility of flesh in hope through ages, so the diverged functions of the psyche throughout the ages must expel the memories of evil imposed to them ... and culminate in God. And they will thus receive back the [God's] strengths in a certain understanding, though not the communion of his excellences, being restored in their initial stage. And thus God will be proved as causeless of sin [and of evil, too]."*[15]

It is clear from this passage that Maximus' understanding of the *logoi* as the ultimate potential of spiritual development is that they ultimately are fulfilled by God's providence and love, in a way that

---

[14] Maximus writes: "*...unify by right faith and spiritual charity those whom vice has sundered in various ways. Indeed for this the Savior suffered—to gather together in one the children of God that were dispersed (John 11:52)*" (*Capitum de Charitate Centuria IV, 17*, in Polycarp Sherwood, *Saint Maximus the Confessor. The Ascetic Life. The Four Centuries on Charity* (Ancient Christian Writers (ACW) 21, New York: The Newman Press, 1995), 194.

[15] Maximus, *Quaestiones et dubia 18*, in Corpus Christianorum Series Graeca (Brepols Turnhout 1953ff, (CCSG) Vol. 19), 18; also PG 90, 796AC.

even "fallen" creatures might still relate to some of God's good qualities (but not of God's *excellences*, namely his highest qualities/*logoi*-as-virtues). Due to the fact that the reality of *one Logos in many logoi* defines the beings from the beginning to their telos, Maximus' ultimate vision of beings is eschatological: this means that the only true "ontology" of all beings refers to the-not-yet-revealed *telos* of the beings. As Loudovikos puts it, *"[t]he end is the ontological beginning; it is a new ontology which is personal and eschatological."*[16] This "end" of course presupposes a different conception of time, the "eternal time," which is at odds with the Kantian dichotomy of presence and appearance, *"that makes us prisoners of a spacious present,"* according to Knight's description of the space-time reality.[17]

It is apparently upon human free will to designate the degree of participation and fulfillment within the divine qualities, of the "eschata," and especially the ultimate *logos* of love. In this journey towards divine love, the beings do not travel alone, Maximus completes his theory of the *logoi*: the beings are always been assisted by the *logoi of providence and love* (λόγοι προνοίας καὶ κρίσεως), which aim at guarding and assisting all beings to walk and progress according to their specific purpose (that their *logos* suggests). Yet, in this long and full of vicissitudes journey, Maximus does not exemplify specifically the degree of one's engagement in social, interpersonal or cultural levels; rather, he implies an ascetic context in which one can advance to the *"well-being"* and then to *"eternally well-being,"*[18] via the virtues of repentance, renunciation and self-judgment culminating in peace, meekness and love.[19]

To conclude, for Maximus, ontology as the reality of the true being is eschatologically defined through the ultimate potential of

---

[16] Loudovikos, *Eucharistic Ontology*, 205.

[17] Douglas H. Knight, *The Eschatological Economy. Time and the Hospitality of God* (Grand Rapids, Michigan, Cambridge UK: William B. Eerdmans Publishing Company, 2006), 22.

[18] See Maximus, *Ambigua* 42, PG 91: 1325BC, 1381D-84A.

[19] See the hierarchical integration of the *logoi*-as-virtues towards love in Maximus, *Ambigua* 21: 1249AB; 41: 1313AB.

the *logoi*, which are principally perceived as virtues. However, and despite some general suggestions, Maximus does not provide realistic examples/incarnations of the actual engagement of these *logoi* in more complex discourses within history and culture, which appear to exceed the boundaries of applied virtues within an ascetic context—such as political decisions, contemporary issues of social equality, cultural challenges, financial problems etc. We need therefore to address this question from different angles and for this purpose we can see now how Hegel articulates his understanding of progress in knowledge towards the real, the Absolute.

## Hegelian progressive consciousness and the *Absolute*

Hegel's phenomenology appears to be the culmination of significant steps in the history of philosophy, following Lock's and Hume's empiricism, Descartes' rationalism and, to some extent, Leibniz's notion of "monads." The latter is the divine sparkle in every being[20] (a remote parallel to Maximus' *logoi*), which also could be seen as an adumbration of Kant's unapproachable "thing-in-itself." Kant, in essence, established a compromise between empiricists and rationalists in his first *Critique of Pure Reason*. Neither the senses nor the reason are valid in establishing a real experience; it is the combination of the sensible and intelligible representations of beings, further synthesized on the level of inner experience and fantasy, that can reach a *reductive realization* of things, rather, but never the *thing-in-itself*. The latter, perhaps aligned with the *eternal well-being* of Maximus' vision of the things/beings on a divine/metaphysical level, is not found within the capabilities of human functions, since, for Kant, it remains unknown. In a similar approach, in his *Religion Within the Boundaries of Mere Reason Alone*, Kant frames more precisely spiritual/religious issues within the concept of two homocentric spheres: "*the wider sphere of faith*," aligned with the unknowable *thing in itself*, and a

---

[20] See Gottfried W. Leibniz, *Monadology and Other Philosophical Essays*, trans. Paul Schrecker and Anne Martin Schrecker (Indianapolis: Bobbs-Merrill Educational Publishing, 1985), § 61–9.

narrower one of *"religion of reason"*[21]—as it is appropriate to expect from a philosophical viewpoint. Subsequent concepts such as Schopenhauer's Will, a potential "thing in itself" according to his vision of the mostly unknown inner will,[22] and prevailing axioms at the time that, *"there are no moral phenomena at all, only a moral interpretations of phenomena...,"*[23] put human experience in contradistinction with metaphysics. It is understood then that the discourse of the reality of things is approached not from an ontological basis, but from an entirely different viewpoint, that is through the inner capabilities of all human functions that comprise human consciousness; namely, from a *phenomenological* viewpoint. The phenomenological approach emphasizes primarily an emerging "self-consciousness" that perceives nature-cosmos "as it appears," contrary to axioms viewed by ontology or religion(s).

"Things" in Kantian reductive realization could be perceived as *phenomena* and *noumena*, but never as *things-in-themselves*, because the latter are unapproachable by human perception. And such a view rendered Kant to be an agnostic. On the contrary, Hegel strongly opposed to the Kantian unknowable "thing-in-itself" and introduced a new approach towards the things-as-appearances. Similarly, Husserl, later on, suggested that *truth-in-itself* has as "ontological" correlate the *being-in-itself*, just as meaning categories have formal-ontological categories as correlates. He thus believed that experience is not limited to empiricism, but is also the source of all knowledge, since objects are perceived through their attributes elaborated by experience and not as objects as such. It is through the so-called *phenomenological reduction* that a subject may come to know directly the "essence" of beings (which however is different from what Maximus defines as

---

[21] Immanuel Kant, *Religion Within the Boundaries of Mere Reason and other Writings*, eds. and trans. Allen Wood, George Di Giovanni (Cambridge: Cambridge University, 1998), 40.

[22] Arthur. Schopenhauer, *The World as Will and Idea*, trans. Jill Berman (London: Everyman, 1819/1995), 87f.

[23] Friedrich Nietzsche, *Beyond Good and Evil. Prelude to a Philosophy of the Future*, trans. R. J. Hollingdale, (Penguin Books, 1886/1974), 78.

a real being defined by its *logos* of essence). Indeed, Hegel's fundamental position was that when the "thing-in-itself" starts to be investigated by human consciousness,

> *"it ceases to be the in-itself, and becomes something that is the in-itself only for consciousness. And this then is the True: the being-for-consciousness of this in-itself. Or, in other words, this is the essence, or the object of consciousness."*[24]

Phenomenology is the philosophy that explores the manners whereby consciousness progressively perceives things and gathers knowledge of things within the broader context of human life and history. R. Norman, one of serious scholars on Hegel's *Phenomenology of Spirit*, describes the six stages of the progressive consciousness towards the Absolute, with the three first of them to refer to self-consciousness and the rest being their social and cultural counterparts. In this way, in terms of *individual experience*, Hegel suggests threes stages of the progressive stages:[25]

A: *consciousness (sense certainty, perception, understanding of the supersensible world)*

B: *Self-consciousness (truth of self-certainty, freedom/independence of self-consciousness)*

C: *Reason (observational reason, self-realization, to be real in and for itself)*

Whereas the respective counterparts-divisions of *social experience* are:

AA: *Spirit (Ethics, Human and Divine Law, Culture and Faith, Evil and forgiveness etc)*

BB: *Religion (Natural Religion, Religion of Art (Spiritual work of Art), Revealed Religion)*

---

[24] Georg W. F. Hegel, *Phenomenology of Spirit*, trans. A. V. Miller, foreword J. N. Findlay (Oxford: Oxford University Press, 1807/1977), 55.

[25] See Richard Norman, *Hegel's Phenomenology. A Philosophical Introduction* (Sussex: Sussex University Press, 1976), 23–4 (in the diagram).

*CC: Absolute Knowledge*

The first stage of phenomenology, "consciousness," is in fact an actual progression of the experience from sense-certainty to perception and to understanding—terms used also by Kant in his process of reduction-realization.[26] On the other hand, the social counterparts serve towards the process of integration of consciousness. Accordingly, the sequence-order of levels of the individual experience is closely correlated with specific features of consciousness-cognitive functions. The latter are not far away from the functions of the Maximian model, that is the aesthesis/senses (both bodily and psychic) and the reason/*logos*, with the important exception of the intellect-nous, able to perceive the ultimate foundations of the things, their *logoi*. Apparently, the social counterparts are not present in Maximus as well as in Kant. In phenomenology, the more aspects of the consciousness are activated the greater is the experience. In the end of this phenomenological process, Hegel suggests, "*appearance becomes identified with essence,*" and consciousness reaches a point that "*will denote the nature of absolute knowledge itself.*"[27]

Hegel's "spirit"/Geist is not something that descends upon the world from without, namely it is not aligned with the divine (*Holy*) *Spirit* or the Maximian *logoi* in a Christian metaphysical sense; rather, it is an "entity" that advances within the world, through human endeavors, even unconscious ones. Indeed, Bykova elucidates, "*Hegel's "spirit" is not a substance or a substrate underlying the concrete individual subject; it is a pure infinite activity of the conscious human individual which gives purpose to itself and to the world.*"[28] Apparently, it is principally upon human effort to progress, understand and experience the spirit of the world, according to Hegel's phenomenology. However, the Hegelian spirit/Geist does not necessarily exclude a metaphysical aspect that might be

---

[26] Hegel, *Phenomenology of Spirit*, 58ff.
[27] Georg W.F. Hegel, *The Phenomenology of Mind*, trans. J. B. Baillie, (London: George Allen and Unwin Ltd.; New York: The Macmillan Co, 2nd edn 1931), 145.
[28] Marina F. Bykova, "Spirit and Concrete Subjectivity in Hegel's Phenomenology of Spirit," in *The Blackwell Guide to Hegel's Phenomenology of Spirit*, ed. K.R. Westphal (Blackwell, 2009), 274.

present within the cosmos, but at the same time is not directly affirmative to that, rather, focuses on the inner capabilities of human consciousness to reach knowledge at the highest possible levels.

It is now understood that the Hegelian synthesis proceeds through the advancing experience of the self-consciousness, consisting of all inner functions. The consciousness thus becomes the defining dimension of human being, able to gradually embrace knowledge and experience from the spirit/Geist that dwells within all beings and constructs (including arts, science and religious knowledge). Everything goes as a *synthesis* of *thesis* and *antithesis*, of "knowledge" and "lack of knowledge," whereas the meeting of opposites leads progressively to a new point, and ultimately to the *absolute*. Taking place in a spatiotemporal continuum, Hegelian synthesis as such includes no metaphysical agent, like Leibniz's *monads*, or Maximus' *logoi*, as a catalyst into the process of attaining knowledge. The spatiotemporal continuum is a manifestation of *the Reason*; but at the same time, Hegel asserts, historical place, which comprises the world or arts, science and religion, is also present in human minds even if is not indented by them. In Hegel's understanding, human history is the work of *the Reason*. Indeed, explains Norman, Hegel seems also *"committed to a stronger thesis, that the reason operative in history is supra-human reason, akin to divine providence."*[29] In other words, Hegel's thesis is that *the Reason* is the world-spirit defining history in all its patterns, and the antithesis to that is that history can deliver a rational meaning.

## Discussion and implications of viewing the real through consciousness

In Hegel's Phenomenology everything has to be experienced by the consciousness, in order to find its unique place in the cosmic space-time continuum. As a result, time and history become the wider context that indicates the ultimate potential of man's activity as well as experience. In Hegel, both the idea of God and religious experience are considered within this continuum in a

---

[29] Norman, *Hegel's Phenomenology*, 114.

manner that serves the higher idea of the Absolute and not as an independent metaphysical category that offers within specific qualities—as in Maximus case—or a dialogue in process, namely a *relational* cooperation of God and man.

In Maximus, on the contrary, the reality of beings, that is their cause, beginning, developmental potential and *telos*, are grounded in the eternal divine principles/*logoi*, which altogether are gathered in the Logos-Christ—as the radius extend from a center and return back to it.[30] God offers to mankind the communion of these *logoi* through, a: the sacraments, which bear the totality of the *logoi*, and b: the ascetic path, comprising spiritual struggle, prayer and contemplation of these *logoi*. For the communion of these *logoi* to be effective it is presupposed that human will cooperates synergistically with the divine will. Due to the fact that this cooperation is not always accomplished, human actions and the consequent historical events are *not always* manifestation of the divine purposes/*logoi*. Despite Maximus' theory of the final restoration as the ultimate manifestation of divine Providence and Love (through the ultimate and all-inclusive divine *logos*), the historical places is the arena within which human choice has the potential either to work alongside with the *logoi*/divine purposes or to go against them.

Compared to the Hegelian synthesis of a constantly evolving self-consciousness (through history, science, the arts, etc.), Maximus' synthesis extends both within space-time and beyond space-time continuum: in essence, it is stretched out towards the ultimate/real ontological potential of beings in their extra-psychic and extra-cosmic dimension. On the other hand, it appears that Maximus does not clearly exemplify how the *logoi* specifically could embrace such external structures as science, arts or, more critically, historical events. In scholars' interpretations of Maximian *logoi* in history, it appears that the distinction between the *logoi*-as-*tropoi* (modes/virtues) implemented *according* to the divine will and the *misused logoi*-as-*tropoi* within human history is

---

[30] See Maximus, *Mystagogia*, PG 90, 668A.

not always convincingly clear.³¹ Whilst Maximus addresses this discourse that embraces man's choices in history within the *logoi of providence and judgment* (which take care of the development of beings), the monastic context that is primarily suggested in Maximus' corpus does not provide specific and convincing examples how these *logoi* could be applied in such complex-critical stages of human behavior as politics, social networks and economics. Maximus' psychic model rather appears to find difficulties to be embedded in the social level or in cultural life in modern terms. This is because to the attitude of renunciation, namely, the detachment of objects through the mystery of the cross, which is necessary to reach the divine love.³²

The progression of the *logoi*-as-virtues towards love/charity is principally based on spiritual struggle and the indispensable attitudes/virtues of *detachment* and *renunciation*. Looking at the Maximian definition of charity as *"the intentional doing of good to one's neighbor and long-suffering and patience; also the use of things in*

---

³¹ There have been thought provoking discussions/interpretations of the Maximian *logoi* in connection with history, which however not always deliver a clear distinction of the decisive role of human choice in historical events. See for instance Dionysis Skliris, "Theologizing on wreckage... with Maximus..." [Θεολογώντας πάνω σὲ συντρίμμια... μαζὶ μὲ τὸν Μάξιμο], in *Synaxis* 123 (2012): 4-14. Skliris gives out an interesting discourse of applying Maximian *logoi* into a postmodern dialogue between God and cosmos and highlights the existing gap in modern theology in discussing the historical embedment of the binary concept "*logos-tropos* (*logoi*-as-virtues)." However, at the same time, he does not efficiently clarify the critical difference between an-according-to-God's-will-incarnation of *logos-tropos* into a historical place/structure via the tropoi of *logoi*/virtues and, conversely, an incarnation of a *misused logos-tropos* in human history as a *failure* resulting from choice *against* the divine will-purposes—that the *logoi* convey. Despite the fact that such a distinction is not always easily applied to historical events and human complex acts, Maximus is clear as to the consequences of a misused *logos-tropos* (*a tropos-virtue never can embrace human failures*). His theory of *final restoration*, nevertheless, ultimately restores man's failures within God's providence and love but under a specific order (not with the sharing of God's *excellences*).

³² "Charity springs from the calm of detachment, detachment from hope in God, hope from patience and long-suffering; and these from all-embracing self-master": Maximus, Capitum de Charitate Centuria I, 2, in Sherwood, Saint Maximus the Confessor, 137.

*due measure,*"³³ the degree of detachment is concretized into the "*due measure*," using the Stoic view of "right reason/*logos*" as the core of virtues.³⁴ That "right reason," Maximus writes, is necessary to avoid the three main vices: ignorance, self-love, and tyranny.³⁵ However, there are no given examples as to how one could implement the "due measure" into contemporary social constructs, technologies, politics and complex human relationships. The wider is the context, as opposed to the narrower monastic/virtuous one, the more difficult appears the understanding and application of Maximian *logoi* into a modern perspective.

On the other hand, Hegel's progressive consciousness is open in investigating—through *thesis* and *antithesis*—the dark moments of human history collectively, such as wars, social or cultural advances and failures, all apparently embraced by the Hegelian *synthesis*. The final synthesis for Hegel is that historical advances do perform changes in consciousness, and the history within is a manifestation of a "*single divine mind.*"³⁶ Yet, it is here that a question is raised: in which ways such "*providential reason*" within history develops when it finds oppositions by human choice. Hegel's mistake, goes on Norman, is to assimilate material and historical changes without criticism to a conceptual progression, which at once defines each individual's spiritual progress within the progressive forms of consciousness.

On the contrary, Maximus contends, human choice is at least as crucial as reason in development of human history. Yet, while Maximus' theory covers theoretically the majority of the

---

[33] Maximus, Capitum de Charitate Centuria I, 40, in Sherwood, Saint Maximus the Confessor, 141-2.
[34] Maximus takes the Stoics concept of "right reason" (ὀρθὸς λόγος) of a sensible handling of all situations, see Diogenes Laertius, SVF 3.473 (Stoicorum Veterum Fragmenta. Collegit Hans Friedrich August von Arnim (ed.). (In aedibus B.G. Tuebneri, Stutgardiae, 1964), but his own application conveys a slightly different connotation: "the use of things with right reason" in Capitum. I, 24-7: Sherwood, Saint Maximus the Confessor, 140; also PG 90: 965AC.
[35] Maximus, Epistulae 2, PG 91, 396D-97A.
[36] Norman, Hegel's Phenomenology, 115.

developmental potentialities, it does not exemplify in which way one should incorporate constructs from socio-cultural realms and historical dynamics. It is questionable whether the Maximian *logoi-*as-virtues are able to address all aspects of psychic development into the personal or the social level, such as Freud's instinctive unconscious,[37] Jungian father/mother archetypes,[38] sexual orientation and human behavior in socio-political dynamics. In other words, it is not clear how one has to implement the "divine purposes" towards parental and interpersonal relationships or participation to social activities that imbed such complex intentions as voting for a government or handling finances. It could be said though, that in a complementary view between Maximus' and Hegel's views, Hegelian synthesis offers this kind of social and cultural embedment that is absent in Maximus, whereas the latter provides a clearer metaphysical perspective of reality.

---

[37] Henri F. Ellenberger explores the origins of the notion of the unconscious long ago before Freud's introduction of the term, in Nietzsche's thought, for which human acts are manifestations of the unconscious realm: "Even the [Freudian] term "id" (Das Es) originates from Nietzsche," in Henri F. Ellenberger, The Discovery of the Unconscious: The History and Evolution of Dynamic Psychiatry (London: Allen Lane, The Penquin Press, 1970), 277, (citing Nietzsche's Zarathustra I, VII, 46-8).

[38] Carl Jung's notion of the archetypes exclusively explains the reason why the psychic energy is formulated and conveyed through certain structured and innate archetypal ideas-images (i.e., mother, father, hero etc.), that are at the same time collective patterns of behaviour and of interaction with others. The ultimate archetype is the Self, the culmination of the individuation process, which "is a union of opposites par excellence ... it represents in every respect thesis and antithesis, and at the same time synthesis" (see Carl G. Jung, Psychology and Alchemy. Collected Works Vol. 12, para. 22 (1944), in The Collective Works of C. G. Jung (CW), eds. Sir H. Read, M. Fordham, G. Adler, W. McGuire, trans. R.F.C. Hull, (London: Routledge & Kegan Paul 1953-1983). Carl Jung, following here Hegel, maintains that "[w]e name a thing, from a certain point of view, good or bad, high or low, right or left ... Here the antithesis is just as factual and real as the thesis," in Carl Jung, Foreword to White's "God and the Unconscious" CW 11 (1952c), para. 457. At these points one can recognize striking similarities between Hegelian and Jungian systems; indeed, Jung later in his life wrote that, there exists "a remarkable coincidence between certain tenets of Hegelian philosophy and my findings concerning the collective unconscious," in Carl Jung, Letters Vol. II: 1951-1961, eds. G. Adler and A. Jaffé, (London: Routledge & Kegan Paul, 1976), 502.

In this complementary approach, we could speak of different levels of life and reality. It might be helpful therefore to consider a multilevel approach to reality, without reducing ontology to phenomenology alone, which, at the same time, would allow space for sub-levels of undeniable human experience to enter. To understand deeper the non-reductionist approaches (that is, e.g., metaphysics/spiritual dimension reduced to psychological experience or self-consciousness alone), we could invite researching tools from other disciplines such as Sociology. For instance, *supervenience*, a notion used in the social sciences, considers certain influences of superior levels/realms on inferior levels as occurring *without* a strong dependency on physical laws.[39] In simple terms, what exists at level A (e.g., the mind or the spiritual) does not necessarily exist at level B (e.g., the body or the psyche). Supervenience could be a useful tool for investigating the "spiritual features" of a system that "inexplicably" affects certain levels but does not subject to the classical reductive analysis.

Christian theologians tend to discuss "the real" within a system that comprises purely ontological principles, about "things as they are" (i.e. doctrines, order and life in Church), rather than as things as they would have been experienced by human consciousness, at times in which our postmodern world appears to be increasingly interested in the *incarnation* and embedment of "the real" in the human reality. To understand how ontology and eschatology would be linked more understandably with history and tangible reality, we could suggest an evolutionary approach from "things as they appear" (perceived by consciousness) towards "things as they are" (in eschatological reality). Such an approach should engage all possible levels of life, namely the bodily, the psychological, the social, the cultural and the spiritual/metaphysical ones. Ontological theories typically define the spiritual/metaphysical dimension from an external perspective (extra-cosmic, divine), whereas phenomenological theories are more affirmative to the

---

[39] Julie Zahle, "Holism and Supervenience," in *Philosophy of Anthropology and Sociology*, Handbook of the Philosophy of Sciences, eds. Stephen P. Turner and Mark W. Risjord, (Amsterdam: Elsevier, 2007).

intra–cosmic reality. Apparently, we need a further step towards integration of these two strands, which is vivid in Maximus' model to a great extent—with the exceptions that already mentioned. To fill this gap we need an approach able to sufficiently incorporate the spatiotemporal historical dimension. Both the fact that certain theories consider the spiritual dimension as an *innate quality* of the psyche related to the potential for something higher, deeper, bigger or future (in line with the *God-image* as Christian anthropology maintains) and the fact that aspects of the spiritual are manifested within the social and cultural realms (e.g. Hegelian *reason* inside all things) advocate an evolutionary viewpoint of the inner-spiritual dimension, from a starting point to an eschatological one.[40] A multilevel approach could incorporate and integrate all levels of reality within the perception of a constantly evolving spiritual/ontological dimension.

Apparently, in fact we speak of interdisciplinary approaches and methods to answer the complex questions that are posed by both theology and philosophy. Since the Hegelian spirit/Geist does not exclude altogether the metaphysical perspective, though it does not principally address clear metaphysics, Maximus' *logoi* and Hegel's *Spirit* could meet at some point. This encounter could give space to the "metaphysical spiritual" to be incarnate into the "spatiotemporal spiritual" that includes all human activities—with the issue of human will/choice sufficiently elaborated. Paul Tillich, for instance, finds in modern culture and particularly cinematic ideas elements of a profound spiritual Revelation.[41] An interdisciplinary approach could provide here new utilities and methodologies to the rather mono-dimensional theological perspective of a man directly related to God.

---

[40] For a multilevel approach see Grigorios Chrysostom Tympas, "The "psychological" and the "spiritual": an evolutional relationship within an ontological framework. A brief comment on Jung's Self," *International Journal of Jungian Studies* (Taylor and Francis), 5 (3, 2013): 193–210, DOI:10.1080/19409052.2013.795181.

[41] See Jonathan Brant, *Paul Tillich and the Possibility of Revelation through Film* (Oxford Theological Monographs, Oxford University Press, 2012).

Does ontology address metaphysics alone? Or does ontology reaches the metaphysical level via other levels/realms of reality, which modern philosophical concepts or psychological ideas address more specifically? Does contemporary science and arts have anything to offer to an ontological inquiry and to convey meaningful understanding, ideas and concepts for the ontological quest to be approach more thoroughly? In this perspective, I hope that I have contributed here some insights for addressing the above questions and discuss further all potentialities of ontological dimensions: a theory of reality within many levels.

## Bibliography

Brant, Jonathan. Paul Tillich and the Possibility of Revelation through Film. Oxford: Oxford University Press, 2012.

Bykova, Marina. F. "Spirit and Concrete Subjectivity in Hegel's Phenomenology of Spirit," in The Blackwell Guide to Hegel's Phenomenology of Spirit, edited by K.R. Westphal. Blackwell, 2009.

Cooper, Adam. G. The Body in St Maximus the Confessor: Holy Flesh, Wholly Deified. Oxford: Oxford University Press, 2005.

Hegel, Georg. W.F. Phenomenology of Spirit, trans. A. V. Miller, foreword J. N. Findlay, Oxford: Oxford University Press, 1977 (originally published in 1807).

Ellenberger, Henri. The Discovery of the Unconscious: The History and Evolution of Dynamic Psychiatry. London: Allen Lane, The Penquin Press, 1970.

Jung, Carl G. The Collective Works of C. G. Jung (CW), edited by Sir H. Read, M. Fordham, G. Adler, W. McGuire, trans. R.F.C. Hull. London: Routledge & Kegan Paul, 1953-1983.

Kant, Immanuel. Critique of Pure Reason, edited and trans. by Paul Guyer and Allen Wood. The Cambridge Edition of the works of Immanuel Kant. Cambridge: Cambridge University Press, 1998 (originally published in 1807).

———. Religion Within the Boundaries of Mere Reason and other Writings, edited and trans. by Allen Wood, George Di Giovanni. Cambridge Texts in History of Philosophy. Cambridge: Cambridge University, 1998 (originally published in 1793).

Knight, Douglas H. The Eschatological Economy. Time and the Hospitality of God. Grand Rapids, Michigan, Cambridge UK: William B. Eerdmans Publishing Company, 2006.

Loudovikos, Nikolaos. A Eucharistic Ontology. Maximus the Confessor's Eschatological Ontology of Being as Dialogical Reciprocity, trans.

Elizabeth Theokritoff. Brookline. Massachusetts: Holy Cross Orthodox Press, 2010.

Nietzsche, Friedrich. Beyond Good and Evil. Prelude to a Philosophy of the Future, trans. R. J. Hollingdale. Penguin Books, 1974.

Norman, Richard. Hegel's Phenomenology. A Philosophical Introduction. Sussex: Sussex University Press, 1976.

Skliris, Dionysios, "Theologizing on wreckage... with Maximus" [in Greek, "Θεολογώντας πάνω σὲ συντρίμμια... μαζὶ μὲ τὸν Μάξιμο:], Synaxis 123 (2012): 4–14.

Sherwood, Polycarp. Saint Maximus the Confessor. The Ascetic Life. The Four Centuries on Charity. Ancient Christian Writers (ACW) 21, New York: The Newman Press, 1995.

Thunberg, Lars. Man and Cosmos: The Vision of St Maximus the Confessor. New York, Crestwood: St Vladimir's Seminary Press, 1985.

Tympas, Grigorios Chrysostomos. Carl Jung and Maximus the Confessor on Psychic Development. The dynamics between the psychological and the spiritual. London and New York: Routledge, 2014.

Yannaras, Christos. Relational Ontology. Brookline MA: HC Press, 2011.

Zahle, Julie. "Holism and Supervenience," in Philosophy of Anthropology and Sociology, Handbook of the Philosophy of Sciences, edited by Stephen P. Turner and Mark W. Risjord. Amsterdam: Elsevier, 2007.

Zizioulas, John. Being as Communion. Studies in Personhood and the Church. Crestwood, New York: St Vladimir's Seminary Press, 1985.

## Chapter 2

# The ontology of mode in the thought of Maximus the Confessor and its consequences for a theory of gender

### Dionysios Skliris

Maximus the Confessor (c. 580-662 AD) lived in a transitional period, during the emergence of Islam and the relative transformation of the Byzantine Empire—the passage from Eastern Late Antiquity to the Middle Ages[1]. These important shifts are indirectly reflected on his thought, where one observes a new thematization of historicity and a greater introspection in anthropological subjects. For the needs of this paper, one can note two of his most crucial contributions which are intrinsically linked. The first is his struggle against the heresies of Monothelitism and Monoenergism, which was validated by the 6th Ecumenical Council (680) after his death. These two movements constituted an imperial effort to achieve a compromise between the Chalcedonians and the Anti-Chalcedonian fractions of the Church, i.e. on the one hand those who stressed the plentitude of Christ's two natures, following the Council of Chalcedon (451 AD), and, on the other, those who conceived of the divine-human union in a different fashion insisting on a natural composition or assimilation of the two natures in Christ. The goal of the imperial policy was to promote peace inside the Empire in view of external attacks through the accommodating formulation that Christ had two natures, but one sole will and operation. Indeed, as it was later to be proven, the alienation of the eastern provinces due to the post-

---

[1] See Walter E. Kaegi, 'Byzantium in the Seventh Century', in *The Oxford Handbook of Maximus the Confessor*, eds. Pauline Allen and Neil Bronwen (Oxford: Oxford University Press, 2015), 84-105.

Chalcedonian conflict was decisive for their secession, for the expansion of Islam and the division of the Mediterranean. On the other hand, Maximus the Confessor did not wish to adhere to a consensus imposed from above. He rather defended an uncompromising Chalcedonian faith in the two full natures of Christ united in the hypostasis of the Logos. At the same time, he did try to integrate in his theology the multitude of the different voices which existed in the Mediterranean world of Late Antiquity, but at a deeper spiritual level which would not betray the Chalcedonian orthodoxy.

Maximus' originality in the exposition of a traditional faith consists in his effort to show that the will and the operation belong to human nature and Christ had thus to receive them in order to heal and save them. Thanks to this effort the will becomes a capacity (δύναμις) and an attribute (ἰδιότης) inherent in human nature probably for the first time in the History of human thought.[2] Before Maximus, the notion of will could be restricted to the external or internal object. But with him the will acquires the character of a faculty of human soul. This necessitated a deep introspection in the human drama. On the other hand, Maximus the Confessor had to balance in the right (Neo-)Chalcedonian way the natural and the personal character of will. He achieved the latter through the use of an elaborate distinction between the *logos* and the mode (*tropos*) of humanity. (In the same way, he had formulated a thorough theory on the relation between nature and energy in order to refute Monoenergism, thus initiating a theology of the energy which was very influential in both East and West). This distinction between the *logos* and the mode did exist in the

---

[2] See Demetrios Bathrellos, *The Byzantine Christ: Person, Nature and Will in the Christology of Saint Maximus the Confessor* (Oxford: Oxford University Press, 2004), 128. Bathrellos is also referring to an evaluation of Maximus by the philosopher Richard Sorabji. It is to be noted that an effort analogous to that of Maximus was performed in the West three centuries earlier by Augustine of Hippo (354-430) but in the different context of the relation between nature and grace.

Cappadocian and Post-Cappadocian tradition[3]. But Maximus had to treat it with greater clarity and thoroughness in order to do justice to all the different natural and personal dimensions of will and energy. In my paper, I will briefly examine the couple *logos*–mode and try to observe if it can be actualized in a post-modern context, in order to contribute to crucial subjects of contemporary political philosophy, such as the theory of gender.

## The importance of the *logos*–mode distinction in the thought of Maximus the Confessor

Both the terms *logos* and *tropos* have a great polysemy and every effort to conceptually exhaust them is futile. We will only try to pinpoint some moments in their evolution. In the Cappadocian tradition the distinction is mainly between the *logos* of nature and the mode of existence (λόγος τῆς φύσεως-τρόπος τῆς ὑπάρξεως). In a Trinitarian theological context, the *logos* refers to the community of nature, whereas the mode to the completely unique way in which the divine Persons exist as the unbegotten Father, the only-begotten Son and the Spirit Who proceeds from the Father. If this distinction is transferred to anthropology, then the *logos* will refer to the logical constitution of the common human nature, whereas the mode to a peculiar modality through which comes to being a personal human hypostasis. The common patristic example, inspired by the biblical narrative is the distinction between on the one hand the common *logos* of human nature and, on the other, the different modes of coming into existence in the cases of Adam, Eve and Seth.

A multitude of different elements was added to this initial distinction. The notion of the *logoi* in the plural is to be found in authors of Late Antiquity, from Philo onwards, including Neoplatonic philosophers, such as Plotinus. Clement of Alexandria

---

[3] For the influence of the Cappadocian tradition on Maximus the Confessor, see for example: George Charles Berthold, "The Cappadocian Roots of Maximus the Confessor", in *Maximus Confessor. Actes du Symposium sur Maxime le Confesseur. Fribourg, 2-5 septembre 1980*, (Paradosis 27), eds. Felix Heinzer and Christoph Schönborn, (Fribourg: Éditions Universitaires Fribourg Suisse, 1982), 51-59.

and ps.-Dionysius offer a Christian version of this doctrine. In the latter, the *logoi* are identified to divine wills for beings. Maximus receives this Dionysian intuition and shapes a notion of *logoi* which is at the same time ontological and gnosiological, rational and volitional. Through his *logoi* God produces beings, but He also wills them to exist in a certain way, leading them to the fulfillment of His will.[4]

Two precisions should be drawn here. Firstly, if the *logoi* are conceived as divine wills, then the distinction between a *logos* referring to the catholicity and a mode referring to the particularity is blurred. In Maximus, the *logoi* as divine wills can refer to the natures and their universality. But they can also refer to personal hypostases, to individuals, to qualities and accidents, or even to events, if these events manifest the Divine Providence for History.[5] We should however keep in mind that the *logos* does seem to retain a sense of catholicity. The *logos* as a divine will confers meaning to a being, attribute or event. It opens it up to a catholicity of a wider horizon which is not lost inside the historical flux. But this catholicity of *logos* is not restricted to natures but it can include particulars and, in general, whatever could be part of God's providence for the evolution of the world. (One should not forget here that the question whether there are ideas of particulars or even individuals was a crucial one also in Neoplatonism).

Secondly, even though the notion of *logos* is transferred from Trinitarian Theology proper to anthropology and cosmology, it does not nevertheless lose its initial Trinitarian signification. In Maximus' thought, there is a great significance ascribed to a certain "psychological" Triadology, where God the Father is the

---

[4] For the evolution of the conceptual couple *logos- tropos* before Maximus, see Polycarp Sherwood, *The Earlier Ambigua of Saint Maximus the Confessor and his Refutation of Origenism*, (Rome: Pontificium Institutum S. Anselmi "Orbis Catholicus", 1955), 155-164.

[5] The distinction between *logos* and *tropos* is not identical to that between universality and particularity. See the important remarks of Jean-Claude Larchet in: Jean-Claude Larchet, *La Divinisation de l'Homme selon Saint Maxime le Confesseur*, (Paris: Cerf, 1996), 141-151; "Introduction" in *Saint Maxime le Confesseur: Ambigua*, trans. Emmanuel Ponsoye (Paris: Ancre, 1994), 20-21. See also the relative passages *Amb.Io.* PG 91,1080A, 1228A-1229A, 1256D, 1313A.

intellect, God the Son is His hypostatical Logos-Reason, the Holy Spirit being His hypostatical Spirit (*Pneuma*).[6] Whereas this psychological Triadology is often a poetical imagery, in Maximus it has many consequences, since it constitutes the archetype also for the human soul, the latter being an "image" of God by equally having intellect, *logos* and spirit. According to this Triadology, God the Father is the One Who has the good will (εὐδοκία), the Son-Logos is the author par excellence (αὐτουργός) of both creation and incarnation, whereas the Spirit is vivifying and bringing creation to its eschatological completion (ζωτικόν, τελοιοῦν). Thus, even though the *logoi* are common wills of God, they are equally "situated" inside the Logos of God. God the Father is the primordial cause of beings through His initial good will, but the Son–Logos is the author of the "logical" character of creation through His incarnation and due to the fact that He is the only one to actually become History. The Spirit of God contributes to this "logical" character of creation by opening History to the eschata and bringing the *logoi* to their eschatological fulfillment.[7] What we wish to show is that Trinitarian theology is never lost in Maximus' thought but continues to fertilize it even when he is indulging in the most contingent details of anthropology and cosmology.

The notion of *logos* has thus in Maximus the following semantical nuances:

(i) It constitutes the meaning of a being (or attribute or even event). The French expression *raison d'être* would arguably convey the richness of this term, since the *logos* entails an opening to a wider catholicity of meaning.

(ii) This meaning is also the will of God for a being. This means that the *logos* of a being is distinguished from the being in itself and its nature. The *logos* is the will of God for the existence of this being in the future. Inside History this *logos* as a will of God might be

---

[6] See, for example, Q.Thal. CCSG 7,161,46-50 (PG 90,332B); CCSG 7,163,72-74 (PG 90,332D); CCSG 7,167,158-159 (PG 90,336C).

[7] See, for example, Q.Thal. CCSG 22,79,94-81,130 (PG 90,624B-625A); Amb.Io. PG 91,1385D-1388A.

cryptic.[8] Hence there is a necessity of purification of the entire human being and especially of the intellect in order to distinguish the *logos* of catholicity inside the chaos of empirical phenomena. If one wishes to indulge in a Neo-Palamite interpretation of Maximus, one could even speak of a distinction between created beings and their uncreated *logoi*. This interpretation does have a ground in Maximian thought since the *logoi* are divine wills for beings and as such they are not identical to beings in themselves.[9]

(iii) The *logoi* of beings retain their Trinitarian character by being linked to the hypostasis of the Logos, Who expresses the good will (εὐδοκία) of the Father–Nous through the co-operation (συνεργία) of the Spirit. The Divine Economy always has a Trinitarian structure, the Father being the initial cause, the Son being the author of both creation and salvation through the incarnation, and the Spirit being the One who opens up creation and History to its eschatological completion. Even though the acts of creation and providence are common to the three persons, they are not impersonal, but connected to particular hypostatical roles of each Person in the divine Economy.

(iv) In this sense, the *logoi* are situated in the Logos[10]. This means that the *logoi* of beings are linked to the way in which they are incorporated in the catholicity of human nature received by the Logos of God. The *logoi* of beings are thus Christological.

(v) The *logoi* as divine wills also have a character of commandment.[11] They constitute calls to man's sense of responsibility to activate nature in a certain way which is in accordance to divine will. Man thus becomes the microcosm and

---

[8] See Nikolaos Loudovikos, Ψυχανάλυση καὶ Ὀρθόδοξη Θεολογία: Περὶ Ἐπιθυμίας, Καθολικότητας καὶ Ἐσχατολογίας (Athens: Armos, 2003), 31.

[9] See, for example, Nikolaos Loudovikos, Ἡ Εὐχαριστιακὴ Ὀντολογία: Τὰ Εὐχαριστιακὰ Θεμέλια τοῦ Εἶναι ὡς ἐν Κοινωνίᾳ Γίγνεσθαι στὴν Ἐσχατολογικὴ Ὀντολογία τοῦ Ἁγίου Μαξίμου τοῦ Ὁμολογητῆ, (Athens: Domos, 1992), 90-96, 151-158. Fr Loudovikos is based mainly on *Amb.Io.* PG 91,1080A-1085.

[10] See *Amb.Io.* PG 91,1077C-1080B, 1156A-B, 1205C, 1285C-1288A; *Q.Thal.* CCSG 7,239,7-24 PG 90,377C.

[11] See *Amb.Io.* PG 91,1085A-B.

*The ontology of mode* 45

mediator of creation as a cosmic "laboratory" (ἐργαστήριον),[12] a universal experiment in which nature will either achieve truth or fail to attain it.

(vi) The *logoi* thus have an eschatological reference. They have a Christological character in a triple way: The many *logoi* are situated "inside" the one Logos as the author of creation and incarnation. As divine wills for beings they denote ways in which these beings will be received by Christ in the catholicity of His human nature in the Incarnation. And since human nature is considered as a microcosm of creation, Christ receives through it the totality of the material and intellectual creation. The ontological consequences of this achievement of *logoi* in Christ are expected to be revealed in all their clarity in the eschatological ever-being after the Second Coming. The *logoi* of beings are thus divine wills which guide beings towards the attainment of their eschatological truth in the future. Through the *logoi* the eschaton "speaks" inside History, *i.e.* the eschatological Christ being the *Logos* of God the Father in the Spirit.

Therefore, the notion of *logos* does not have an autonomous value. It coexists with the notions of mode (τρόπος) and end (τέλος). In the Trinity there is a common *logos* that is nevertheless "situated" par excellence in the Logos of God. This common *logos* coexists with the three modes of existence, even though primarily referring to the mode of Son the *Logos*. (This Trinitarian treatment of the notions of *logos* and mode is of course a very difficult theological issue which should be treated with the necessary apophatic respect). In creation, each being has a *logos* meaning the way in which God desires this being to exist, as well as a particular mode through which this being actually exists inside History. There is thus a dialogue taking place between man and God. This dialogue takes place at the level of an exchange of uncreated and created *logoi* between respectively God and man.[13] But it equally takes place at the level of *tropos* that is of the modification of nature. God creates nature proposing His *logoi* to it, i.e. intentions

---

[12] See *Amb.Io. PG* 91,1305A.
[13] See Nikolaos Loudovikos, Ἡ Εὐχαριστιακὴ Ὀντολογία, 70-76.

about how this nature could exist in the future. Man enters into dialogue with this divine desire which is at the same time enigmatical but also very tangible in the flesh of the incarnated *Logos*. In this dialogue, the human being uses the natural capacities, such as the created intellect, reason (*logos*) and spirit, which are according to Maximus in the image of the Trinity.[14] The created intellect researches God's cryptic *logoi* inside beings, the created *logos* expresses and activates this created intellect in dialogue with God's *Logos* and the created spirit accompanies the human *logos* through its vivifying "breath." But this dialogue also happens at a more ontological level, in which the human person cannot but modify her nature in one way or another.

A triple schema that is very crucial for Maximian thought is the distinction between "*according to nature*" (κατὰ φύσιν), "*contrary to nature*" (παρὰ φύσιν) and "*above nature*" (ὑπὲρ φύσιν). It is worth to be noted that the κατὰ φύσιν ("according to nature") refers to the *logos*, whereas the other two refer to modes that are either contrary to or above nature. In other words, the κατὰ φύσιν does not refer to nature in itself and to its static character, but to its logical dynamism towards its Christological and eschatological goal.[15] However, the reception of the created nature and its integration in the hypostasis of the *Logos* of God transcends the *logoi* of nature, since it is "*above nature*" (ὑπὲρ φύσιν). There is no *logos* of nature for the divinization and the union with the *Logos*.[16] This union is hypostatical and at the same time supernatural. There is of course a certain thirst of the nature and of the soul, a drive (ὄρεξις)[17] or urge (ἔφεσις)[18] for immortality and existential fulfillment. But this desire is infinite in both the senses of the word, *i.e.* both without end and indefinite. This incessant thirst can be fulfilled only by a Person, that is by the Person of the *Logos* Who will offer concrete novel modifications to the *logoi* of nature. But in

---

[14] *Amb.Io.* PG 91,1088A, 1196A.

[15] See John D. Zizioulas, *Communion & Otherness: Further Studies in Personhood and the Church* (London and New York: T&T Clark, 2006), 64.

[16] See *Op.Th.Pol.* 1 PG 91,33C.

[17] See, for example, *Op.Th.Pol.* 1 PG 91,12C-D.

[18] See, for example, *QThal.* CCSG 22,53,128-134 (PG 90,608D).

human nature, the παρὰ φύσιν, i.e. man's failure to respond to the *logoi* and his distance from the goal they point to. The term *tropos* is used by Maximus in order to denote two extremes: On the one hand evil, which consists in an irrational cutting off of the way suggested by the *logos*. On the other hand God's grace which is above both nature and the *logoi* pertaining to it. The divine grace responds to a deep thirst of nature, but in ways which are always surprising and paradoxical, and as such beyond the *logoi*.

The extremes of the two modes, that of the irrational and that of the supra-rational, however distant, might meet since God responds to the irrationality of human sin by His grace. The Paulinian notion that "where sin increased, grace increased all the more" (*Romans* 5:20) is not developed by Maximus into a full-blown theory of *felix culpa*. It does nevertheless lead him into a consideration of the divine-human drama in which a supernatural mode comes to find man in whatever mode of sin he has fallen. The *logos* is thus confirmed but through modes which are "more divine and paradoxical."[19] In order to bring an example which shall make this dialectic more comprehensible, the *logos* of human nature is infinite life. After the Fall, this *logos* has received the mode of selfishness (φιλαυτία) and of survival at all costs even at the detriment of others. In Christ, the *logos* of desire for infinite life is confirmed but in another mode, which is the communion through the sacrifice and the resurrection. By His prayer in the agony at Gethsemane,[20] Christ confirms the *logos* of human desire for life, i.e. the will not to die. Nevertheless, this *logos* is modified by an alternative mode, that of a body which is broken in order to be given as life for all.

The mode thus activates the *logos*. The latter does not have an autonomous value but awaits a concrete *tropos* in order to be activated. Inside History this mode is very often a mode of sin which is attached to the *logos* like a parasite. For this reason evil is

---

[19] *Amb.Io.* PG 91,1097C-D.
[20] For the theme of the Agony in Gethsemane in Maximus' thought, see: François-Marie Léthel, *Théologie de l'Agonie du Christ: La Liberté Humaine du Fils de Dieu et Son Importance Sotériologique Mises en Lumière par Saint Maxime le Confesseur* (Paris: Beauchesne, 1979); Demetrios Bathrellos, *The Byzantine Christ*, 140-147.

termed as a "mode of parhypostasis" by Maximus.²¹ Evil does not exist in an autonomous way, but draws its power from the "logical" character of nature, which it undermines as a parasitical mode. But evil does not have the last word inside History. God comes to find man where he had fallen and to reactivate his nature through new modes of supernatural grace. These include miraculous interventions and the transformation of divinization. But they also include the assumption of pain and death. In Maximus Crucifixion is not described in terms of *logos*, since it does not constitute God's primordial will. God is not a sadomasochist; He does not wish the death of His Son or of His adopted sons by grace. It is a will according to dispensation (κατ' οἰκονομίαν),²² that is a will according to mode and not according to *logos*. And it is the paradoxical character of the mode of crucifixion which paves the way for the even greater paradox of the Resurrection, the latter fulfilling nature's craving for immortality, but in a new personal mode.

## The actuality of the ontology of mode for political philosophy

Through the couple of *logos* and *tropos*, Maximus the Confessor articulates an ontology of dialogue which expresses the historical adventure of humanity. We are thus given the opportunity to comprehend a dialogue between God and man, where God proposes His *logoi* to humanity, the human being activates nature in a certain way, and God comes in Christ to find humans in whatever historical mode they are led by the historical adventure of their freedom. This ontology of mode gives the opportunity to articulate not only the dialogue between God and man but also a space, which is transitional and liminal between, on the one hand, the full communion of nature, and, on the other, the absolute otherness of personhood. The mode is a historical modification of

---

²¹ *Op.Th.Pol.* 1 PG 91, 24B.

²² For Maximus the Confessor the divine will is distinguished in will according to εὐδοκία (good will), according to οἰκονομία (dispensation) and according to συγχώρησις (concession). See *Qu. Du.* 83 *CCSG* 10, 66 (*PG* 90,801B).

nature, which is however committed by the human person in dialogue with God's *logoi*. The mode is related to nature, since it consists in a modification of nature in its actualization in the Aristotelian sense of a passage from potency to act. It is nevertheless a modification which bears the stamp of personhood and freedom. However, in comparison to the notion of personhood as an absolute otherness, the concept of mode has a porous character. It thus allows the thematization of common modalities, i.e. common historical modes, as well as an interpenetration (περιχώρησις) of modes, when one person interiorizes the mode of another person in the context of a contingent historical dialectic. This dialectic brings about a meeting of the uncreated *logos* of God with the created *logos* of man. The latter can be closed in its self-referentiality and turn into an idol. But the possible idolatrous character of human *logoi* can be undermined by new modifications which aim at the eschatological end in dialogue with the divine *logos*. The historical drama does continue even if there are ossifications in modes of sin or a certain self-reference of the human *logos*. The reason is that there is always the possibility of new historical modifications, which break the petrification of a sinful historical mode or the closedness of a self-referential *logos*.

What is important about the Maximian theory of *tropos* is that it helps us avoid two extremes in our postmodern age: The one extreme is abstract universalism, where we have a common humanity without historical modifications. And the other extreme is a total fragmentation of the social body either with a retirement into the sphere of the private or with a strengthening of particularistic communities which indulge into their proper parallel monologues. These phenomena of fragmentation and particularism could receive the Maximian name of "gnomic will" in the sense that in Maximus the "gnome" constitutes a rupture in the catholicity of nature.[23] In our post-modern age these two extremes, namely the abstract universalism and the fragmentation of particularism often feed and reinforce each other. For this reason it is crucial to articulate an intermediary space of

---

[23] See *Epistola 2* PG 91,400C.

communion, for which I think that a new interpretation of the Maximian notion of the historical mode could prove crucial. The historical drama between *logos* and *tropos*, as developed by Maximus the Confessor, could thus be actualized in the direction of a post-modern political philosophy. I will give an important example drawn from the theory of gender.

## The theory of gender in Maximus the Confessor

Maximus the Confessor has a very peculiar view on genders and sexuality.[24] It could be summed up in the position that both the sexual reproduction and the genders do not belong to the *logos* of human nature. This position is repeated in many passages.[25] It is of course to be noted that the issue of genders is not the same as that

---

[24] For an analysis of Maximus the Confessor's view on issues of sexuality and gender, see: Damien Casey, "Maximus and Irigaray: Metaphysics and Difference", in *Prayer and Spirituality in the Early Church* 4, *Liturgy and Life*, eds. Wendy Mayer, Pauline Allen and Lawrence Cross, (Sydney: St Paul's Publications, 2006), 189-198; Cameron Partridge, *Transfiguring Sexual Difference in Maximus the Confessor*, PhD Thesis, Harvard University, 2008; Verna Harrison, "Women in the *Philokalia*?", in *The Philocalia: A Classic Text of Orthodox Spirituality*, eds. Brock Bingaman and Bradley Nassif (Oxford and New York: Oxford University Press, 2012), 252-261; Doru Costache, "Living above Gender: Insights from Saint Maximus the Confessor", *Journal of Early Christian Studies* 21/2 (2013), 261-290; Kostake Milkov, "Maximus and the healing of the sexual division of creation", in *Knowing the purpose of creation through the resurrection. Proceedings of the Symposium on St Maximus the Confessor. Belgrade, October 18-21, 2012*, ed. Maxim Vasiljević (Alhambra, California and Belgrade: Sebastian Press, 2013), 427-436.

[25] See *Amb.Io*. PG 91, 1305C: "τὴν μηδαμῶς ἠρτημένην δηλαδὴ κατὰ τὸν προηγούμενον λόγον τῆς περὶ τὴν γένεσιν τοῦ ἀνθρώπου θείας προθέσεως κατὰ τὸ θῆλυ καὶ τὸ ἄρσεν ἰδιότητα." Later in 1316A-1321B, he considers sexual reproduction as something exterior to the *logos* of nature through the use of expressions like "ἐπίρρυτος τῆς σπορᾶς τρόπος" and "ἐπείσακτος γέννησις," which are opposed to the *logos* of becoming ("λόγος τῆς γενέσεως"). See also 1341B-C. Besides, in a slightly different context, in *Op.Th.Pol*. PG 91, 240C, sexual reproduction is considered as a mode of birth which is introduced to nature *a posteriori* ("ἐπεισαχθεὶς τῇ φύσει τῆς γεννήσεως τρόπος") in contradistinction to the ineffable *logos* of the birth of Christ ("ἄρρητος τῆς γεννήσεως λόγος"). The same expression ("ἐπεισαχθεὶς τῆς φύσεως τρόπος") also appears in *Op.Th.Pol*. PG 91, 61B.

of sexual reproduction. For the latter Maximus gives a multitude of reasons why he excludes it from the *logos* of humanity:

(i) Maximus thinks that sexual reproduction constitutes a regression to animality. It is important to make a distinction here: Maximus does not think that sexual reproduction is something unnatural which was introduced by man in an original way after the Fall. He rather considers it as something contrary to the *logos* (ἄλογον). In other words, even if the sexual reproduction does have a natural character for animals, man had received the vocation to transcend it.[26] The fact that he did not overcome it meant a regression to the level of the irrational animal as well as a subordination (ὑπαγωγή)[27] to the animal elements which he should have assumed in a direction of self-transcendence.[28]

(ii) Besides, sexual reproduction is linked to "succession,"[29] that is to the substitution of hypostases by other hypostases. But this entails a certain vicious circle where man strives in vain to overcome death through the sexual reproduction which only perpetuates mortality.[30]

(iii) In a similar way, there is a vicious circle between pleasure and pain (ἡδονή–ὀδύνη, see *QThal.* 21[31] and 61[32]). The two vicious circles are usually linked in that pleasure precedes birth and is thus considered as constitutive of man's fallen condition. Pleasure means a demand for absolute existential independence of which pain seems to be the inherent limit. The vicious circle consists in man's vain effort to avoid pain through greater pleasure, not realizing that as a matter of fact pain is the interior limit of pleasure. In this fallen way, man perpetuates pain through

---

[26] In *Amb.Io. PG* 91,1320D, man's mode of birth (γέννησις) is "post-lapsarian" and it is compared even to the mode of reproduction of plants, for example to herbs which are reproduced by seed.

[27] This is a frequent Maximian term, see, for example, *Amb.Io. PG* 91,1305D.

[28] See *Amb.Io. PG* 91,1276B: "ἡ ἁμαρτία διὰ τῆς παρακοῆς τὴν αὐτὴν τοῖς ἀλόγοις ζώοις τοὺς ἀνθρώπους ἔχειν τῆς ἐξ ἀλλήλων διαδοχῆς ἰδιότητα κατεδίκασε."

[29] *Amb.Io. PG* 91, 1276B.

[30] See John D. Zizioulas, *Being as Communion: Studies in Personhood and the Church* (London: Darton, Longman and Todd, 1985), 50-53.

[31] *Q.Thal., CCSG* 7,127-133 *PG* 90,312B-316D.

[32] *Q.Thal., CCSG* 22,85-91,108 *PG* 90,628A-632A.

pleasure in the same way that he perpetuates death through sexual reproduction (γέννησις).

A further question that arises is whether genders in themselves are also not part of the *logos* of humanity. This question is not redundant, since one could arguably conceive of a distinction between on the one hand the genders which are part of human *logos*, and, on the other, the actual sexual reproduction which is not a part of this *logos*. However, Maximus the Confessor is quite explicit that the genders as well, namely the male and the female (ἄρρεν, θῆλυ) are not part of the *logos*, since they constitute a division. This is mainly observed in a schema of five divisions which are eventually overcome by Christ, whereas Adam had previously failed to achieve this transcendence. The five divisions are in descending order (i) the one between the uncreated and the created, (ii) the intelligible and the sensible realm, (iii) heaven and earth, (iv) Paradise and the inhabited part of the earth, and (v) male and female. In the ascending order of man who is called to transcend these divisions the order would of course be the inverse. In this schema the division of genders is presented as the opposite of the *logos*. Whereas the *logos* unites the divided realities and refers them to a wider catholicity, the distinction between the genders is considered as a division in the heart of human existence. It is that contrary to the *logos* in the sense that it constitutes a division against the unitary movement that the *logos* inaugurates. Of course, it is to be noted that certain of the divisions of the fivefold schema, like the one between the intelligible and the sensible realm, or, even more, between the created and the uncreated, constitute natural distinctions which are saved in Christ according to the Chalcedonian dogma. In a similar way, it would be possible to conceive of the genders surviving as mere distinctions, in spite of the overcoming of their divisive character in Christ. Nevertheless, Maximus states emphatically that it is the difference of genders in itself which is in no way founded ("μηδαμῶς ἠρτημένη"[33]) on the *logos* of nature. Man is thus called to *"shake it*

---

[33] *Amb.Io.* PG 91, 1305C.

*off"* of his nature as a mode of division (τρόπος τῆς διαιρέσεως[34]). In the whole passage *Amb.Io.* PG 91,1304D-1312A Maximus is very resolute in his affirmation that the distinction of the genders is not a *logos*, but a *tropos*, rather in the sense of a historical mode of "parhypostasis," i.e. of a mode which claims a parasitical sort of existence drawing its vitality from the *logos*.

The thematization of the difference between the two genders in terms of *logos* and *tropos* becomes explicit in *Amb.Io.* PG 91,1309A, where Maximus writes that Christ becomes a perfect man without being in need of the sequence of sexual reproduction, thus showing that there could be another mode of multiplication of human beings, had there been no Fall.[35] The *logos* as a divine will thus refers to the multiplicity of the human hypostases and their increase, whereas the sexual reproduction is only a particular mode in view of that goal, *i.e.* a mode which is due to the bad use of man's natural capacities. And since these modes are contingent, Maximus envisages other possible modes for the multiplication of human hypostases, if the Fall had not taken place. This mode is termed *"divine and spiritual growth into a multitude"* ("θεία καὶ πνευματικὴ εἰς πλῆθος αὔξησις").[36] According to a common Maximian methodology, we can understand what Adam failed to do by comparing it with what Christ had eventually achieved. And what Christ does is, in a Maximian idiom, to save the *logos* of nature but through another mode. The *logos* is the genesis, *i.e.* the coming into existence of the psycho-corporeal ensemble;[37] the new Christological mode is a mode which assumes certain aspects of

---

[34] *Amb.Io.* PG 91,1309D-1312A.
[35] *Amb.Io.* PG 91,1309A: "γίνεται τέλειος ἄνθρωπος [...] τῆς κατὰ φύσιν ἀκολουθίας γαμικῆς οὐδόλως εἰς τοῦτο προσδεηθείς, ὁμοῦ τε καὶ κατὰ τὸ αὐτὸ δεικνύς, ὡς οἶμαι, τυχὸν ὡς ἦν καὶ ἄλλος τρόπος τῆς εἰς πλῆθος τῶν ἀνθρώπων αὐξήσεως προεγνωσμένος Θεῷ, εἰ τὴν ἐντολὴν ὁ πρῶτος ἐφύλαξεν ἄνθρωπος καὶ πρὸς κτηνωδίαν ἑαυτὸν τῷ κατὰ παράχρησιν τρόπῳ τῶν οἰκείων δυνάμεων μὴ κατέβαλε, καὶ τὴν κατὰ τὸ ἄρρεν καὶ θῆλυ διαφοράν τε καὶ διαίρεσιν τῆς φύσεως ἐξωθούμενος, ἧς πρὸς τὸ γενέσθαι, καθάπερ ἔφην, ἄνθρωπος, οὐδόλως προσεδεήθη, ὧν δὲ ἄνευ εἶναι τυχόν ἐστι δυνατόν. Ταῦτα εἰς τὸ διηνεκὲς παραμεῖναι οὐκ ἀνάγκη. Ἐν γὰρ Χριστῷ Ἰησοῦ, φησὶν ὁ θεῖος Ἀπόστολος, οὔτε ἄρρεν οὔτε θῆλυ (Gal. 3:28)."
[36] *Amb.Io.* PG 91,1341C.
[37] The whole problematic is developed in *Amb.Io.* PG 91,1316-1349.

Adam's fallen mode of reproduction, namely the gestation and the parturition, but does not include others like the pleasure and the corruption. According to the Maximian schema, Christ has assumed the "γέννησις," *i.e.* birth through labor, in order to save the "γένεσις" (1317B), *i.e.* the coming into being of a unitary and coherent psycho-corporeal being. This schema is a parallel of the corresponding schema that Christ had assumed the pain and the death of the Cross, in order to save life. We could arguably understand Maximus' rationale if we changed the phrase of the Orthodox troparion of the Resurrection "trampling death by death" into "trampling birth by birth." In other words, Christ received elements of the fallen mode of reproduction, such as the gestation and the parturition, but only in order to remove from the inside its sinful character residing in the vicious circle between pleasure and pain as well as between birth and death (1317B).

In 1317D-1320B, Maximus proceeds to a more cataphatic theology of mode by distinguishing between the "previous *logos* of the genesis of man" and the "*tropos* of birth" of Christ "*according to pedagogical dispensation because of sin*." The genesis refers to the initial plan of God's good will for the Incarnation of the Logos through the reception of the psycho-corporeal ensemble. As such it constitutes a *logos* of the good will of God. The gennesis (γέννησις, with double "n") refers to the mode of dispensation (τρόπος τῆς οἰκονομίας), that is to a modification of the divine plan due to the Fall, by which God did not abandon man but found a new pedagogical mode (τρόπος παιδαγωγίας), teaching him how to utilize pain and death. This pedagogical mode comprises on the one hand the pain and the death of the Cross, and, on the other, birth[38] through the gestation and parturition of Virgin Mary. The latter are the results of the divine-human dialogue, in which God did not assume sin, but certain results of the sin, in order to save man from the interior of his condition.

To recapitulate, one can distinguish between four dimensions: (i) The *logos* of the genesis (λόγος γενέσεως), which refers to the simultaneous coming of the soul and the body into being. (ii) This

---

[38] See *Amb.Io. PG* 91,1320D-1321A.

*logos* might receive different modes, like in the examples of Adam, Eve and Seth, which are inspired by the Bible. When Maximus speaks about genesis after the Fall, he is rather referring to the "conception" which in the fallen man is linked to pleasure, whereas in the case of Christ it denotes a new and paradoxical mode of conception without corruption. (iii) The gennesis (with a double "n") comprises gestation and parturition and could be considered as a mode of the genesis. (iv) But the genesis itself can receive different modes. In Christ there is a new mode of genesis without corruption.

The comprehension of these complex relations can help us raise some apparent contradictions of the Maximian text, such as between *Amb.Io.* 1340B-C and 1341C. In the first, Maximus criticizes harshly those who depreciate "marriage" (the term "gamos" can signify both the marital institution and sexual intercourse), considering them as blasphemous against God. But later on (1341C) he repeats his firm conviction that sexual reproduction is not primordial. Maximus seems to imply that the fact that sexual intercourse and hence the institution of marriage are introduced *a posteriori* should not lead us into a depreciation of "genesis," i.e. of the simultaneous coming into being of the human soul and body. Such a depreciation would entail a blasphemous moralism that would smack of Manicheism. According to the general Maximian schema, the mode, *i.e.* the "gamos" (=marriage, sexual intercourse) and the "gennesis" (birth) do not annul the *logos*, *i.e.* the "genesis" (=the coming into being of the psycho-corporeal ensemble). Besides, Maximus' general stance consists in considering sexual reproduction as a historical mode. The latter does not however entail a depreciation of sexual intercourse since it is also a "νόμος γενέσεως," that is a law or, more likely, a habit according to which the hypostases are multiplied inside History. The latter is also considered as an institution promulgated by God even if it is more a *"will according to dispensation"* (θέλημα κατ' οἰκονομίαν) and not an initial good will (θέλημα κατ' εὐδοκίαν).

In the thought of Maximus the Confessor both the genders and the actual sexual reproduction constitute a mode. The Virgin birth of Christ liberates man from the mode of division[39] and elevates him in the unity of his *logos* according to the Paulinian diction: *"there is neither male nor female, for you are all one in Christ Jesus"* (Gal. 3:28). This is the first stage in the series of divisions which include the ones between paradise and the inhabited world, heaven and earth, the intelligible and the sensible realm, and, finally, the created and the uncreated. The dogmatic issue of the virgin birth of Christ must be examined in the context of the transcendence of every division, including egoism (φιλαυτία) and death, in order to manifest the unity of the *logos*. This ontological achievement is transmitted to the faithful through baptism. Baptism is for the faithful the equal of the Virgin birth for Christ, that is a new mode of birth. The characteristics of this new mode of birth are developed in *Amb.Io. PG* 91,1345C-1349A and in *QThal.* 61.[40] Baptism is defined as a "birth in a spiritual adoption,"[41] which is undergone by Christ before its transmission to the faithful. This new birth annuls the corporeal birth ("εἰς ἀθέτησιν τῆς ἐκ σωμάτων γεννήσεως").[42] There is thus a radical opposition between the new birth of baptism and the biological one, as we also witness in *QThal.* 61,[43] where Maximus makes a contrast between, on the one hand, the new birth and the mystical adoption of the New Adam, and, on the other, the law of becoming introduced by the old Adam.[44] Maximus remarks that the baptism utilizes death as it was assumed by Christ in the sense of a mortification of sin. Baptism turns thus against the previous mode of birth in order to annul its sinful character. This dialectic between History and the eschaton is fundamental for comprehending the distinction between the *logos* and the *tropos*. One could arguably say that eschatology is the criterion for distinguishing *logos* from *tropos*. Whatever survives in eschatology belongs to the *logos* of humanity. Whatever does not survive, as is the case with sexual reproduction and the genders, in

---

[39] *Amb.Io. PG* 91,1309D-1312A.
[40] *CCSG* 22, 97,216-99,260; *PG* 90,636B-637A.
[41] *Amb.Io. PG* 91, 1348B.
[42] *Amb.Io. PG* 91, 1348B.
[43] *CCSG* 22,97,216-99,244; *PG* 90,636B-D.
[44] See John D. Zizioulas, *Being as Communion*, 53-59.

one of their senses, is a mode relative to man's historical itinerary. In eschatology there is also a mode which modifies human nature, but this is the supernatural mode of the new birth of Christ.

## Maximus the Confessor's theory of gender in the context of a post-modern political philosophy

What would be the contemporary significance of a theory of gender based on the intuitions of Maximus the Confessor? We can sum up three points.

(i) The fact that the genders do not belong to the *logos* of humanity entails a rejection of heteronormativity. There is not one single anthropological norm which would include the dyad of the genders, namely the male and the female. This paves the way for an *apophaticism of gender and of the unchartered human body*.

(ii) However, the ontology of mode means that even though the gender is not regarded as a part of the *logos* of humanity, it could be considered as a *historical* mode. The fact that for Maximus gender is not a part of the *logos* means that it is a historical mode. As such it could be a mode of division and thus of sin. But it can also be a mode which bears the stamp of the person. In general, the fact that an element belongs to the *tropos* and not to the *logos* does not necessarily mean that it does not survive in the eschaton. There are modes which do not belong to the *logos* and yet they survive in eschatology, such as the stigmata of the martyrs. The cross, the martyrdom, the assumption of pain do not belong to the *logos*, that is to God's good will, but they do belong to the divine economy, that is to the soteriological utilization of the results of sin. In this sense, the fact that the gender may not belong to the primordial *logos* does not necessarily mean that it is totally indifferent and to be rejected. It can be significant if it is assumed inside History in a personal way and if it becomes part of a soteriological narrative. In this case, one could conceive of a survival of gender, even though one should be very apophatic in this regard and not impose our own preconceptions on God. In any case, Maximus seems to conceive of a spiritual notion of gender, when he links the genders to different parts of the soul.⁴⁵ The allegorical and spiritual value of the genders points to a direction of an ontological valorization of them as modes.

(iii) When we speak of mode in Maximus the Confessor, we do not mean a Post-modern constructionism, but rather a historical work on nature and its transformation in view of the eschatological future. This work on the gender might happen in the context of a dialectic, where the human historical mode might respond to a divine *logos* or to a human created one. In the second case, we might have an undermining of an idolatrous dominant created *logos* through a mode that is oriented to the future. Gender as a historical mode survives only as a part of a personal narrative. Hagiology is full of such examples, where a historical mode of gender acquires significance for the personal evolution of a saint. What is important is that the ontology of mode gives us the possibility to avoid both an abstract universalism and a fragmentation in our anthropology. It also evades the dominant normativity which is used in order to avoid such fragmentation. The ontology of mode offers the possibility to conceive of an intermediary space, which is neither the universalistic human nature in its abstractness nor a divisive otherness. Without the ontology of mode, there would be the following options: Either the gender would be suppressed from anthropology as something indifferent. But this would alienate us from an important part of our experience. Or it would be conceived as a divisive factor. But the transcendence of the division of genders would then happen in the way of a dominant normativity, as is the case with heteropatriarchy. On the contrary, the notion of *tropos* means a liminal condition through which both the catholicity of humanity and its particularities are saved.

By these, I have tried to show one of the cases where there can be a fertile application of the ontology of mode in political

---

[45] The male gender is linked to the intellect, whereas the female one to sensation in *QThal. CCSG* 7,161,34-167,159 (*PG* 90,332A-336C). The male gender (παῖς) is linked to the irascible part of the soul, while the female one (παιδίσκη) to desire in *QThal. CCSG* 7,499,302-501,334 (*PG* 90,548C-549B).

philosophy, broadly conceived. It could be argued that this ontology can be utilized in every domain and subject, where there is a need of an intermediary between full universalism and absolute otherness.

## Bibliography

Primary Sources

Maximus the Confessor. Ambigua ad Iohannem [Amb.Io.]. Edited by François Combefis. Patrologia Graeca 91:1061–1424.

———.Opuscula theologica et polemica [Op.Th.Pol.]. Edited by François Combefis. Patrologia Graeca 91:9–286.

———. Epistolae. Edited by François Combefis.
    Patrologia Graeca 91:363-650.

———. Quaestiones ad Thalassium [Q.Thal.]. Edited by Carl Laga and Carlos Steel. CCSG 7:3–539; 22:3–325.

———. Quaestiones et Dubia [Qu.Du.]. Edited by José Declerck. CCSG 10: 3-171.

Secondary Literature

Bathrellos, Demetrios. The Byzantine Christ: Person, Nature and Will in the Christology of Saint Maximus the Confessor. Oxford: Oxford University Press, 2004.

Berthold, George Charles. "The Cappadocian Roots of Maximus the Confessor." In Maximus Confessor. Actes du Symposium sur Maxime le Confesseur. Fribourg, 2-5 septembre 1980, (Paradosis 27), eds Felix Heinzer and Christoph Schönborn, 51–59. Fribourg: Éditions Universitaires Fribourg Suisse, 1982.

Casey, Damien. "Maximus and Irigaray: Metaphysics and Difference." In Prayer and Spirituality in the Early Church 4, Liturgy and Life, eds. Wendy Mayer, Pauline Allen and Lawrence Cross, 189–98. Sydney: St Paul's Publications, 2006.

Costache, Doru. "Living above Gender: Insights from Saint Maximus the Confessor." Journal of Early Christian Studies 21/2 (2013), 261-290.

Harrison, Verna. "Women in the Philokalia?" In The Philocalia. A Classic Text of Orthodox Spirituality, eds. Brock Bingaman and Bradley Nassif, 252–261. Oxford and New York: Oxford University Press, 2012.

Kaegi, Walter E. "Byzantium in the Seventh Century." In The Oxford Handbook of Maximus the Confessor, eds. Pauline Allen and Neil Bronwen, 84–105. Oxford: Oxford University Press, 2015.

Larchet, Jean-Claude. "Introduction" in Saint Maxime le Confesseur: Ambigua, trans. Emmanuel Ponsoye, 9–84. Paris: Ancre, 1994.

———. La Divinisation de l'Homme selon Saint Maxime le Confesseur. Paris: Cerf, 1996.

Léthel, François-Marie. Théologie de l'Agonie du Christ: La Liberté Humaine du Fils de Dieu et Son Importance Sotériologique Mises en Lumière par Saint Maxime le Confesseur. Paris: Beauchesne, 1979.

Loudovikos, Nikolaos. Ἡ Εὐχαριστιακὴ Ὀντολογία: Τὰ Εὐχαριστιακὰ Θεμέλια τοῦ Εἶναι ὡς ἐν Κοινωνίᾳ Γίγνεσθαι στὴν Ἐσχατολογικὴ Ὀντολογία τοῦ Ἁγίου Μαξίμου τοῦ Ὁμολογητῆ. Athens: Domos, 1992.

———. Ψυχανάλυση καὶ Ὀρθόδοξη Θεολογία: Περὶ Ἐπιθυμίας, Καθολικότητας καὶ Ἐσχατολογίας. Athens: Armos, 2003.

Milkov, Kostake. "Maximus and the healing of the sexual division of creation." In Knowing the purpose of creation through the resurrection. Proceedings of the Symposium on St Maximus the Confessor. Belgrade, October 18-21, 2012, ed. Maxim Vasiljević, 427–436. Alhambra, California and Belgrade: Sebastian Press, 2013.

Partridge, Cameron. "Transfiguring Sexual Difference in Maximus the Confessor." PhD diss., Harvard University, 2008.

Sherwood, Polycarp. The Earlier Ambigua of Saint Maximus the Confessor and his Refutation of Origenism. Rome: Pontificium Institutum S. Anselmi "Orbis Catholicus", 1955.

Zizioulas, John D. Being as Communion: Studies in Personhood and the Church. London: Darton, Longman and Todd, 1985.

———. Communion & Otherness: Further Studies in Personhood and the Church. London and New York: T&T Clark, 2006.

Chapter 3

# The communo-centric political theology of Christos Yannaras in conversation with Oliver O'Donovan

Jonathan Cole

## Introduction

Christos Yannaras (b. Athens, 1935) is one of the Orthodox world's most important intellectuals.[1] He has written over 50 books in philosophy, theology, and politics, and has been a regular and high profile political commentator in the Greek media (television, radio, and print) since the 1970s. Yet, in spite of this remarkable output and his influential voice in Greek political discourse, Yannaras' work is still not particularly well known in the West.[2] This may, to some extent, be attributable to the fact that only eleven of his books have been translated into English, and most of those only recently.[3] The acerbic critique of Western Christianity and

---

[1] For an introduction to Yannaras, see Norman Russell, "The Enduring Significance of Christos Yannaras: Some Further Works in Translation," *International Journal for the Study of the Christian Church* 16, no.1 (2016); Norman Russell, "Christos Yannaras," in S. J. Kristiansen and S. Rise, eds., *Key Theological Thinkers: From Modern to Postmodern* (Surrey: Ashgate, 2013); and Andrew Louth, "Some Recent Works by Christos Yannaras in English Translation," *Modern Theology*, 25, no.2 (2009).

[2] Russell notes that *"serious philosophers in Western Europe and North America have begun to take notice of him and to respond to him."* Russell, "The Enduring Significance of Christos Yannaras," 59.

[3] Sotiris Mitralexis notes that some of Yannaras' most important works are yet to be translated into English. Sotiris Mitralexis, "Person, Eros, Critical Ontology: An Attempt to Recapitulate Christos Yannaras' Philosophy," *Sobornost* 34, no.1 (2012), 33–34.

civilization that runs through many of his books might also have attenuated his appeal in the West.[4]

Nevertheless, there is no gainsaying his significance, particularly within the realm of political discourse in Greece.[5] Yannaras' indomitably independent (he is a lay theologian and not tied to any political party) and critical analysis of Greek culture, history, religion, and politics, which often contravenes conventional wisdoms and cherished ideals, makes him a highly original and unique thinker among Greek intellectuals. These qualities carry through into his theology and philosophy, which, in spite of the influence of a firm Orthodox ecclesial commitment and a "neo-patristic" theological foundation, can be highly original and even adventurous.

This essay will provide an exposition of Yannaras' political theology. It will then bring Yannaras into critical dialog with one of the leading Protestant political theologians, Oliver O'Donovan (b. London, 1945). This will be done to help advance a critical engagement with Yannaras' political theology, and also to demonstrate why Yannaras could be an invaluable dialog partner for Western (Protestant and Catholic) political theologians, who have historically dominated English literature in the field.

## Theophilosophical Foundations

It is difficult to categorize Yannaras' thought.[6] His work proceeds as if there were little distinction in practice between theology and philosophy, and even political theory. In that sense he transcends what can still be in the West rather rigid conventional boundaries between disciplines. Norman Russell aptly describes Yannaras'

---

[4] Russell, "The Enduring Significance of Christos Yannaras," 59. It is important to recognize that Yannaras is also critical of the Eastern Orthodox Church, and his newspaper columns in particular can contain scathing, even inflammatory, criticism of the Greek Orthodox Church to which he belongs.

[5] Mitralexis notes that while Yannaras is best known in the West for his philosophical and theological contributions, he is best known in Greece for his political commentary. Mitralexis, "Person, Eros, Critical Ontology," 33.

[6] Russell, "The Enduring Significance of Christos Yannaras," 59.

method as *"theological philosophy,"*[7] which we have rendered in adjectival form as "theophilosphical." Yannaras' main interest is ontology. However, since reality has its source in the Trinitarian God of the Christian church, ontological inquiries necessarily involve discussion about God, i.e., theology. So Yannaras' philosophical inquires often stray deep into the traditional territory of theology, and often involve discussion of the church and even exegetical analysis of Scripture.

There is an unusual (by modern standards) unity to Yannaras' voluminous work. A consistent conceptual framework guides his inquiries into ontological, epistemological, theological, ecclesiological, and political questions. As a consequence, it is difficult to examine one particular aspect of his thought, such as politics, without some prior understanding of this conceptual framework.

Yannaras has produced a detailed discussion of the concepts that govern his thought in the untranslated work *Six Philosophical Pictures*.[8] The preface to the second edition, provides a very useful short summary of the framework, which we will use as the basis for an overview below.[9] Our overview will be augmented by reference to other works where clarification is necessary or helpful.[10]

*Apophaticism*

The self-declared starting-point for Yannaras' conceptual framework is *"apophaticism."*[11] Yannaras defines apophaticism as

---

[7] Ibid.

[8] Christos Yannaras, Ἔξι φιλοσοφικὲς ζωγραφιές: Σύνοψη εἰσαγωγικὴ καὶ πάντως αὐτεξεταστικὴ (Athens: Ikaros, 2011). Mitralexis has aptly described this book as a *"philosophical autobiography."* Mitralexis, "Person, Eros, Critical Ontology," 34.

[9] Christos Yannaras, Ἔξι φιλοσοφικὲς ζωγραφιές, 3–11. The overview of Yannaras' conceptual framework is taken from this preface. Yannaras does not use the word *"framework"* to describe the conceptual scheme he outlines in the preface. However, he indicates that the concepts are presented in their logical and developmental order, and it is on this basis that we have characterized it as a framework.

[10] For a more detailed discussion of these concepts, see Mitralexis, "Person, Eros, Critical Ontology."

[11] Christos Yannaras, Ἔξι φιλοσοφικὲς ζωγραφιές, 3.

*"the refusal to exhaust knowledge in its articulation."*[12] Apophaticism expresses the idea that while concepts can convey reliable *"knowledge"* (gnosis) about reality, they cannot exhaust the reality that they signify. In apophaticism Yannaras sees something of a *via media* between the pitfalls of *"relativism"* and *"agnosticism"* on the one hand, and *"ideology"* and *"dogmatism"* on the other.[13] Although Yannaras does not mention it in the booklet, apophaticism also characterizes his biblical hermeneutic. Scripture is the apophatic testimony to the real historical encounter of the creator with humankind, firstly with Israel, and subsequently with the church.

### Communal epistemology

The second concept is the *"communal verification"* of knowledge, which we will call *"communal epistemology."*[14] Knowledge, according to Yannaras, begins with subjective experience of reality. However, this subjective experience can only be translated into *"truth"* when it is verified by the communal experience, through a process of critical dialectic.[15] To return very briefly to Yannaras' hermeneutics, Scripture provides the *"communally verified"* testimony of Israel and the church's encounter and relationship with God. The *"communal verification"* is the source of its authority, its *"truth."*

### Relational ontology

The third concept is *"relational ontology."* At the core of Yannaras' communal epistemology is the notion that knowledge is relational. The human subjective experience of reality that is the foundation of truth comes as a product of human beings' direct participation

---

[12] Ibid. Another formula Yannaras uses to define apophaticism is *"the refusal to conflate understanding of signifiers with knowledge of the signified."*

[13] Ibid.; Christos Yannaras, Ὀρθὸς λόγος καὶ κοινωνικὴ πρακτική (Athens: Domos, 1984), 277.

[14] Yannaras, Ἕξι φιλοσοφικὲς ζωγραφιές, 4. Mitralexis also uses this term to describe Yannaras' epistemology along with *"apophatic epistemology."* Mitralexis, "Person, Eros, Critical Ontology," 36.

[15] Ibid., 4.

in reality.¹⁶ It is through our relationships with other humans, animals, objects, and ultimately with God that we can begin to build a reliable, if not exhaustive, picture of reality. Reality is fundamentally a constellation of complex and dynamic relationships, rather than a static object which humans investigate externally.

## Person(hood)

"*Person*" or "*personhood*"[17] expresses Yannaras' anthropology. "*Person*" describes the "*unique, dissimilar, and unrepeatable otherness*" of every human.[18] But the heterogeneous consciousness or subject is not an "*individual*" in the sense of an autonomous, self-determining entity. Rather, the human person is "*referential*" and "*relational.*"[19] Yannaras explains the "*referential*" aspect of personhood by drawing attention to the etymological root of the Greek word for "*person*" (prosopon). Prosopon is a combination of the preposition *pros* (towards) and the noun *ops* (eye).[20] The word thus originally conveyed the sense of "*I have my face turned towards someone or something; I am opposite someone or something.*"[21] This ties the identity of the heterogeneous human subject to other human subjects and objects. The key idea is that the "*absolute existential otherness*" of each human can only emerge, take on meaning, and ultimately develop in relationship with other persons.[22]

Personhood expresses humankind's *imago Dei*, according to Yannaras. As Yannaras explains: "*The testimony of the ecclesial experience points to a personal first cause of creation...and to the parousia*

---

[16] Ibid., 5.
[17] There is no Greek work for "*personhood*." The term Yannaras uses is simply "*person*" (prosopo). However, in some contexts the English term "*personhood*" seems to better capture the connotations of the Greek term prosopo(n) as used by Yannaras.
[18] Yannaras, Ὀρθὸς λόγος καὶ κοινωνικὴ πρακτική, 283.
[19] Christos Yannaras, *Person and Eros*, trans. Norman Russell (Brookline: Holy Cross Orthodox Press, 2007), 5.
[20] Ibid.
[21] Ibid.
[22] Christos Yannaras, Ἡ ἀπανθρωπία τοῦ δικαιώματος (Athens: Domos, 1998), 201.

*of a particular historical person, Jesus of Nazareth, whose freedom from the existential constraints of human nature...reveal the freedom of God...the freedom of love which is identified with a mode of existence and which makes his incarnation possible, without alteration or change to his being."*[23] Personhood thus provides the ontological grounds for a relationship (*theosis*) with God.

*The Trinity*

This brings us to the Trinity. Yannaras identifies *"love"* as the ultimate cause of existence.[24] But love is not a quality, attribute, or behavior or God.[25] Rather, it describes the very *"mode of existence"* of God: the *"loving existential community of three persons."*[26] He interprets the statement in 1 John 4:16 that *"God is love"* ontologically, i.e., God's *"own Being is love."*[27] The loving community of the Trinity is constituted by free will rather than any necessity.[28] Human personhood, and therefore human community, finds its origin in the Trinity.

This is admittedly little more than a schematic overview of Yannaras' conceptual framework. The concepts surveyed receive far more elaborate and nuanced treatment in book-length studies. However, the overview does provide a useful and necessary

---

[23] Yannaras, Ἔξι φιλοσοφικὲς ζωγραφιές, 8.
[24] Ibid.
[25] Ibid.
[26] Ibid.
[27] Yannaras, *Elements of Faith: An Introduction to Orthodox Theology*, trans. Keith Schram (Edinburgh: T&T Clark, 1991), 59.
[28] Yannaras, Ἔξι φιλοσοφικὲς ζωγραφιές, 8–9.

foundation for a discussion of Yannaras' political theology, to which we now turn.[29]

## Communo-centric politics

None of Yannaras' substantive work in political theology has been translated into English.[30] This may in part explain why comparatively little has been written on it in English, and why Yannaras is a relatively unknown figure in English-language theopolitical discourse.[31] Our exposition of Yannaras' political theology is drawn from two untranslated works, *The Inhumanity of Right*[32] and *Rationality and Social Practice*.[33]

*Individual right*

*The Inhumanity of Right* consists of both a critique of Western liberal political order and a proposal for its redemption.[34] The core

---

[29] Yannaras does not refer to his political thought as a *"political theology"* per se. He describes, for example, *The Inhumanity of Right* as a work in *"political theory."* Yannaras, Ἡ ἀπανθρωπία τοῦ δικαιώματος, 8. However, the book's discussion of the Trinity, the Incarnation, the church, and its biblical exegesis bring it within the scope of *"political theology"* using English categories. Daniel Payne and Aristotle Papanikolaou both describe Yannaras' political thought as a *"political theology."* Daniel P. Payne, *The Revival of Political Hesychasm in Contemporary Orthodox Thought: The Political Hesychasm of John S. Romanides and Christos Yannaras* (Lanham: Lexington Books, 2011), 240. Aristotle Papanikolaou, *The Mystical as Political: Democracy and Non-radical Orthodoxy* (Notre Dame: Notre Dame University Press, 2012), 46.

[30] Two very short essays on political theology by Yannaras are available in English: Christos Yannaras, "A Note on Political Theology," translated from French by Steven Peter Tsichlis, *St Vladimir's Theological Quarterly* 27, no.1 (1983); and Christos Yannaras, "Human Rights and the Orthodox Church," in Emmanuel Clapsis ed., *The Orthodox Churches in a Pluralistic World: An Ecumenical Conversation* (Geneva: WCC Publications, 2004).

[31] For a discussion of Yannaras' political theology in English, see Kristina Stoeckl, "The "We" in Normative Political Philosophical Debates: The Position of Christos Yannaras on Human Rights," in *Orthodox Christianity and Human Rights*, eds. Alfons Brüning and Evert van der Zweerde (Leuven: Peeters, 2012); Payne, *The Revival of Political Hesychasm in Contemporary Orthodox Thought* (Chapter 6); and Papanikolaou, *The Mystical as Political* (Chapter 3).

[32] Christos Yannaras, Ἡ ἀπανθρωπία τοῦ δικαιώματος (Athens: Domos, 1998).

[33] Christos Yannaras, Ὀρθὸς λόγος καὶ κοινωνικὴ πρακτική (Athens: Domos, 1984).

[34] In the context of this critique Greece is regarded by Yannaras as *"Western."*

of Yannaras' critique is that Western liberal political order is founded on the flawed notion of *"individual right,"* and that this has led to widespread *"alienation."*[35] Yannaras defines individual right as the *"authority to demand satisfaction of a particular private or public (collective) interest."*[36] The authority of individual right is vested in a *"system of law,"* which allows each individual to exact his or her private interest.[37] Western liberal political order is therefore little more than a mechanism for managing competing individual interests, and the role of government in this context is merely to balance and manage those interests.[38]

Even collective political action, according to Yannaras, is in reality driven by individual self-interest. Individuals with common interests form political parties, industry associations, lobbies, and unions to advance the interest of their individual members, which are threatened or impinged by the individual interests represented by other organizations.[39]

The fundamental problem with the politics of self-interest (individual rights) is that it is based on the false anthropology of *"individualism."* Individual right, and the legal and political order to which it has given rise, construes *"human existence as a unit of*

---

[35] It is common in the English literature on Yannaras' political thought to translate the title of this book as *The Inhuman Character of Human Rights* and to discuss Yannaras' critique of *"human rights."* However, a literal translation of the title is *The Inhumanity of Right*, and the Greek term for *"human rights"* (anthropina dikaiomata) nowhere occurs in the book. Yannaras discusses *"individual rights"* (atomika dikaiomata) which he often abbreviates simply to *"right"* (dikaioma). His use of the term *"individual right"* can reasonably be construed as including what is connoted by the English term *"human rights."* But it has a wider scope than merely the rights recognized in law. *"Individual right"* also captures the cultural, anthropological, and philosophical ethos of the West, including its conventions and customs.

[36] Yannaras, Ἡ ἀπανθρωπία τοῦ δικαιώματος, p. 15.

[37] Ibid. The Greek term translated *"system of law"* here is *dikaio* and its semantic field includes what might be more appropriately termed *"conventions"* or *"customs"* in English. Yannaras clarifies, for example, that by *dikaio* he means both *"written"* and *"unwritten"* laws.

[38] Ibid., 28.

[39] Ibid., 232–233.

*interests, a unit of self-determination and self-interest."*[40] This erroneous view of the human makes a travesty of personhood in Yannaras' view. This is what is meant by the provocative title *The Inhumanity of Right*—individual right dehumanizes the human person. Given that the person *relates to* and *references* other persons, creatures, things, and ultimately God, it is deeply connected to and dependent on community, and hence communal interests.

Yannaras thinks the concept and priority of individual right in Western political culture has perverted its understanding of community. This is particularly evident in the concept of the *"social contract,"* which has as its premise the notion of the *"common action of individuals."* [41] Community ends up being defined in terms of *"quantitative size"* and as *"an abstract total of undifferentiated individuals"* instead of a *"community of persons"* i.e., a community of relationships as Yannaras thinks it should.[42]

The legal system required to give authority to individual right is also fundamentally inimical to community, according to Yannaras.[43] The *"unique, dissimilar, and unrepeatable mode of existence"* of the *"person"* gives community an indefinable quality because of the unpredictability and uniqueness inherent in each relationship.[44] This, he thinks, makes it impossible to translate the *"interpersonal relationship"* that is constitutive of community into an objective body of law.[45] However, an objective body of law is precisely what the authorization of private interest requires. Individual right has therefore given rise to the concept of the *"legal person"*: an *"a-personal and undifferentiated unit of a common species."*[46] The problem is that a legal system founded on the concept of individual right is incapable of recognizing and contending with the otherness at the heart of what it means to be a person.

---

[40] Ibid., 16.
[41] Ibid., 21.
[42] Ibid.
[43] Ibid., 15–19.
[44] Ibid., 17.
[45] Ibid.
[46] Ibid., 18.

The absolute priority of individual right in Western political order, culture, and law is harmful to community in other respects too. It severs, for example, the organic bond between the citizen and the community. Governments and institutions function autonomously from the citizens they are supposed to serve. They function rather like individuals, more interested in survival and self-satisfaction than in performing a *"communal function."*[47] In turn, individuals perceive governments, institutions, and even the community writ large, as threats to their self-determination.[48] This is one of the ways that individual right subverts community, by transforming it from the common human struggle of persons in relationship into a competition of private interests.

### Freedom and Alienation

*"Alienation"* is the tragic legacy of the West's adoption of individual right as its governing principle. Alienation is closely connected to the concept of freedom in Yannaras' political theology, so it is best to analyze them together. Yannaras construes freedom as the ability to be one's true, authentic self, i.e., a *"unique, dissimilar, and unrepeatable subjectivity."*[49] As the heterogeneous person can only emerge and flourish in relationship, freedom relates to the ability to *"form relationships."*[50] Once again, this orientates the focus to community.

Individual right, however, produces a conception of freedom that is fundamentally alienating. It construes freedom in terms of *"possession"* and *"disposal"*: the ability of the individual to have authority over the self and the self's activity.[51] This orients the focus of freedom towards the concept of *"choice,"* thus connecting the individual right to *"freedom of choice."*[52]

---

[47] Yannaras, Ὀρθὸς λόγος καὶ κοινωνικὴ πρακτική, 321, 323.
[48] Yannaras, Ἡ ἀπανθρωπία τοῦ δικαιώματος, 45, 52.
[49] Ibid., 283; Yannaras, Ὀρθὸς λόγος καὶ κοινωνικὴ πρακτική, 283.
[50] Yannaras, Ἡ ἀπανθρωπία τοῦ δικαιώματος, 29.
[51] Ibid., 23–24.
[52] Yannaras, Ὀρθὸς λόγος καὶ κοινωνικὴ πρακτική, 279.

Yannaras sees two adverse and somewhat paradoxical consequences of the modern Western conception of freedom founded in individual right. The first is that it inevitably leads to competition, particularly in the economic sphere, as individuals strive to satisfy their personal choices, aspirations, and interests. The second consequence is pervasive central government intervention in an effort to guarantee that all individuals can satisfy their free choices.[53]

Alienation is a *"failed"* relationship, one lacking the *"love"* and *"freedom"* that are constitutive of personhood, community. Examples of alienating relationships include those defined by *"dependence, subjugation, necessity, and...authority."*[54] Individual right does not just alienate persons from other persons and community. It alienates the worker from the creative output of their work, and persons and community from their natural environment.

*Politics as authentic existence*

Yannaras' conception of politics is closely tied to the conceptual framework we summarized above. He conceives politics as the pursuit of *"authentic existence."*[55] As he describes it, politics is *"the organic consequence of the participation of the citizen in the common struggle of a community of relationships."*[56] We recall that the attainment of truth depends on *"communal verification,"* a process dependent on the *"common struggle of a community of relationships."* This makes politics fundamentally about truth.

This conception also brings politics within the scope of theology. In fact, it brings it right into the center. For the *"prototype of truth (the reality of real existence) is the logos of the personal otherness of a creative loving communion of Persons who form the Trinitarian first cause*

---

[53] Ibid., 280.
[54] Ibid., 283, 299.
[55] Literally *"existential authenticity"* (ὑπαρκτικὴ γνησιότητα). This idea has its genesis in the Ancient Greek conception of *"politics"* which Yannaras argues was adopted and *"Christianized"* by the Byzantine Empire. Yannaras, Ἡ ἀπανθρωπία τοῦ δικαιώματς, 49–50.
[56] Ibid., 69.

*of what exists.*"⁵⁷ In other words, what Yannaras sometimes calls *"the Trinitarian prototype"* of human existence is both the origin and telos of politics.

However, humankind rejected communion with God for a life of selfish individualism. The consequence of this fateful rejection is alienation from God, human solidarity, and nature. As Yannaras explains:

> "God offered to the first formed people the possibility of life, of "real life," of incorruptibility and immortality, giving them the world, nourishment, as an event of communion with Him. But the realization of life as communion and relationship is nevertheless a fruit of freedom—there is no necessary or compulsory communion or relationship of love. This means that the life of paradise of those first-formed people included even the possibility of a different use of freedom: the possibility of human existence to be realized, not as an event of communion and relationship with God, but to be realized by itself alone, drawing existential strength from itself, from its created nature alone."⁵⁸

Western liberal political order therefore embodies humankind's original alienation from God (its original sin). It has embedded this alienation in its political and legal structures, perpetuating our alienation from the true telos of political life: authentic (communal) existence in communion with the Trinitarian mold of existence.

### The politics of relationship

The solution that Yannaras proposes for rescuing Western liberal political order from its alienation is a move to a *"communo-centric"* political order.⁵⁹ A *communo-centric* political order is one in which

---

⁵⁷ Ibid., 71–72.
⁵⁸ Christos Yannaras, *Elements of Faith*, 77.
⁵⁹ Yannaras, Ἡ ἀπανθρωπία τοῦ δικαιώματος, 186.

"*relationship*" would take precedence over "*individual right.*" By focusing on relationships Western liberal political order would be able to better promote the flourishing of human personhood, a prerequisite for authentic existence in communion with God. Yannaras does not go into great detail about the full range of institutional arrangements, or reforms to existing arrangements, that a *communo-centric* political order might entail or necessitate. He does, however, provide insight into how he envisages a *communo-centric* politics of relationship might function in specific areas of political life.

In *The Inhumanity of Right*, he gives consideration to what a shift of priority from individual right to relationship might mean for the legal system in Western liberal political order. His main criticism with respect to Western legal systems is that they ignore the otherness that is constitutive of personhood.[60] As a consequence, laws focus on *individual* action and behavior, treating people as "*abstract standardized individuals*" rather than taking into account the context of "*real human relationships.*"[61] In contrast, a legal system that prioritized relationships would "*define and judge interpersonal relationships and not impersonal individual actions.*"[62] This would have as its principal goal distinguishing "*just*" from "*unjust*" relationships, with a view to preventing alienation.[63]

In *Rationality and Social Practice* Yannaras explores the impact a priority on relationships might have on "*ownership*" and "*work.*" Eschewing the simplistic ("*Manichean*") dichotomy of "*bad private ownership*" and "*good common ownership,*" Yannaras recognizes that ownership can either promote relationships or cause alienation, depending on the circumstances.[64] There is, he says, ownership that is the result of personal creative effort and which serves a

---

[60] Ibid., p. 17. Yannaras argues that the contract at the heart of contractarianism is the "*giving up of the ontological otherness of every social participant.*" p. 19.

[61] Ibid., 17. Yannaras' argument is not that behavior is irrelevant or unimportant in the context of law, but rather that behavior is referential and can only be properly judged in the context of the relationships that define it.

[62] Ibid., p. 37, 95.

[63] Ibid., 35.

[64] Yannaras, Ὀρθὸς λόγος καὶ κοινωνικὴ πρακτική, 307–308.

communal function. However, on the other hand, there is ownership that is exploitative and selfishly unproductive.[65] Yannaras suggests that alienation might serve as a *"criterion"* for judging ownership, with the implication that forms of ownership that lead to the alienation of personhood might be outlawed or restricted.[66]

It is important to clarify that Yannaras does not propose that Western liberal political order should abolish or abandon the concept of individual right all together.[67] The point is to transform individual right from an end unto itself into a means to the end of an authentic politics of relationship. Yannaras aspires to a *"political practice which has as its goal the communo-centric version and exercise of individual rights."*[68] He suggests, for example, that *"respect of the rights of the individual could form a positive impulse towards the realization of that equality that is a necessary...condition for making relationships of community a reality."*[69] However, the precise function of individual right in a *communo-centric* political order is not developed in any detail.

### Direct democracy

In *Rationality and Social Practice*, Yannaras argues that *"direct democracy,"* construed as *"the greatest possible participation of citizens in taking responsibility for their common life,"* is the model that best expresses the aspirations of a *communo-centric* politics.[70] Direct democracies are self-governing communities. However, Yannaras acknowledges that a direct democracy would necessitate small communities that *"are not always feasible."*[71] Nevertheless, he suggests this obstacle might be overcome by a network of self-

---

[65] Ibid., 307.
[66] Ibid., 309.
[67] Yannaras, Ἡ ἀπανθρωπία τοῦ δικαιώματος, 186.
[68] Ibid., 9.
[69] Ibid., 186.
[70] Yannaras, Ὀρθὸς λόγος καὶ κοινωνικὴ πρακτική, 285.
[71] Ibid., 286.

governing communities bound together under some form of *"central authority."*[72]

The role Yannaras envisages for such a central authority is *"coordination," "security"* (from external threats), and *"service."*[73] Its sole focus would be facilitating the self-governing communities that that would possess the real executive power. The genesis of Yannaras' proposal about direct democracies is the democratic Greek city-state and the self-governing communities of the Byzantine and Ottoman Empires. In that sense, Payne is correct to characterize Yannaras' proposal as a retrieval rather than an innovation.[74]

Although Yannaras does not provide much detail about how the direct democracies he envisages might be organized and function in practice, he does provide some interesting detail about how he thinks they can be brought into existence. In the first instance, this is through a process he describes as *"the dynamic of revolutionary aspiration."*[75] In fact, the term that recurs throughout the discussion of direct democracies is *"communal dynamic."* This is a difficult concept to grasp, as Yannaras does not define it with any precision.[76] This is because it is a concept that, in some respects, defies precise definition. *"Communal dynamic"* does not refer to a technique, program, or policy.[77] It is an *"organic"* force for change

---

[72] Ibid., 286 & 292. Interestingly, Yannaras does not describe this *"central authority"* as a government, possibly to avoid any connotation of the type of strong central executive governments we see in Western federations such as the United States and Australia, with their large bureaucracies and pervasive powers.

[73] Ibid., 293. Yannaras does not mean *"service"* in the sense of the provision of services, such as Welfare, but rather serving the goal of autonomous communal self-governance.

[74] Payne, *The Revival of Political Hesychasm in Contemporary Orthodox Thought*, 252.

[75] Yannaras, Ὀρθὸς λόγος καὶ κοινωνικὴ πρακτική, 287.

[76] Ibid., 301. Yannaras says that the term *"retains the indeterminacy of the freedom of relationships."*

[77] Ibid., 300.

driven by the *"creative character of catholic community demands."*[78] It is, as Yannaras says, *"a fruit of freedom."*[79]

*"Communal dynamic"* is activated by *"common needs"* which transform into demands.[80] *"Needs"* translated into *"demands"* can in turn prompt *"practice."*[81] *"Communal dynamic"* is thus that natural or organic impetus to communal political action that cannot be controlled or manipulated, but that can only arise organically from genuine communal needs. So the establishment of *communo-centric* political order can only occur when relationships become the common demand of the community, sparking into operation the engine of *"communal dynamic."*

No doubt these proposals will strike some as naïve and short on detail. But it is important to understand the apophatic nature of Yannaras' thought. These proposals are not offered as a political manifesto or ideological dogma. He acknowledges himself at many points that his proposals will sound *"utopian"* and at times he describes them as *"general"* and *"simplistic."*[82] They are offered in a heuristic vein, in the hope that they might spark thought and discussion.[83]

### The church as political role-model

Yannaras' conception of politics as authentic existence (communion with God) and his vision for a *communo-centric* political order founded on a Christian person-centric anthropology has interesting implications for the role of the (Orthodox) church. In effect, it makes the church the political community *par example*.

---

[78] Ibid., 301.
[79] Ibid. Yannaras suggests that the communal demands energized by *"communal dynamic"* can take various forms, such as legislative reforms, passive resistance, strikes, and even revolutionary uprising and *"violent confrontation."*
[80] Ibid.
[81] Ibid.
[82] Ibid., 293, 303.
[83] In the final analysis, a political proposal must be subjected to the test of *"communal verification"* and will only prompt coordinated political action if it becomes a *"truth"* for the community.

To appreciate this implication, it is necessary first to provide some elaboration of Yannaras' ecclesiology.

Yannaras is fond of talking about the church in terms of the *"ecclesial event."*[84] The foundational *"event"* that gave birth to the church is the incarnation of God in the *"historical person"* Jesus Christ.[85] As the focal point for communion with God, the church functions like a living organism. It is not a *"religion"* or *"metaphysical ideology,"* nor an *"institution, "governing hierarchy,"* or *"buildings."*[86] The church is *"a community which paves the way in the struggle of communal life, the realization of the trinitarian model of real existence."*[87] The Eucharist, for Yannaras, is the quintessential expression of human personhood in the image of, and in relationship with, God: *"In the Eucharist meal, the Church realizes an approach to life radically opposed to that of those who were first formed. She takes nourishment not within the framework of the individual demand for life, but in order to realize life as a reference to God and communion with him."*[88]

Given the telos of politics is authentic existence in communion with God, and that this is precisely what the church seeks to achieve in its own internal life, Yannaras appears to make the church the ideal political community, or at least the model *par excellence* of an authentic political practice. It also appears to place an onus on the (Orthodox) church to function in the current context as a catalyst for change, as it is the only repository of the person-centric anthropology and true understanding of ontology and the purpose of politics. This notion of the church as the political community *par example* does not presuppose any institutional involvement in the exercise of political authority, and Yannaras does not advocate for such a thin. The church's role is more social, bearing in mind that Yannaras' expansive conception

---

[84] For a detailed discussion of the church, see Christos Yannaras, *Against Religion: The Alienation of the Ecclesial Event*, trans. Norman Russell (Brookline: Holy Cross Orthodox Press, 2013).

[85] Yannaras, Ἡ ἀπανθρωπία τοῦ δικαιώματος, 114.

[86] Yannaras, *Elements of Faith*, 121–122.

[87] Yannaras, Ἡ ἀπανθρωπία τοῦ δικαιώματος, 114.

[88] Yannaras, *Elements of Faith*, 125.

of politics in many respects collapses the distinction between society and politics in the more restricted sense of things pertaining to governments).

However, in reality the picture is far more complicated. Yannaras believes that the Orthodox Church has been infected by the pathology of individualism with all of its toxic consequences: *"the priority of ideology," "moralism,"* and *"psychological individualism."*[89] It too has therefore become alienated.[90] So how can the alienated Orthodox Church save Western liberal political order from its own alienating political order? This is an unresolved tension in Yannaras' political theology. He does believe that Christianity's person-centric anthropology and its conception of life as authentic existence in communion with God lives on in the Orthodox Church's *"theology," "liturgy,"* and *"monasticism,"* if not in the lives of the majority of its clergy and members.[91] So in theory, at least, it has the resources to once again to lead the common struggle for authentic existence, as Yannaras believes it did during the Byzantine era.[92] But Yannaras does not provide a roadmap to how the Orthodox Church might revive in practice its true life and purpose as the authentic political community *par excellence*.

## Christos Yannaras in Conversation with Oliver O'Donovan: a Critical Ecumenical Dialog

Our exposition of Yannaras' political theology has thus far been descriptive, and it is now time to move to a more critical footing. We will do so by bringing Yannaras into dialog with one of the most highly regarded and influential Protestant political

---

[89] Yannaras, Ἡ ἀπανθρωπία τοῦ δικαιώματος, 138.
[90] The Western churches have been alienated from the true meaning and function of the *"ecclesial event"* since Augustine, according to Yannaras.
[91] Ibid., 125. Yannaras regards the Orthodox monastic community as a *"socio-political example"* of authentic Trinitarian Christian life, though in his own admission, this idea requires a more specialized study for substantiation.
[92] Ibid., 224–225, 251–252. Yannaras cites the institutions of self-management in the areas of production and local governance in Byzantium as evidence.

theologians, Oliver O'Donovan (b. London, 1945).[93] O'Donovan is an Anglian priest and Professor Emeritus, Christian Ethics and Practical Theology at the University of Edinburgh. He and Yannaras have not directly engaged each other's work. In fact, it is interesting to note that Yannaras does not engage any contemporary Protestant or Catholic political theology at all. And while O'Donovan's work displays a deep and sympathetic engagement with Catholic political thought (medieval and contemporary), he does not engage substantively with either contemporary Orthodox political thought or Byzantine political thought. This makes the pair ideal dialog partners.

*Divine rule, political authority, and judgment*

O'Donovan believes the central task of political theology is to expound *"an account of the reign of God."*[94] Indeed, *"divine rule"* functions as the controlling concept in his political theology. He perceives an inextricable connection between *"political history"* and *"the history of divine rule,"* the former falling within the scope of the latter.[95] As such, politics and theology are both *"concerned with the one history that finds its goal in Christ, "the desire of the nations.""*[96]

---

[93] Nicholas Wolterstorff described O'Donovan's book, *The Desire of the Nations: Rediscovering the Roots of Political Theology*, as the twentieth century's *"most important contribution to political theology."* Nicholas Wolterstorff, "A Discussion of Oliver O'Donovan's *The Desire of the Nations*," *Scottish Journal of Theology* 54, no.1 (2001), 100. Philip Lorish and Charles Mathewes believe *The Desire of the Nations "inaugurated a new era in theological thinking on politics."* Philip Lorish and Charles Mathewes, "Theology as Counsel: The Work of Oliver O'Donovan and Nigel Biggar," *Anglican Theological Review* 94, no.4 (2012), 725. The idea for this critical ecumenical dialog comes from Yannaras. He supports an ecumenism that respects the otherness of different Christian experiences (traditions), but which equally recognizes that truth is only attainable through a communal dialectic. See Christos Yannaras, "Towards a New Ecumenism," *Sourozh* 70 (1997).

[94] O'Donovan, *The Desire of the Nations: Rediscovering the Roots of Political Theology* (Cambridge: Cambridge University Press, 1996), 19.

[95] Ibid., 2.

[96] Ibid.

O'Donovan *"postulates an analogy...grounded in reality—between the acts of God and human acts."*[97] *"Divine rule"* therefore provides *"the ground for speaking of human political authority."*[98] Human political authority begins with *"a human act, the "political act""* (which we will call the *"human political act"*).[99] The *"human political act"* is a *"divinely authorized act,"* which *"witnesses faithfully to the presence and future of what God has undertaken for all."*[100] O'Donovan further maintains that *"the history of divine rule is presented to us as a revealed history which takes form quite particularly as the history of Israel."*[101] Israel is the location where divine rule and the divinely authorized *"human political act"* coalesce in human history in a normative pattern.[102]

Scripture provides an account of God's reign, thus making political theology fundamentally an *"exegetical task,"* according to O'Donovan. The task is to identify *"true political concepts"* that are authorized in Scripture.[103] Only political concepts authorized by Scripture can be properly characterized as *"politico-theological."* [104]

*"Divine kingship"* forms the foundational biblical concept in O'Donovan's political theology. He identifies, via an exegesis of the Old Testament, three *"affirmations"* commonly associated with Yahweh's kingship: *"salvation," "judgment,"* and *"possession."*[105] From his analysis of the way these three *"affirmations"* forge Israel's distinctive political identity and express how God ruled over Israel as its king, he develops a normative conception of *"political authority"*: *"Political authority arises where power, the execution of right and the perpetuation of tradition are assured together in one coordinated*

---

[97] Ibid.
[98] Ibid., 20.
[99] Ibid.
[100] Ibid.
[101] Ibid., 21.
[102] Ibid., 27, 45.
[103] Ibid., 15–16.
[104] Ibid.
[105] Ibid., 36.

*agency.*"¹⁰⁶ To this he adds the following dictum: *"That any regime should actually come to hold authority, and should continue to hold it, is a work of divine providence in history, not a mere accomplishment of the human task of political service."*¹⁰⁷

O'Donovan contends that Christ's exaltation at the right hand of the father represents a *"victory won...over the nations' rulers."*¹⁰⁸ The impact of this victory is a *"re-authorization"* of political authority. Christ's triumph gives secular governments (secular in the temporal sense) a new, more restricted function: the exercise of *"judgment."*¹⁰⁹ Secular governments mediate God's judgments, and this is the only task remaining to them following Christ's victory. O'Donovan defines judgment as *"an act of moral discrimination that pronounces upon a preceding act or existing state of affairs to establish a new public context."*¹¹⁰ So the sole, legitimate function of secular political authority in the present era of salvation-history is the mediation of God's *"judgments."* O'Donovan defines politics as *"those activities with a direct relation to government."*¹¹¹ As the sole legitimate function of government is the performance of judgment, politics is in effect about judgment.

O'Donovan, contra Yannaras, considers Liberal Western political order an *"achievement...won by Christ over the nations' rulers."*¹¹² He contends that Christ's victory helped Christianity to develop political ideals, such as responsible government, that have come to define Western liberal political order.¹¹³ On this basis, the *"Christian*

---

¹⁰⁶ Ibid., 46. *"Right"* in this context means judgment (i.e. an act of moral discrimination) and should not be conflated with the *"right"* that Yannaras critiques.

¹⁰⁷ Ibid.

¹⁰⁸ Ibid., 229.

¹⁰⁹ Ibid., 151. It is important to clarify that O'Donovan conceives *"judgment"* in this context as having wider scope than the strictly judicial sense of the word, although it certainly includes this. *"Judgments"* denote a range of government decisions, policies, and actions.

¹¹⁰ O'Donovan, *The Ways of Judgment: The Bampton Lectures, 2003* (Grand Rapids: Eerdmans, 2005), 7.

¹¹¹ Ibid., 56.

¹¹² O'Donovan, *The Desire of the Nations*, 229.

¹¹³ Ibid., 231.

*theologian can venture to characterize a normative political culture broadly in continuity with the Western liberal tradition.*"[114] However, the separation of theology and politics in the *"late-modern liberal"* era severed Western liberal political order from its mooring in *"Christian liberalism."*[115] *"Modernity,"* O'Donovan writes, *"is the child of Christianity"* but *"it has left its father's house and followed the way of the prodigal."*[116] By severing its genetic link to Christianity, Western liberal political order runs the risk of developing into an *"Antichrist, a parodic and corrupt development of Christian social order."*[117]

The role of the church vis-à-vis politics is to *"represent…God's Kingdom by living under its rule, and by welcoming the world under its rule."*[118] O'Donovan believes that Christ's kingly rule *"is visible in the life of the church."*[119] But the church and state have distinct roles. The state cannot perform the church's mission of proclaiming the kingdom of God, for it is not *"consecrated"* for such a task. Its task is to make judgments, which is not the task of the church.[120] O'Donovan contends that *"church and society are in a dialectical relation, distant from each other as well as identified."*[121]

*The Trinity versus divine kingship*

Space prohibits us from offering a more detailed and nuanced exposition of O'Donovan's political theology, and it is important to

---

[114] Ibid., 230.
[115] Ibid., 9, 278.
[116] Ibid., 275.
[117] Ibid.
[118] Ibid., 174.
[119] Ibid., 146.
[120] Ibid., 217.
[121] Ibid., 251.

recognize that it is not without its Protestant critics.[122] However, the above synopsis amply demonstrates that in O'Donovan we have a very different approach to political theology from Yannaras. Whereas Yannaras' political theology finds its foundation in the Trinity, O'Donovan's finds it in divine kingship. Whereas Yannaras defines politics as authentic existence in communion with the Trinitarian God, O'Donovan's definition centers on the mediation of God's judgments. The core politico-theological concepts in Yannaras' political theology are *"person," "relationship,"* and *"community."* For O'Donovan, they are *"act (divine and human)," "authority,"* and *"judgment."* Yannaras believes Western liberal political order alienates humans from communion with God, where O'Donovan believes it is the product of Christ's victory.[123] Finally, while Yannaras conceives the church as the political community *par example,* O'Donovan conceives it as the model of obedience to Christ's rule.[124]

Comparing these contrasting conceptual matrices reveals some interesting lacunae in Yannaras and O'Donovan's political theologies respectively. *"Divine kingship," "the political act," "political authority,"* and *"judgment"* play no significant role in Yannaras' political theology. In fact, O'Donovan's foundational concept of

---

[122] For a critical Protestant engagement with O'Donovan's political theology, see Wolterstorff, "A Discussion of Oliver O'Donovan's *The Desire of the Nations.*"; William Schweiker, "Freedom and Authority in Political Theology: A Response to Oliver O'Donovan's *The Desire of the Nations,*" *Scottish Journal of Theology* 54, no.1 (2001); Stanley Hauerwas and James Fodor, "Remaining in Babylon: Oliver O'Donovan's Defense of Christendom," *Studies in Christian Ethics* 11, no.2 (1998); Craig Bartholomew et al., eds., *A Royal Priesthood?: The Use of the Bible Ethically and Politically, A Diaologue with Oliver O'Donovan* (Carlisle, Cumbria: Paternoster, 2002).

[123] O'Donovan's affirmation of Western liberal political order and Yannaras' critique of it should not be misconstrued as representative of *all* Protestant and Orthodox political theology respectively. For an example of a Protestant critique of Western liberal political order, see Stanley Hauerwas and William Willimon, *Resident Aliens: A Provocative Christian Assessment of Culture and Ministry for People Who Know that Something is Wrong* (Nashville: Abingdon, 1990). Conversely, for an Orthodox defense of Western liberal political order, see Papanikolaou, *The Mystical as Political.*

[124] In truth, the church has the function of role-model to secular society in both Yannaras and O'Donovan. However, what they role model is very different.

divine kingship is virtually absent from Yannaras' political theology. Similarly, the Trinity is all but absent from O'Donovan's political theology. And while there is discussion on the nature and function of community, it is not foundational in the way it is for Yannaras. Moreover, personhood and relationship do not play significant roles in O'Donovan.

These respective lacunae are not the result of ignorance or oversight. They reflect theological choices. There is a section in *The Inhumanity of Right*, for example, that examines some of the key New Testament passages on political authority. Yannaras concludes that Rom. 13:1–8[125] establishes that *"all existing forms of political authority, without exception, are appointed by God,"* and *"political authority exists, because there is evil in the world."*[126] However, the ultimate purpose of restraining evil via political authority is to *"make possible the co-existence that is a prerequisite for life as a community of relationships, in imitation of the Trinitarian prototype."*[127] And the whole section functions more as an excursus than an integral step in the development of Yannaras' critique of individual right and his argument for a *communo-centric* politics.

In the prologue to *The Desire of the Nations*, O'Donovan argues that *"theology is political simply by responding to the dynamics of its own proper themes,"* and he names the Trinity as one such theme.[128] In *The Ways of Judgment* he goes so far as to state that political theology also *"has a trinitarian shape."*[129] However, in reality there are no more than a handful of references to the Trinity in either book, and none of these plays an integral role in the thesis O'Donovan develops about God's reign, political authority, and judgment. The *persons* of the Trinity, as distinct from the *community* of the Trinity, each have distinct, albeit complementary, roles in the drama of human politics. *"Yahweh"* rules over Israel

---

[125] Rom. 13:1–7 for Protestants.
[126] Yannaras, Ἡ ἀπανθρωπία τοῦ δικαιώματος, 123.
[127] Ibid.
[128] O'Donovan, *The Desire of the Nations*, 3.
[129] O'Donovan, *The Ways of Judgment*, 239.

and then Christ, following his exaltation, *"mediates"* God's rule.[130] The Holy Spirit does not ostensibly play any formal role in mediating God's rule or judgments.[131]

There is a certain internal logic to the matrix *"Trinity-person-relationship-community"* and *"kingship-political-act-political-authority-judgment"* respectively, which gives both matrices a degree of internal coherence. It is possible that Yannaras' matrix militates against the elevation of divine kingship as a central politico-theological concept as it does not ostensibly illuminate the concepts person and community. Similarly, it is possible that O'Donovan's matrix militates against elevating the Trinity as a central politico-theological concept as it does not prima facie appear particularly germane to an elucidation of God's kingly rule over history.

*Points of convergence*

In spite of the very profound conceptual differences evident in Yannaras and O'Donovan's political theologies, there are many interesting points of conceptual convergence. But these points of convergence also bear the imprint of the different conceptual matrices at work in each of their political theologies.

Freedom is one such concept. It plays an important role in both O'Donovan and Yannaras' political theologies. However, whereas

---

[130] O'Donovan, *The Desire of the Nations*, 133. It is interesting to note that O'Donovan refers to God as *"Yahweh"* throughout his discussion of God's reign over Israel, but *"God"* when discussing Christ's reign i.e., as the mediator of *"God's"* rule.

[131] The Holy Spirit is not absent from O'Donovan's political theology. The Spirit *"authorizes"* the church, *"giving legitimacy to its existence, effect to its mission, right to the various relations it comprises."* Ibid., 174. Given one of the church's functions is to proclaim Christ's rule to secular governments, the Holy Spirit can be construed as having an indirect political role. It is worth noting that Yannaras says virtually nothing of the Holy Spirit in his political theology. However, like O'Donovan, he believes the Holy Spirit *"is the foundational and constitutive event of the Church."* He further believes that the Holy Spirit brings about the *"existential change"* (through the Eucharist) which enables authentic existence, i.e., communion with God. Given Yannaras' conception of politics as authentic existence, the Holy Spirit implicitly takes on a significant indirect role in political life. Yannaras, *Elements of Faith*, 128–129.

Yannaras conceives freedom as the ability to be one's true authentic self through relationships, O'Donovan connects freedom to authority and act. He says *"authority is the objective correlate of freedom,"* because it *"evokes free action, and makes free action intelligible."*[132] O'Donovan's construal of freedom reflects his overriding interest in what legitimizes the human political act in light of God's sovereign rule. Yannaras, by way of contrast, is concerned with explaining how humans can live out their *imago Dei* as persons in the context of politics.[133]

Another interesting point of convergence is the issue of community. O'Donovan approaches community through the lens of *"communication,"* which he explains as follows:[134]

> *"To "communicate" is to hold some thing as common, to make it a common possession, to treat it as "ours," rather than as "yours" or "mine." The partners to a communication form a community, a "we," in relation to the object in which they participate."*[135]

This particular conception of community finds its origin in Augustine.[136] With Augustine, O'Donovan believes that what binds

---

[132] O'Donovan, *The Desire of the Nations*, 30. This idea is first explored in Oliver O'Donovan, *Resurrection and Moral Order: An Outline for Evangelical Ethics* (Grand Rapids: Eerdmans, 1986), 122.

[133] These differences notwithstanding, there are points of genuine convergence in the pair's account of freedom. O'Donovan, for example, says that *"the rationale of political structures is not to preserve private freedoms, though they will also be preserved, but to preserve public freedoms, i.e., the free communications that we undertake simply because we are, as human beings, helplessly social."* O'Donovan, *The Ways of Judgment*, 55.

[134] It is interesting to note that O'Donovan grounds the notion of *"communication"* in Paul's use of the term *koinonia*. This is the Greek term at the heart of Yannaras *"communo-centric"* (koinoniokentriki) political theology. Ibid., 242.

[135] Ibid.

[136] O'Donovan has identified Augustine as the single greatest influence on his theology. "Oliver O'Donovan and Joan Lockwood O'Donovan," in *God's Advocates: Christian Thinkers in Conversation*, ed. Rupert Shortt (London: Darton, Longman and Todd, 2005), 267.

a community together is its *"common objects of love."*[137] O'Donovan's emphasis on *"objects"* and *"things"* as the focal point of community once again reflects his preoccupation with human agency. He articulates the problematic of community in the following indicative manner: *"It is the question of what unifies a multitude of human agents into a community of action and experience sustained over time."*[138] We recall that Yannaras' conception of community focuses on *"interpersonal relationships"* united by the common struggle for authentic existence.[139]

### Theological anthropology

The contrasting construals of freedom and community identified point to a fundamentally different theological anthropology at work in Yannaras and O'Donovan's political theologies. In turn, these different theological anthropologies appear to be the product of Yannaras and O'Donovan's different starting points: The Trinity and divine rule respectively. We recall that *"otherness"* and *"relationship"* are the constitutive components of Yannaras' theological anthropology. O'Donovan's theological anthropology, in contrast, centers on the *"individual"* rather than the person in Yannaras' sense, with the constitutive components being *"agency"* and the *"act."*

It is interesting to note the ease with which O'Donovan's employs the term *"individual"* in contrast to Yannaras' disease. O'Donovan

---

[137] Oliver O'Donovan, *Common Objects of Love: Moral Reflection and the Shaping of Community* (Grand Rapids: Eerdmans, 2002), 22.

[138] Ibid., 1.

[139] Again, it is important to note that there are genuine points of convergence on the issue of community. O'Donovan says, for example, says that it would be a mistake to construe *"private interest"* as either the *"foundation or...the goal of communication* [i.e., community]" and that *"the social use of goods cannot be constructed out of individual interests in things."* O'Donovan, *The Ways of Judgment*, 249. We also recall that Yannaras' relational conception of community includes relationships with *"things,"* not just persons.

argues, for example, that it is *"individual persons...who have direct standing before God...Classes, communities, and other collectives have no such standing."*[140] He also maintains, in a section of *The Desire of the Nations* fittingly titled *"The individual,"* that, although *"in the Hebrew Scriptures the holy community is the prior original fact...the individual becomes...load-bearing"* in the First Temple Period *"so that at the exile the future of the nation has come to depend on individual faithfulness."*[141]

These different theoanthropological perspectives may help to shed some light on the different conclusions Yannaras and O'Donovan draw about Western liberal political order. For O'Donovan, the problem is not the West's view of the person *per se*. His conception of the person as an individual moral agent sits comfortably within the orbit of the prevailing Western conception of the person as an individual. He is much more concerned with Western liberal political order recognizing God's divine rule and the potential dangers that arise from not doing so.

Yannaras, on the other hand, contends that his conception of the person is radically different to and incompatible with the Western conception of the individual, which finds its most inimical expression in the notion of individual right. While he would no doubt agree with O'Donovan that Western liberal political order is *Western* Christianity's child, he would likely add that both the prodigal son and the father are hopelessly alienated from the God in whose image they were created, and that much more is required to fix the situation than simply acknowledging God's kingship.

*Probing questions*

The critical dialog we have conducted between Yannaras and O'Donovan has not proceeded on the presupposition that their respective views form a mutually exclusive dichotomy. It is, after all, difficult to impugn the theological legitimacy and pedigree of both the Trinity and divine kingship. Moreover, both Yannaras and O'Donovan recognize as much, even though their respective

---

[140] Ibid., 50.
[141] O'Donovan, *The Desire of the Nations*, 73.

political theologies emphasize one at the expense of the other. This difference of emphasis may in actual fact reflect a tension at the heart of political theology that is rarely brought to the surface or addressed directly. This is the tension between the conception of God as a communion of three persons and as a king, and the relationship of both images to politics. The fundamental difference between Yannaras and O'Donovan might stem from a focus on the immanent and economic Trinity respectively as the point of departure for Christian political theology.

Reading Yannaras and O'Donovan side by side can leave one with a sense of incompleteness in relation to their respective accounts of politics, for all the genuine insightfulness, subtlety, and richness that is regularly on display in both. The searching question they pose to each other is whether a Trinity-centric and divine kingship-centric political theology respectively can provide a sufficient basis for a *complete* political theology.

It is difficult to escape the sense that each points to something lacking in the other. Reading O'Donovan with Yannaras, for example, reveals that it is very much what we *do* as humans, rather than who we *are* as humans, that is of political significance in O'Donovan's view. A corollary of this is that community appears to lack intrinsic political value. It merely forms the necessary context or backdrop in which the real drama of politics takes place: individual divine and human political acts of judgment. The way Yannaras connects the Trinity to personhood, community, and authentic existence might give O'Donovan a means of broadening and enriching his conception of politics so that the flourishing of communities and persons can also be brought within the scope of the telos of politics and the purposes of salvation-history.

Reading Yannaras with O'Donovan reveals that Yannaras does not have an account of political history. Yannaras focuses on historical "*events*" (gegonota) rather than historical "*narrative*." It is seminal events such as the ecclesial event and the Incarnation event that define and shape history. Politics has its own narrative. Regimes and civilizations rise, survive, change, and develop in specific times and places and in specific ways in a discernable pattern that allows us to talk about their histories, their stories. However, Yannaras' emphasis on authentic existence in communion with the Trinitarian community can make political history appear to lack any kind of theological meaning or significance. Moreover, it can also make God feel somewhat remote from *actual* human political developments. There is a sense in which in spite of the ability of humans to realize communion with God, the struggle to establish and maintain a political order is very much left to their own devices, without any specific guidance or intervention from God. There is no sense that history forms the "*theatre*," to borrow O'Donovan's term, for the shared *personal* story of God and humankind. O'Donovan's understanding that human political authority and human political acts find their legitimacy in God's sovereignty over history might give Yannaras a way to find theological significance in the *narrative* of political history, thus broadening his conception of God as merely the telos of politics to also taking on an active role in the movement of political history towards that telos.

## Conclusion

Yannaras has already cemented his reputation as one of the Orthodox world's most important thinkers. What we hope to have demonstrated in this essay, with the detailed exposition of his political theology from untranslated Greek sources, and by bringing him into critical dialog with a leading Western political theologian, is that he could be an invaluable and stimulating dialog partner for Western Christian reflection on politics, which is, as he points out, a perpetual *catholic* human struggle.

# Bibliography

Bartholomew, Craig, Jonathan Chaplin, Robert Song, and Al Wolters, eds. *A Royal Priesthood?: The Use of the Bible Ethically and Politically: A Dialogue with Oliver O'Donovan.* Carlisle, Cumbria: Paternoster, 2002.

Hauerwas, Stanley, and James Fodor. "Remaining in Babylon: Oliver O'Donovan's Defense of Christendom." *Studies in Christian Ethics* 11, no.2 (1998): 30–55.

Hauerwas, Stanley, and William H. Willimon. *Resident Aliens: A Provocative Christian Assessment of Culture and Ministry for People Who Know that Something is Wrong.* Nashville: Abingdon, 1990.

Lorish, Philip, and Mathewes, Charles. "Theology as Counsel: The Work of Oliver O'Donovan and Nigel Biggar." *Anglican Theological Review* 94, no.4 (2012): 717–736.

Louth, Andrew. "Some Recent Works by Christos Yannaras in English Translation." *Modern Theology*, 25, no.2 (2009): 329–340.

Mitralexis, Sotiris. "Person, Eros, Critical Ontology: An Attempt to Recapitulate Christos Yannaras' Philosophy." *Sobornost* 34, no.1 (2012): 33–40.

O'Donovan, Oliver. *Common Objects of Love: Moral Reflection and the Shaping of Community.* Grand Rapids: Eerdmans, 2002.

———.*The Desire of the Nations: Rediscovering the Roots of Political Theology.* Cambridge: Cambridge University Press, 2003.

———.*Resurrection and Moral Order: An Outline for Evangelical Ethics.* 2nd ed. Grand Rapids: Eerdmans, 1994.

———.*The Ways of Judgment: The Bampton Lectures, 2003.* Grand Rapids: Eerdmans, 2005.

Papanikolaou, Aristotle. *The Mystical as Political: Democracy and Non-radical Orthodoxy.* Notre Dame: Notre Dame University Press, 2012.

Payne, Daniel P. *The Revival of Political Hesychasm in Contemporary Orthodox Thought: The Political Hesychasm of John S. Romanides and Christos Yannaras.* Lanham: Lexington Books, 2011.

Russell, Norman. "Christos Yannaras." In S J Kristiansen and S Rise, eds. *Key Theological Thinkers: From Modern to Postmodern.* Surrey: Ashgate, 2013.

———."The Enduring Significance of Christos Yannaras: Some Further Works in Translation." *International Journal for the Study of the Christian Church* 16, no.1 (2016): 58–65.

Schweiker, William. "Freedom and Authority in Political Theology: A Response to Oliver O'Donovan's *The Desire of the Nations.*" *Scottish Journal of Theology* 54, no.1 (2001): 110–126.

Shortt, Rupert, ed. *God's Advocates: Christian Thinkers in Conversation.* London: Darton, Longman and Todd, 2005.

Stoeckl, Kristina. "The "We" in Normative Political Philosophical Debates: The Position of Christos Yannaras on Human Rights." In *Orthodox Christianity and Human Rights*, edited by Alfons Brüning and Evert van der Zweerde, 187–198. Leuven: Peeters, 2012.

Wolterstorff, Nicholas. "A Discussion of Oliver O'Donovan's *The Desire of the Nations.*" *Scottish Journal of Theology* 54, no.1 (2001): 87–109.

Yannaras, Christos. *Against Religion: The Alienation of the Ecclesial Event.* Translated by Norman Russell. Brookline: Holy Cross Orthodox Press, 2013.

———.*Elements of Faith: An Introduction to Orthodox Theology.* Translated by Keith Schram. Edinburgh: T&T Clark, 1991.

———."Human Rights and the Orthodox Church," in Emmanuel Clapsis ed., *The Orthodox Churches in a Pluralistic World: An Ecumenical Conversation.* Geneva: WCC Publications, 2004.

———."A Note on Political Theology," translated by Steven Peter Tsichlis, *St Vladimir's Theological Quarterly* 27, no.1 (1983): 53–56.

———.*Person and Eros.* Translated by Norman Russell. Brookline: Holy Cross Orthodox Press, 2007.

———. "Towards a New Ecumenism," *Sourozh* 70 (1997):

———.Ἡ ἀπανθρωπία τοῦ δικαιώματος. Athens: Domos, 1998.

———. Ἔξι φιλοσοφικὲς ζωγραφιές: Σύνοψη εἰσαγωγικὴ καὶ πάντως αὐτεξεταστική. Athens: Ikaros, 2011.

———.Ὀρθὸς λόγος καὶ κοινωνικὴ πρακτική. Athens: Domos, 1984.

# Chapter 4

# An ontology of the historico-social: Christos Yannaras' reading of European history

Sotiris Mitralexis

In chapter three of this book, Jonathan Cole masterfully summed up the main points of Christos Yannaras' political theology, thus providing us with an introduction to it: (a) Yannaras' communal epistemology, (b) his relational ontology of the social, (c) his critique of rights due to (d) the conception of agency as personhood, (e) his dialectics of freedom and alienation, (f) his focus on direct democracy, as well as (g) the distinctly ontological nature that is ascribed to politics, i.e. politics as authentic existence rather than simply co-existence, and so on. Cole is right in recapitulating Yannaras' politically relevant thought as "communo-centric politics," a term that Yannaras himself uses (κοινωνιοκεντρικὴ πολιτική[1]). In this chapter,[2] I will provide some background for a notion central to Yannaras' thought, that of the "West" and of its difference to the Graeco-Roman, ecclesial world of what would be later called "Byzantium."

---

[1] Christos Yannaras, *Κοινωνιοκεντρικὴ Πολιτική: Κριτήρια* [*Communo-Centric Politics: Criteria*] (Athens: Estia, 2005); Christos Yannaras, "«Κοινωνιοκεντρικὴ» Πολιτική: Τί Σημαίνει; ['Communo-Centric' politics: What Would This Mean?]," *Kathimerini*, June 16, 2002, sec. Feuilleton, http://www.kathimerini.gr/688373/opinion/epikairothta/arxeio-monimes-sthles/koinwniokentrikh-politikh-ti-shmainei.

[2] I am grateful to the German Research Foundation (DFG), which provided me with the means necessary for conducting the research behind this paper through *Forschungsstipendium* MI 1965/2-1.

"West" is a primarily geographical term; however, its semantic content is not geographical in character, but rather civilizational and political. And if the term retains some remnants of "geographicality" in its rendition as descriptive of the modern culture of (western) Europe, North America and perhaps Australia—but not Africa, which would be equally "Western" to Europe from a geographical point of view—it resists these remnants when defined in its full historical depth, whatever this may be. In spite of the polysemy attributed to the term "Western civilization" and of the debates concerning its exact meaning, received wisdom has it that it refers to a historical and civilizational trajectory beginning with classical Greece (or even the earliest Mesopotamian cultures) and Rome i.e. the Roman empire, acquiring Christianity as one of its constitutional elements, evolving into the Renaissance and, later, the Enlightenment and concluding in (Western) Modernity—which may or may not include "the End of History."

Of course, this is not to mean that there is any substantive homogeneity in the various definitions of Western civilization; disagreements, divergences, and contradictions abound. For example, R. R. Palmer in his *History of the Modern World* conceives of a Western World beginning with the Greeks and centered around the Mediterranean, but then breaking apart into three segments in the early Middle Ages—while Frank Roy Willis defines the West as "that civilization that developed in the continent of Europe and was carried to [...] areas in other parts of the globe that were colonized by people from Europe," which may or may not include the Greeks and the Romans. On the other hand, Edward Burns, Robert Lerner and Standish Meacham hold that "among all peoples of the ancient world, the one whose culture most clearly exemplified the spirit of Western society was the Greek or Hellenic," *but* "by about 700 AD, in place of a united Rome, there were three successor civilizations that stood as rivals [...] the

Byzantine, the Islamic and the Western Christian."[3] However, we can safely say that the lowest common denominator of most, if not all, definitions of Western civilization, popular and scholarly alike, revolve around the axes of classical Greece, Rome, Christianity, Renaissance, Enlightenment and Western Modernity.

Christos Yannaras sees the question of the "West" in a very different light, and discerns the basis and precondition for civilizational differences at the level of ontology and epistemology. A central aspect of Yannaras' vision is the enquiry into the differences between Western civilization and the Greek-speaking civilization in which the Church, undivided at first but Orthodox later on, initially blossomed. This is not mere *Kulturkritik*, as it evolves into a comprehensive contradistinction of *modes*: not of secondary differences, but on diverging *stances* towards being, knowledge, history, and the Church. It is of utmost importance, however, to clarify that this contradistinction is *internal* rather than *external*: it consists in the *self-criticism* of a Western thinker in a culturally wholly Western world, not in the comparison of today's West to today's Orthodox Church or, much less, to today's Greece. Yannaras laments a past, non-Western paradigm and approach to reality, the *criteria* of which are long gone in East and West alike. In his words:

> *Let me therefore make one thing absolutely clear. The critique of western theology and tradition which I offer in this book does not contrast "Western" with something "right" which as an Orthodox I use to oppose something "wrong" outside myself. I am not attacking an external Western adversary. As a modern Greek, I myself somebody both the thirst for what is "right" and the reality of what is "wrong": a contradictory and alienated survival of ecclesiastical Orthodoxy in a society radically and unhappily Westernised. My critical stance towards*

---

[3] The views quoted in this paragraph are cited in Lawrence Birken, "What Is Western Civilization?," *The History Teacher* 25, no. 4 (1992): 451-52, doi:10.2307/494353.

> the West is self-criticism; it refers to my own wholly
> Western mode of life. I am a Western person searching for
> answers to the problems tormenting Western people
> today.[4]

This is a hermeneutical key. Without this, Yannaras makes no sense; an approach of his stance as "Anti-Western" would make his texts woefully impenetrable and his contribution out of the reader's reach.

While Yannaras makes frequent references to his understanding of the "West" in his many writings, providing short definitions thereof, the most potent recapitulation of his understanding of the "West" (which, interestingly, is not juxtaposed to any "East") is to be found in his recent treatise *The Schism Engendered Europe*,[5] the title referring to the East–West Schism of 1054 AD, i.e. the break of communion between what are now the Eastern Orthodox and Roman Catholic churches. In spite of appearances, the book does not focus on the Great Schism, or on denominational differences between Orthodox Christianity and Western Christianity, i.e. Catholicism and Protestantism, or in religious matters *per se*; rather, the book focuses on what Yannaras reads as a fundamental difference in each culture's *approach* towards things—towards knowledge, reality, science, society, politics and human relationships—and historical development behind each approach respectively. And the cultures in question are, on the one hand, the Greek classical world and its Christian ecclesial continuation in the Eastern Roman Empire, a culture now extinct as a distinct civilizational entity; and, on the other hand, its historical deviation/inversion, resulting in a culture (the "West") bearing the potential and momentum of geographical universality, of civilizational globalization.

---

[4] *Orthodoxy and the West: Hellenic Self-Identity in the Modern Age*, trans. Peter Chamberas and Norman Russell (Brookline, Mass.: Holy Cross Orthodox Press, 2006), viii–ix.

[5] Christos Yannaras, Ἡ Εὐρώπη Γεννήθηκε Ἀπὸ Τὸ Σχίσμα [*The Great Schism Engendered Europe*] (Athens: Ikaros, 2015).

Yannaras' narrative is in many ways precisely the polar opposite of that of Samuel P. Huntington, according to which "the legacies of the West from Classical civilization are many, including Greek philosophy and rationalism, Roman law, Latin, and Christianity. Islamic and Orthodox civilizations also inherited from Classical civilization but nowhere near to the same degree the West did."[6] For Yannaras, the differentiating mark of the "West" is precisely that it *does not* derive from classical civilization, Greek philosophy or Christianity, but that it survives from their extinction as civilizational modes discernible as representative of what we would today term as state entities, a point to which we shall return. However, these differences do not pertain exclusively to the history, culture, politics or religion, but directly to *ontology*— the question concerning being *qua* being and its implications—and *epistemology*—the question concerning the criteria for the validity of knowledge, the nature of truth. As such, Yannaras' attempt at a comprehensive narrative on European history, leading to a political theology, can be categorised as *an ontology of the historico-social*.

A crucial *caveat:* it is important to understand that Yannaras does not claim that he does *history*: contrary to that, his claim is that, in a way which draws from but should not be conflated with the *data* the science of history brings into the discussion, a hermeneutical *synthesis* of those data is pending, a hermeneutical *approach* to their aggregation (i.e., precisely what in the social sciences would term as a *narrative*, a notion without any *per se* evaluative charge). He sets to propose such a hermeneutic *synthesis*, examining the societal and historical domain through the lens of ontological "traditions," of discernible patterns in each peoples' way of looking at the primary questions of being, meaning, and knowledge—and of the way their implicit answers influence and transform *civilization*: politics, society, religion, art, architecture, scientific enquiry (a process that can run both ways) .

Yannaras begins the book by articulating the need for a hermeneutic proposal that will connect the pieces of the historical

---

[6] Samuel P. Huntington, *The Clash of Civilizations and the Remaking of World Order* (New York: Simon & Schuster, 1996), 69–70.

puzzle that are the relations between "European West" and the "European East"—the relations of the "post-Roman" societies of Western Europe with *Hellenism*, which is the name he uses for the now extinct Eastern Roman civilization that was a particular kind of classical Greece's Christianized continuation.[7] Focusing on Modern Greece, the author expresses his dissatisfaction with what he diagnoses as the current state of affairs: the European West sees itself as the heir to the legacy of classical Greece, Roman universality (οἰκουμενικότητα) and Christianity, while Greece— and post-Byzantine societies in general—out of a perceived inferiority to the advances of the West hastens to boast about its classical Greek predecessors engendering Western civilization; Yannaras, however, declares that he will formulate a different approach to the relations between post-Roman West and Hellenism—and by extension, today's post-Byzantine and Westernized Greece.[8] As stated therein, the book intends to be in implicit conversation with Jacques Le Goff's *Europe est-elle née au Moyen Age?* [*Was Europe Born in the Middle Ages?*][9]—to provide both a supplement and an alternative to Le Goff's historical vision. Yannaras notes that in spite of the Le Goff's inquisitive title, what is taken for granted when one refers to "Europe" is that this actually commences with the birth of the "post-Roman West," i.e.

---

[7] Yannaras, *The Great Schism Engendered Europe*, 13. Yannaras proposes a rather original schematization of continuity-in-discontinuities (see, e.g., Ibid., 76): classical Greece and the Eastern Roman ("Byzantine") empire have a radically different *ontology*—in spite of the fact that the latter built upon the advances of the former—but share the same *epistemology*, the apophatic and communal epistemology of *participation*. We see in historical practice, he argues, that a discontinuity in *ontology* does not necessarily effect a cultural discontinuity (and vice versa, that possessing the same ontology does not guarantee cultural commonality); on the other hand, even cultures with different *ontologies*/metaphysical traditions/axes of meaning can demonstrate continuity *if* their epistemology, their criteria for the validity of truth and knowledge, remain the same. This bold position of Yannaras' is elaborated and analyzed in Dionysios Skliris, "Review Article: Christos Yannaras, The Great Schism Engendered Europe," *Theologia*, no. 3 (2015): 379–90.

[8] Yannaras, *The Great Schism Engendered Europe*, 14–15.

[9] Jacques Le Goff, *Europe est-elle née au Moyen Age?* (Paris: Éditions du Seuil, 2013); English edition, *The Birth of Europe*, trans. Janet Lloyd (Oxford: Wiley-Blackwell, 2006).

of the new state of affairs in Europe as shaped by the core Migration Period (*Völkerwanderung*, mainly from the fourth to the sixth century AD),[10] the Barbarian Invasions which themselves mark the end of the Western part of the Roman world—and the fall of Rome itself. Agreeing with Le Goff, Yannaras asserts that it is indeed from these developments, from the overthrow of the Roman *ordo rerum* by new peoples, that the illustrious civilization that is today a global and globalized paradigm emerged. However, it is precisely the peculiarity of these developments and of the civilizational evolutionary trajectory they entailed that radically differentiate this Western, European civilization both from what preceded it in the European continent, i.e. the classical Greek and the Roman world, and from the continuation of this civilization in the Eastern part of the Roman empire, which developed into a distinct civilizational entity[11]—a reality which Samuel P. Huntington emphatically asserts, as Yannaras is keen to remind us.

Following this introduction, the author proceeds to an exposition of what he picks out as the hallmarks of Graeco-Roman antiquity, its distinctive characteristics, i.e. the *unity* and *identity* of this world. These comprise (i) the birth of critical enquiry in the Greek world, (ii) a peculiar *relational* empiricism (which will be later contrasted to intellectualism and the absolutisation of the Cartesian *cogito*), (iii) the communal (and apophatic) verification of knowledge, i.e. this civilization's distinct yet implicit epistemological *stance* and general *tendency*[12] (iv) truth as a *mode of existence* rather than as a correct formulation, and (v) politics as a collective endeavor for iconizing *truth*, and not merely usefulness, in a society.[13] For the "internationalization" of these Greek

---

[10] Yannaras, *The Great Schism Engendered Europe*, 16.
[11] Ibid., 16–17.
[12] Remarks made in Sotiris Mitralexis, "Person, Eros, Critical Ontology: An Attempt to Recapitulate Christos Yannaras' Philosophy," *Sobornost* 34, no. 1 (2012): 33–40 on Yannaras' communal verification of knowledge, as well as in Sotiris Mitralexis, "Activity and Otherness in Christos Yannaras' Propositions for a Critical Ontology," in *Christos Yannaras: Polis, Philosophy, Theology*, ed. Mary Cunningham and Andreas Andreopoulos (London: Ashgate, 2017), could prove helpful in elucidating this concept.
[13] Yannaras, *The Great Schism Engendered Europe*, 21–35.

hallmarks in the Graeco-Roman world comprising most of the then known *ecumene*, two factors played a decisive role: (vi) the implementation of Greek as a *lingua franca, de facto* at first—to the extent that the New Testament gospels *had* to be written in Greek—and much later *de jure* as well, which forms a linguistically defined mode of thinking, and (viii) the constitution of, firstly, Alexander the Great's empire—e.g., the Hellenic cities, with *agora* and *theatre*, that he founded and which by far outlived the empire itself—and, then, of the Roman world as a civilizational *ecumene* at first, an *ordo rerum* with a *religio imperii*: the internationalization of a Hellenic cultural *mode*.[14]

From the dawn of critical enquiry in the Ionian coast to the maturity of the Roman empire, it is not the *political* changes that disrupted the continuity of a civilizational *paradigm* that can be clearly discerned—a *paradigm* that had nothing to do with race as it expanded to a staggering number of races, Yannaras contends. However, the immense changes in the European continent effected by the Barbarian Invasions, the *Völkerwanderung*, particularly from the fourth to the sixth century with the Fall of Rome as its high point, had among other things the impact of gradually creating a second, parallel grand civilizational paradigm, which in time became antagonistic to the Graeco-Roman one. Yannaras bases his insights on a number of historical studies,[15] but centers on J.M. Wallace-Hadrill's *The Barbarian West—the Early Middle Ages, 400-1000 AD*.[16] "Barbarian" here stands for precisely non-Graeco-Roman, but Yannaras sees this difference as a predominantly cultural one.

Drawing on Wallace-Hadrill, the author notes how the new peoples of Europe, with the help of missionary activity, saw Christianisation as a *sine qua non* precondition for entering mainstream Graeco-Roman civilization and its organized societies, i.e. for being considered as civilized. Christianity in the European space, however, had developed on a number of *preconditions* offered by Hellenic antiquity and its achievements in intellectual

---

[14] Ibid., 36–46.
[15] expounded in ibid., 49–50 fn. 1.
[16] J. M. Wallace-Hadrill, *The Barbarian West 400-1000* (Oxford: Wiley-Blackwell, 1996).

refinement. The Gospel had been articulated in the Greek language, with its vertiginous ability for discerning subtle nuances, while the Church's doctrine as it developed during the first Christian centuries was formulated on the basis and principles of the categories (though not of the philosophical content) of Greek philosophical thought (e.g., the full semantic content of the distinction between οὐσία and ὑπόστασις is not directly approachable even in Latin, where both *essentia* and *substantia* had been used for οὐσία, leading to profound confusion even today). Mass Christianization rendered the proper reception of this philosophical and theological legacy, which was itself a prerequisite for a full adoption of Christianity, impossible for the newly baptized peoples. Yannaras sees this process as a *religionization* of Christianity, as a gradual transformation of the *ecclesial event,* a reality fundamentally different from religion which itself presupposes a liberation from the preconditions of religion, into merely another *religion,*[17] with a God/"supreme being," faith as the acceptance of convictions, and morality as a law—all this constituting the polar opposite of the ecclesial event, in which God constitutes freedom from necessity and relational self-transcendence, calling humanity to reflect this divine mode of being.[18]

While the ecclesial event is fundamentally a communal event and constitutes/reflects a communo-centric paradigm (κοινωνιο-κεντρικὸ παράδειγμα), a religionized Christianity marks an individualistic paradigm, the primacy of the natural subject. The fragmentation that this tendency engenders, the fragmentation effected in the Barbarian post-Roman world and the multitude of Barbarian races, paved the way for the emergence of what would be later called feudalism. A watershed moment for the developments in the European space was the emergence, after centuries of fragmentation, of a leader who could unite the races

---

[17] This view and difference has been elaborated in Christos Yannaras, *Against Religion: The Alienation of the Ecclesial Event,* trans. Norman Russell (Brookline, Mass.: Holy Cross Orthodox Press, 2013).

[18] Yannaras, *The Great Schism Engendered Europe,* 53–63.

and kingdoms of this new, Barbarian post-Roman European reality around the Franks: Charles the Great, *Charlemagne* (742–814 AD).

As a political entity, the Roman Empire had fully survived in its Eastern part with New Rome–Constantinople as its capital; the political and administrative capital of the Empire had been transferred to Constantinople since Constantine the Great's time, and as tragic as the Fall of Rome was, it did not change that reality for the Romans, who would never identify themselves otherwise (the use of the name "Byzantium" for the empire and its subjects was introduced as late as the sixteenth century AD by Hieronymus Wolf and implemented precisely in order for it not to be referred to as "Roman," a name reserved for Charlemagne's empire). Yannaras portrays Charlemagne as a man who understood the need for creating an imperial political unity for the Franks and Europe's post-Roman peoples, united in peace (pax romana) and religion (religio imperii): an entity *distinct from* the Roman empire in the East, which would be its main adversary. This entity *could not* be Roman and Christian in the way that the Roman empire of Constantinople was, for it would thus lose the ability to maintain its distinctiveness. However, Yannaras contends, this entity *had to* be Christian, which was by then the "ticket to civilization," and it *had* to be Roman, for this was the only known "imperial civilization" in Europe and the only grand legacy to draw from. This gives birth to the need for a *second* Roman empire, with a *different* version of Christianity. Combined with the political interests of the papacy, the coronation of Charlemagne on 25 December 800 AD by Pope Leo III in St Peter's Basilica in Rome as the "Holy Roman Emperor" of another Roman empire, distinct from the active Roman empire in the East and the Roman Empress Irene of Athens, formed the symbolic epitome of the creation of this new, second, parallel Roman empire, with its own version of *ordo rerum,* a discernibly different Christian *religio imperii* and a *pax romana/christiana.*[19]

Yannaras is primarily interested in the civilizational *priorities* in collective outlook that emerge as the distillates of such historical

---

[19] Ibid., 67–80 and further on.

processes: he sees *utilitarianism* (χρησιμοθηρία), the priority of being *useful* (rather than, for example, existentially true—and certainly in contrast to commune-centric criteria, to the priority of relationship and communion), as the primary differentiating mark of this *new* civilization that emerged out of Europe's Barbarian invasions. Yannaras considers this priority as a *pre-political* one, i.e. as one which presupposes a stage of political evolution *prior* to the one achieved by Athenian democracy and the *polis*.[20] "To seek for utility everywhere is entirely unsuited to men that are great-souled and free," as Aristotle would hasten to remind us.[21]

Subtle differences in language, religion, art, or architecture signify much greater and crucial civilizational differences. For Yannaras, the difference between approaching things as a dynamic "how," i.e. as a *mode*, a *mode of existence*, marks a fundamentally different outlook when compared to one that asserts *entities*, that enquires into a static "what" rather than a dynamic "how":

> *In Greek, the word οὐσία derives from the feminine present participle of the verb to be [εἶναι], ὤν, οὖσα, ὄν; it signifies the event of participation in being, [...] the mode of participation. In the West, essence-nature (essentia-natura) signifies a quidditas (from quid: which, something); it does not refer to an active mode of existence but to a "something," to a definitive and stable given of an existent's existence, to something with permanent attributes allowing accidental differentiations. The West had and has an ontic understanding of essence: it accepts essence as a being, an entity, a "what"—not a "how."*[22]

It should be noted that there is indeed a basis in Greek patristic tradition for an exorbitant focus on this modal "howness": again,

---

[20] Ibid., 85–87.
[21] Aristotle, Politics, Book 8, section 1338b: "τὸ δὲ ζητεῖν πανταχοῦ τὸ χρήσιμον ἥκιστα ἁρμόττει τοῖς μεγαλοψύχοις καὶ τοῖς ἐλευθέροις."
[22] Yannaras, *The Great Schism Engendered Europe*, 81.

Maximus the Confessor's corpus shall serve as a witness to that.[23] This *modal* difference in approach forms the focal point of Yannaras' ontologically-inspired hermeneutic proposal on "Greece" and "West," rather than on "East" and "West."

As soon as the West's claim (i.e., the claim of this *new* Western Europe as formed and transformed by Charlemagne's historical presence) to being Roman and to constituting a Roman empire materialized, "Greece" or rather "the Greeks" emerged as a negatively loaded term for the Roman East—a way to refer to the "other" Roman empire without granting it with the all-important name of "Roman." Yannaras names about ten different books under the common title *Contra Errores Graecorum*, "against the errors and fallacies of the Greeks" (or similar titles: *Adversus Graecos*, "against the Greeks," *Contra Graecos* etc.), which emerged and circulated from the ninth to the thirteenth century—with Thomas Aquinas' own *Contra Errores Graecorum* (1263 AD) being the most famous of them. During that crucial historical period, the author sees *religious* differences (which, for him, signify the deviation from the ecclesial event that is the gradual emergence of a new, distinct Western Christian *religion*) morphing into *political* differences—or rather the other way around: the Western European political need for civilizational differentiation from the Roman East as turning into religious divergence.[24] This climaxed in the addition to the Nicaean Creed of the *filioque*, "and the Son," concerning inter-Trinitarian relations, i.e. the procession of the Holy Spirit by the Son—a fundamental yet gradual change to which the Western Church itself protested, as is the case with Pope Leo III's silver plates on the walls of St' Peter's Basilica with the original Creed inscribed on them, before Benedict VIII's official inclusion of *filioque* in the Creed (1014 AD). Yannaras recognizes the political value and, perhaps, rationale of such moves, but at the same time he ascribes ontological content to them; he considers them as

---

[23] For an example of this Maximian *topos,* see Sotiris Mitralexis, "Ever-Moving Repose: The Notion of Time in Maximus the Confessor's Philosophy Through the Perspective of a Relational Ontology" (PhD diss., Freie Universität Berlin, 2014), 172–83.

[24] Yannaras, *The Great Schism Engendered Europe*, 85, 91–94.

signifying deep and very real differences in how each civilization, the post-Roman West and what would later be called the "Byzantine" East i.e. the late antique and mediaeval Graeco-Roman world, approached the fundamental questions of existence: the implications of, or behind, such historical events are read as ontological, theological, and epistemological.[25] Political changes, changes in church organization, church life, and theology, as well as the new directions of mediaeval Western art and architecture, gradually create an immense rift, only a symbolic moment of which would be the Great Schism of 1054 AD. Yannaras contends that the core difference which these differences circumscribe is the introduction of an understanding of salvation as an *individual* event (pending, for example, on religious morality) rather than as an *ecclesial*, communal event.[26] The theological root for these developments is to be found *a posteriori* in Augustine,[27] the fourth/fifth century Latin Church Father who centuries later rose to become a foundational figure for Western Christianity, Roman Catholic and (much later) Protestant as well. Yannaras studies the teachings that derive from Augustine's thought, which he sees as conducive to the religionization of the ecclesial event,[28] and points out the later impact of the distinctive characteristics of his thought in intellectual domains, even modern and contemporary ones, seemingly wholly unrelated to church, theology, and Christianity.[29] In doing this, the author highlights the particularity of post-Roman Western civilization, of the civilizational trajectory that began with late antiquity's *Völkerwanderung* to end up being a culture with an unprecedented dynamics of universality, albeit a civilization of utilitarianism instead of communion, in stark contrast to its great historical adversary, the Graeco-Roman, and later *ecclesial*, civilization's otherness[30]—the capability for the historical survival

---

[25] Ibid., 95–97.
[26] Ibid., 98–117.
[27] It should be noted, however, that Augustine was always cited in the East as one of the most important Church Fathers; for example, Maximus the Confessor names him as one of the pillars of the church's doctrine.
[28] Yannaras, *The Great Schism Engendered Europe*, 21–156.
[29] Ibid., 157–86.
[30] Ibid., 189–213.

of which was crucially, if not in essence definitively, undermined in 1204 AD, with the Sack of Constantinople that formed part of the Fourth Crusade. Yannaras' analysis of how this civilizational difference begins *from* ontology (from a difference in *modes* of approach, *modes* of existence) *through* history, i.e. historical realization, *to* the organization of the social (politics, society, institutions)[31] forms a particularly original contribution to the litany of readings of mediaeval history through an East-West perspective.

The latter part of the book deals with the further development of this dichotomy in modernity and its history, and particularly on how the Modern Greek state is far from being a continuation of the Graeco-Roman, *ecclesial*, "Byzantine" civilization, being just another modern Western nation-state instead—a reality which reaffirms the extinct character of this other, communo-centric civilization that materialized in the European East.[32] Of particular interest is Yannaras' analysis on how the Modern Greek state was founded precisely as a *pre*-Byzantine, neo-classical "Athenian-centred" state (while Athens played an extremely minor role in previous centuries, compared to other cities), with more care for restoring the names of classical antiquity's famous cities than for the restoration of the collective life of the newly liberated Greek people, echoing the romanticism of the Philhellenic movement and confirming a reading, according to which the legacy of classical antiquity was preserved in the *West*, and not in the Christianised Roman empire's Eastern continuation.[33] The official Modern Greek *intelligentsia* adopted this scheme, with Adamantios Korais' *metakenosis* doctrine being iconic of this development.[34] In a

---

[31] Ibid., 217–35.
[32] Ibid., 239–330.
[33] Ibid., 239–45.
[34] Alexandros Papaderos, *Metakenosis: Griechenlands Kulturelle Herausforderung Durch Die Aufklärung in Der Sicht Des Korais Und Des Oikonomos* (Meisenheim am Glan: Verlag Anton Hain, 1970); and Sotiris Mitralexis, "Ἡ Κοραϊκὴ «Μετακένωσις» Σύμφωνα Μὲ Τὴ Διδακτορικὴ Διατριβὴ Τοῦ Ἀλέξανδρου Παπαδεροῦ Στὸ Mainz Τὸ 1962 [Korais' 'Metakenosis' According to the Doctoral Thesis of Alexander Papaderos in Mainz, 1962]," in *Πολιτικὴ Ἀδολεσχία I [Political Contributions I]* (Athens: Manifesto, 2011), 103–20.

scathing critique of nationalism as guaranteeing the annihilation of true *catholicity* and civilizational universality, Yannaras also criticizes the violent formation of a Greek state Church, later recognized as autocephalous (i.e. self-governing), by ecclesiastically cutting the Greeks away from the Ecumenical Patriarchate in Constantinople,[35] in a move of "ecclesiastical nationalism" that further estranged Modern Greece from its Hellenic legacy.[36] Thus, the most potent proof of the historical extinction of the "Hellenic *mode*" as a mode of a communo-centric organization of collective life is Modern Greece itself.

\*

In recapitulating Yannaras' hermeneutic proposal, we would say that, together with his other writings, Yannaras' reading of European history implies a political theology as its corollary which centres on the notion of *mode* (τρόπος). The semantic content of *mode* (τρόπος) is foundational for Yannaras' thought *mode* and signifies a fluid and dynamic tendency within history, neither a self-sufficient entity, a *res*, nor a finite category or an isolated quality; as such, Yannaras' approach resist a categorization thereof as *essentialist*, for it does not identify an objectifiable essence of what *is* and what *isn't* "Western."

Implicitly, Yannaras' notion of *mode*, a certain *howness*, draws heavily upon Maximus the Confessor's ontological triad of historicisation (λόγος–τρόπος–τέλος, i.e. *logos*, mode and end).[37] Dionysios Skliris, himself a Maximian scholar, notes in a review article that is perhaps the most serious engagement with Yannaras' *The Schism Engendered Europe* to date that this way of

---

[35] On this, see Sotiris Mitralexis, "The Liberation of Church from State in Greece, and the Administrative Fragmentation of Ecclesial Jurisdictions," in *Ex Oriente Lux*, ed. Anna Zhyrkova and Martha Małecka-Kuzak (Cracow: Wydawnictwo Ignatianum, 2016), forthcoming.

[36] Yannaras, *The Great Schism Engendered Europe*, 246–49.

[37] cf. Dionysios Skliris, "Le Concept de Tropos Chez Maxime Le Confesseur" (PhD diss., Université Paris IV-Sorbonne, 2015).

seeing a civilizational paradigm as a *mode* entailing a primarily ontological content can be traced back to Yannaras' early works, for example in his *Person and Eros* (1976)

> but gradually comes to the forefront of [Yannaras'] thought, completing as a third axis his ontology along with the notions of "person" [πρόσωπο] and "relation." In speaking of a mode, we are referring to "that" which is not an idea or ideology, but to what is transmitted independently of conceptual understanding from one generation to another, from the teacher to the pupil, from the master to apprentice, from the Elder to the younger monk, from a spiritual or biological parent to a child; we are referring to a gift by a person we love. One could say that the mode is what remains when one forgets the totality of the particular content of a teacher's teaching and we remain solely with the teacher's way, the teacher's mode, with a universal ethos or character transmitted imperceptibly and which is ultimately what is of essence, while we were thinking that we would simply learn a particular craft.[38]

Skliris notes how this "Hellenic mode" is not another name for nationalism, but the very annihilation of the possibility of nationalism, which would require a clearly deniable, reified "*ellinikotita*" and, above all, a historically tangible subsistence. Not only does Yannaras' "Greek mode" defy such subsistence, but it emerges *precisely when* this subsistence is nowhere to be found, in the utter absence of any historically distinct *Greek* state—or imperial—entity:

> Insisting on the mode, the author wants to juxtapose the Hellenic mode to a nationalistic and ideological understanding of Hellenism that would shrink it either to an ethno-racial heritage enclosed within a modern

---

[38] Skliris, "Review Article: Christos Yannaras, The Great Schism Engendered Europe," 379–80.

> national state or to a coherent ideology and the illusory attempt to hold on to it through force and power that would be its corollary. On the contrary, the Greek mode is considered by Yannaras as having survived, flourished and borne fruit precisely when it was non definable in state sovereignty or other varieties of sovereignty, as was the case during the Roman Empire, the Ottoman occupation or during other periods of Hellenism's creative indefinability.[39]

Yannaras notes how this Greek *mode* is decisively undermined by Greek nationalism, how it perishes historically precisely when, and to the extent that, Greek nationalism prevails. Both in his treatises as well as in his weekly newspaper articles, Yannaras condemns Greek nationalism as a grave danger to any valuable alterity discernible within Greek culture, as the primary threat even to *patriotism*: "Nationalism is a disaster, a false perversion of patriotism, which it alienates and turns into an ideology. [...] Nationalism substitutes life's experience with a narcissistic psychological stubbornness which it displays as convictions enforceable on everyone. Nationalism implements a propagandistic use of history towards an illusionary 'high.' Nationalism equals boasting and hollow conceit, it claims the feats of ancestors for one's ego, as well as the privileges that follow from them."[40] Consistently throughout his *corpus*, Yannaras identifies nationalism as the primary threat to any fecund civilizational otherness: "Hellenism [...] ended in 1922. Naturally, the mourning for the disaster and the pain for the definitive loss gave way to delusions. The novel historical prime matter for these delusions of survival was *nationalism*. Nationalism is patriotism, when it is turned into an ideology, the psychological overcompensation for the inferiority complex emerging from adopting a second-hand

---

[39] Ibid., 380.
[40] Christos Yannaras, "Τὸ «ὅραμα» Νὰ Γίνει Ἡ Ἑλλάδα Σιγκαπούρη... [The 'Vision' of Turning Greece into Singapore...]," *Kathimerini*, November 28, 2010, http://www.kathimerini.gr/722944/opinion/epikairothta/arxeio-monimes-sthles/to-orama-na-ginei-h-ellada-sigkapoyrh.

identity."[41] And he chooses to identify with those representatives of Modern Greek intellectual legacy that have first taken up the battle against nationalism as a ideologically formulated perversion of being a Greek: "A hundred years since the imposition of state nationalism [...] were needed before a current of fecund resistance to the transformation of *ellinikotita*[42] into a state nationalist ideology could emerge within Greek society; a current by intellectuals and artists, the 'Generation of the '30s.'"[43]—Yorgos Seferis, Odysseas Elytis, Yannis Ritsos et al.

To return to the question of his *modal* understanding of Greek otherness, and apart from its fundamental juxtaposition to nationalism, *mode* also eludes reification as a *concept*—and as such escapes both the Scylla of essentialism and the Charybdis of nominalism. In the same way that Greek nationalism guarantees the eradication of the Greek *mode*, conceptualizing this mode, i.e. turning it into an ideology or a belief system, annihilates it, robs it of its very modality (τροπικότητα); Skliris notes that

> *by approaching the meaning of the "Greek mode," one can easily fall prey to contradiction, since from its very nature a mode is not a concept. We can say that a mode is precisely the opposite of a concept, and that by approaching it conceptually we are depriving it of its deeper dynamics. In contrast to any concept, a mode consists in acquiring an ethos, perhaps by granting it with a special personal modification, without an a priori intention to control what one acquires through concepts or to impose it as an ideology. What can be achieved, however, and what this book attempts, is to point out a posteriori certain moments/milestones of this transmitted mode and their significance. Certain*

---

[41] Yannaras, *The Great Schism Engendered Europe*, 284.
[42] I will be retaining the Greek word "*ellinikotita*" instead of translating it, as a number of translations will not do: "Greekness" identifies a property or substance, which is precisely the opposite of Yannaras' *modal*, experiential understanding; "Hellenicity" has essentialist undertones as well, etc.
[43] Yannaras, *The Great Schism Engendered Europe*, 255.

> *formulations that signify the experience of the mode, without claiming to exhaust it, can be considered as such landmarks.*[44]

This indefinability of the *mode*, which only emerges visibly as *points* in history, constitutes a peculiar kind of history as philosophical poetry, which in turn introduces fertile ground for a political theology aimed at reclaiming history's yet unattained *ecclesial* mode in the *Eschaton*, beyond nations, but *not* beyond the historically incarnated *mode* of civilizational particularity. For, while "in Christ Jesus neither Jew nor Gentile, for you are all one" (Gal. 3:28), *historicity* entails saving what has been loved; such a view resonates in a remark by Georges Florovsky, "What shall pass from history into eternity? The human person with all its relations, such as friendship and love. And in this sense also *culture*, since a person without a concrete cultural face would be a mere fragment of humanity."[45] Yannaras' contribution to this is, in many ways, a different yet related matter, full with potential fecundity—to which we shall return.

## Bibliography

Baker, Fr Matthew. "The City of Cain and the City of Jesus." *Orthodox Christian Network*, March 5, 2015. http://myocn.net/city-cain-city-jesus/.

Birken, Lawrence. "What Is Western Civilization?" *The History Teacher* 25, no. 4 (1992): 451–61. doi:10.2307/494353.

Huntington, Samuel P. *The Clash of Civilizations and the Remaking of World Order*. New York: Simon & Schuster, 1996.

Le Goff, Jacques. *Europe est-elle née au Moyen Age?* Paris: Éditions du Seuil, 2013.

———. *The Birth of Europe*. Translated by Janet Lloyd. Oxford: Wiley-Blackwell, 2006.

Mitralexis, Sotiris. "Activity and Otherness in Christos Yannaras' Propositions for a Critical Ontology." In *Christos Yannaras: Polis,*

---

[44] Skliris, "Review Article: Christos Yannaras, The Great Schism Engendered Europe," 380.

[45] Cited by the late Florovsky scholar, Fr. Matthew Baker, in a sermon he would deliver on March 5, 2015. Fr. Matthew Baker, "The City of Cain and the City of Jesus," *Orthodox Christian Network*, March 5, 2015, http://myocn.net/city-cain-city-jesus/.

*Philosophy, Theology*, edited by Mary Cunningham and Andreas Andreopoulos. London: Ashgate, 2017, *forthcoming*.

———. "Ever-Moving Repose: The Notion of Time in Maximus the Confessor's Philosophy Through the Perspective of a Relational Ontology." PhD diss., Freie Universität Berlin, 2014.

———. "Person, Eros, Critical Ontology: An Attempt to Recapitulate Christos Yannaras' Philosophy." *Sobornost* 34, no. 1 (2012): 33–40.

———. "The Liberation of Church from State in Greece, and the Administrative Fragmentation of Ecclesial Jurisdictions." In *Ex Oriente Lux*, edited by Anna Zhyrkova and Martha Małecka-Kuzak, *forthcoming*. Cracow: Wydawnictwo Ignatianum, 2016.

———. "'Ἡ Κοραϊκὴ «Μετακένωσις» Σύμφωνα Μὲ Τὴ Διδακτορικὴ Διατριβὴ Τοῦ Ἀλέξανδρου Παπαδεροῦ Στὸ Mainz Τὸ 1962 [Korais' 'Metakenosis' According to the Doctoral Thesis of Alexander Papaderos in Mainz, 1962]." In *Πολιτικὴ Ἀδολεσχία I [Political Contributions I]*, 103–20. Athens: Manifesto, 2011.

Papaderos, Alexandros. *Metakenosis: Griechenlands Kulturelle Herausforderung Durch Die Aufklärung in Der Sicht Des Korais Und Des Oikonomos*. Meisenheim am Glan: Verlag Anton Hain, 1970.

Skliris, Dionysios. "Le Concept de Tropos Chez Maxime Le Confesseur." PhD diss., Université Paris IV-Sorbonne, 2015.

———. "Review Article: Christos Yannaras, The Great Schism Engendered Europe." *Theologia* 2015, no. 3 (2015): 379–90.

Wallace-Hadrill, J. M. *The Barbarian West 400-1000*. Oxford: Wiley-Blackwell, 1996.

Yannaras, Christos. *Against Religion: The Alienation of the Ecclesial Event*. Translated by Norman Russell. Brookline, Mass.: Holy Cross Orthodox Press, 2013.

———. *Orthodoxy and the West: Hellenic Self-Identity in the Modern Age*. Translated by Peter Chamberas and Norman Russell. Brookline, Mass.: Holy Cross Orthodox Press, 2006.

———. *Ἡ Εὐρώπη Γεννήθηκε Ἀπὸ Τὸ Σχίσμα [The Great Schism Engendered Europe]*. Athens: Ikaros, 2015.

———. *Κοινωνιοκεντρικὴ Πολιτική: Κριτήρια [Communo-Centric Politics: Criteria]*. Athens: Estia, 2005.

———. "«Κοινωνιοκεντρικὴ» Πολιτική: Τί Σημαίνει; ['Communo-Centric' politics: What Would This Mean?]." *Kathimerini*, June 16, 2002, sec. Feuilleton. http://www.kathimerini.gr/688373/opinion/epikairothta/arxeio-monimes-sthles/koinwniokentrikh-politikh-ti-shmainei.

———. "Τὸ «Ὄραμα» Νὰ Γίνει Ἡ Ἑλλάδα Σιγκαπούρη... [The 'Vision' of Turning Greece into Singapore...]." *Kathimerini*, November 28, 2010. http://www.kathimerini.gr/722944/opinion/epikairothta/arxeio-monimes-sthles/to-orama-na-ginei-h-ellada-sigkapoyrh.

Chapter 5

# Symphonia as a social ethic: toward an Orthodox Christian multiculturalism

Chris Durante

Since the onset of modernity the Orthodox Christian world has experienced many of the tensions that have come to characterize our current historical age, including the tensions between: religion and secularism, ethnicity and religion, and inter-ethnic as well as inter-religious conflict. In the contemporary era, these tensions continue to persist as scholars, policy-makers and the general public alike attempt to arrive at a means of resolving them. Given our current situation, how might the Orthodox Christian tradition make sense of its place within this pluralistic era? I would like to propose that the Byzantine religio-political ideal of symphonia might be able to speak to such issues. In Byzantium, symphonia was enacted as a basic model of Church-State relations between the Patriarchate of Constantinople and the Emperor and has been continually invoked and implemented throughout various historical periods yet was never fully developed as the basis of either a robust political theology or social ethic.

The primary task of this study is to re-examine the applicability of the historical concept of symphonia in our contemporary context and to explore ways in which it might be capable of serving as the foundation of a multicultural social ethic for Orthodox Christianity. As an ethical ideal grounded in the pursuit of social harmony and concordance amongst distinct voices, symphonia can be re-conceptualized as implying a more robust and polyphonic understanding of its purview, whereby it would seek to foster a concordance amongst a variety of ethnic and linguistic cultural identities and perspectives within its own canonical fold as it strives for ecumenical unity and may eventually serve as a means of fostering interfaith amicability and cooperation as it seeks to ensure peaceability and solidarity in global society. For the sake of brevity and precision, this study will focus its attention on the internal ethno-cultural pluralism of the Orthodox Church. Drawing primarily upon the work of Charles Taylor, this study will provide an analysis of the socio-ontological and ethical dimensions of the concepts of symphonia and ethnos. It will be argued that symphonia may be implemented as the foundation of an Orthodox Christian ethics of multiculturalism.

## Symphonia beyond Church-State relations

As a religio-political concept, symphonia was developed by the Byzantine Emperor Justinian in the 6$^{th}$ century as a means of promoting lasting and harmonious relations between the Imperial throne and the Patriarchate of Constantinople in an era in which the relations between Church and State, and issues of social and political authority pertaining to the two, were being questioned. Symphonia was established as an ideal social situation in which the Church and the Imperial throne remained socially distinct institutional entities harmoniously co-existing in their pursuit of common moral and spiritual aims for the imperial community. Justinian's ideal of symphonia builds upon the Emperor Constantine's notion of "One Empire, One Emperor, One Faith" in an ad hoc attempt to postulate a social ideal that could simultaneously promote a formal unity between the Emperor and the Church while recognizing their uniqueness in the social arena. The Church readily adopted the ideal of symphonia yet, did so without ever developing any robust theological or philosophical treatises on the subject.

Grounded in the notion of "One Empire, One Emperor, One Faith," symphonia came to embody a diaphonic understanding of the social world in which only the religious and the political were represented. As a term, "symphonia" implies a coming together of voices and hence, necessarily entails the idea of polyphonia. In a musical sense, symphonia entails distinct notes and instruments coming together to produce a sonorous and harmonious convergence of unique sounds; "harmony in difference" is implicit within the concept itself. As a social concept, symphonia implies the existence of harmonious relations between a number of distinct perspectives and points of view being voiced and hence, again inherently contains difference within it. Historically, those voices might have been the ecclesial authorities and those of the State. Yet, symphonia, and the concordance of voices it implies, need not be restricted to the binary model implemented by the Byzantines. To reduce symphonia to a diaphonic paradigm is to strip this ethical concept of its full potential. Recovering the notion of symphonia in our contemporary era would have to entail picking up where the Byzantines left off and hence, would require further analysis of the underdeveloped aspects of this social ideal.

Simply attempting to apply an unmodified notion of symphonia to current social realities would be to overlook the fact that the enactment of the ideal of symphonia was itself a response to a particular set of socio-historical circumstances and hence, today it must be refashioned as a response to our contemporary circumstances if it is going to retain its ability to pursue its initial purpose of helping the Church make sense of its place in a novel social situation. In our culturally pluralistic age, the voices being sounded are far more numerous and do not simply represent the political and religious spheres of society. Hence, the ethical ideal of symphonia must be developed beyond the confines of Church-State relations. The two primary types of pluralism that the Orthodox Christian tradition must cope with in our contemporary era are: (1) its own internal cultural pluralism and (2) the heightened religious pluralism that has now become a feature of societies across the globe. When taken as a historical ideal of social harmony and community-building, rather than as an imitate-able practice of a medieval era, symphonia can become a social ethic that can enable a greater sense of unity amongst the various cultural communities of the Orthodox world as well as open the Orthodox Christian tradition to establishing amicable relations amongst the diverse faith groups within global society. In order for symphonia to be adopted as a social ethic today I would first like to begin by briefly examining the role that the ideal of symphonia can play in our contemporary paradigms of social thought.

As we engage the social realm we first experience an immediate community of others whom imbue us with our sense of self-identity; while each person is indeed unique, the community of others in which a person's self-identity takes shape is an integral part of each individual's social ontology. As the philosopher and social psychologist George Herbert Mead argued, "The self-conscious human individual, then, takes or assumes the organized social attitudes of the given social group or community to which he belongs...[by which] he governs his own conduct accordingly."[1] Drawing upon Mead, Charles Taylor writes,

> *"The general feature of human life that I want to evoke is its fundamental dialogical character. We become full human agents, capable of understanding ourselves, and hence of defining an identity, through our acquisition of rich human languages of expression...I want to take "language" in a broad sense, covering not only the world we speak but also other modes of expression whereby we define ourselves...No one acquires the languages needed for self-definition on their own. We are introduced to them through exchanges with others who matter to us— what George Herbert Mead called "significant others." The genesis of the human mind is in this sense not "monological,"...but dialogical...We define this [our identity] always in dialogue with, sometimes in struggle against, the identities our significant others want to recognize in us."*[2]

---

[1] George Herbert Mead, *Mind, Self, and Society: From the Perspective of a Social Behavioralist.* Ed. Charles W. Morris. (Chicago: University of Chicago Press, 1934), 156

[2] Charles Taylor, *The Ethics of Authenticity.* (Cambridge, Mass: Harvard University Press, 1991), 32–33.

Communities come to share a social identity and collectively possess a framework for understanding and making sense of reality when persons come together because of a common condition, similar circumstances, and parallel experiences that shape their attitudes and direct their points of view in a common direction, so that they share a perspectival gaze which conditions the way they reason about particular topics and respond to situations of varying kinds. These shared perspectives provide persons with epistemic maps that enable them to navigate the terrain of the social circumstances they find themselves in what Charles Taylor often calls a "social imaginary." Taylor explains writing,

> *"the social imaginary is that common understanding which makes possible common practices, and a widely shared sense of legitimacy...Our social imaginary at any given time is complex. It incorporates a sense of the normal expectations that we have of each other; the kind of common understanding which enables us to carry out the collective practices which make up our social life. This incorporates some sense of how we all fit together in carrying out the common practice...the social imaginary extends beyond the immediate background understanding which makes sense of our particular practices...[It is] an implicit "map" of social space...[that] is unlike a theoretical description of this space...The understanding implicit in practice stands to social theory the way my ability to get around a familiar environment stands to a (literal) map of this area."[3]*

A social imaginary tends to work precisely because it is shared by the other members of the community to which a person belongs. When communities not only share perspectives but—as a result of having to act and live together in shared circumstances—have also developed and established shared sets of norms, ideals of

---

[3] Charles Taylor, *A Secular Age*. (Cambridge, Mass: The Belknap Press of Harvard University 2007), 172-173

excellence and modes of reasoning to guide personal and social behavior, what emerges is a robust cultural community that becomes narratively, normatively and epistemically bound. Such a community becomes narratively bound through shared personal and ancestral histories as well as the stories of the community's ancestral and intellectual forefathers; it becomes normatively bound through a shared ethos, socio-historical teleology, and ideals of excellence that guide collective behavior, personal conduct and shape personal strivings; and epistemically bound through the shared modes of uncovering meaning in experiences, events, phenomena and relations as they collectively construct entire paradigms of symbols and signifiers to produce mutually intelligible ways of making sense of and communicating understandings of lived reality.

Unlike the social imaginary of our contemporary circumstances, which Charles Taylor has described as "unenchanted," the social imaginary of the Byzantine Medieval era was not only one that was "enchanted," or more appropriately a world in which immanence and transcendence were intimately linked, but it was also a social imaginary in which social life was deeply connected to either imperial and or phyletic (tribal) modes of sociality. In such circumstances symphonia was the Church's way of making sense of its role in an imperial civilization that had become amicable, where it was once hostile, toward its existence. For the Church, *symphonia was a response to a particular historical need*: namely, responding to the question of how the Church can remain an active force of social transformation and personal spirituality in an age in which the imperial state promotes its existence as a means of ensuring the bonds necessary for a common collective identity. While this might have been the socio-historic situation that gave rise to symphonia as a social concept, the current socio-historical circumstances are such that the Orthodox Church must address the issue of pluralism and find ways of being an active social presence of peace and transcendence in an era in which diverse identities have been vying for recognition within an immanent social frame. As such, one of the main obstacles facing Orthodox Christianity today is the task of finding ways in which a sense of ecclesial unity can be cultivated yet, to do so without eradicating the particularities of the various ethno-cultural communities of which its global ecumene is comprised. It must find a way in which it can recognize and respect the unique cultural identities of its members, and continue to enable them to congregate as distinct cultural communities while simultaneously cultivating a sense of shared faith and common moral mission in the world.

In the pre-modern times of Byzantium, notions of transcendence and immanence were intimately interwoven in the social imaginary of the era whereby conceptions of lingua-cultural unity, religio-political unity and divine-human unity all intermingled in personal and communal strivings for human flourishing. A prominent aspect of what Charles Taylor calls our "secular age" is that the transcendental dimensions of existence have become marginalized. He argues that we now begin our lives situated within an "immanent frame" in which it is possible to imagine our place within social life without any reference to the transcendent. This is one of the problems of "secularity" that all religious traditions face and have been grappling with in their attempts to make sense of their role in our current historical period. If Taylor's thesis is correct, that which has become marginalized in a secular age is a person's ability to pursue vertical transcendence and hence, because of this deprivation, we are witnessing a revival of personal and communal strivings for "spiritual" transcendence—the quest to transcend the immanence of the natural world itself—as we begin to enter an epoch in which religion has re-emerged in the public sphere, and which some are referring to as "post-secular." While such a revival of transcendental strivings may indeed be evident in the contemporary era as evidenced by a renewed interest in various forms of mysticism and contemplative spirituality, there is still a sharp divorce in our social imaginary between that which is considered "transcendent," and or "sacred," and that which is thought to be "immanent," or "profane."

In our era one of the tasks of symphonia will be to reconcile the binary that has been constructed between the transcendent and the immanent. If we turn to the Hegelian roots of Taylor's thought, we will discover a dual conception of transcendence: that of vertical transcendence and horizontal transcendence.[4] Our age begins within the "immanent frame," to borrow Taylor's phrase, and hence, calls for a re-conceptualization of transcendence from within the frame of immanence. What we might refer to as a "post-secular," or "post-modern," (for lack of a better phrase) understanding of transcendence overcomes the antagonism between the immanent and transcendent by attempting to recognize and harmonize the vertical and horizontal dimensions of transcendence. Therefore, symphonia as a social ethic calls for a form of transcendence within immanence whereby the transcendental ceases to be conceptualized as being solely a "vertical" movement and comes to include a "horizontal" transcendence of the reified identity constructs that we have built in our secular age.

In its original religio-political usage, symphonia indicated the harmony between two distinct social entities in which both remained recognizably unique. Likewise, in the Orthodox theological discussions of theosis, or divine-human communion, a person's uniqueness is not lost into the divine as s/he undergoes self-transcendence—both the divine and the human person retain their uniqueness in a process of union. The pursuit of horizontal transcendence is predicated upon the capacity for inter-personal communion as well as inter-group communion whereby the uniqueness of both particular persons and/or uniqueness of distinct communities is recognized and respected as people attempt to move beyond individualistic and collectivistic forms of self-enclosure. An ethic of symphonia recognizes the possibility of bringing forth an intercultural harmony whereby religious unity is not predicated upon cultural uniformity and solidarity does not require homogeneity.

As a result of overly collectivist and extreme forms of homogenizing universalism, we tend to conceptualize solidarity as being predicated on the annihilation of our differences and hence, we have been neglectful of diversity to the point where we seek

---

[4] Georg Wilheim Fredrick Hegel, *Phenomenology of the Spirit.* trans. A.V. Miller. (Oxford: Clarendon Press, 1807).

the homogenization of cultures in our attempts to proclaim a single shared tradition as the sole possessor of truth. Yet, there is a middle way between the extremes of divisive diversity and unifying homogeneity. The Orthodox Church is capable of finding a uniquely Orthodox and indigenous means of coping with the pluralism of our contemporary world that will neither lead it down the path of exclusivistic particularism nor toward an extremist universalism that seeks to eradicate the ethno-cultural customs and heritages that have helped carry the faith through history. This is where an ethic of symphonia may be able to resolve the internal divisiveness that currently exists within the global Orthodox Church as well as eventually provide a means for responding and relating to the social world outside of its own canonical fold.

## Ethnicity, religion & recognition

During the height of modernity, the Orthodox world experienced an era in which secularism's "disenchanting" of society gave rise to a social imaginary in which the ontological aspirations of peoples were expected to be realized in immediate historical circumstances and in which cultural teleologies of flourishing were politicized into nationalistic aspirations for political sovereignty. As a result, ethno-nationalism emerged as a perceived means of providing onto-historical fulfilment through political ends and hence, secular nationalism became wedded to ethno-cultural narratives that eventually served as a historically divisive force that weakened the social unity of the larger Orthodox Christian religious community.

Through the "secularization" of social life that occurred during modernity, notions of the "sacred" and "profane" became altered to the point where valuing historically contingent yet useful human social constructs morphed into a reverence for them as if they were timeless and eternal transcendental phenomena. The sociologist of religion, Jose Casanova, has claimed that in the secular age we have come to sacralize a variety of secular phenomena, including: the nation, citizenship and human rights.[5] I

---

[5] Casanova, José. *The Secular and Secularisms,* Social Research 76.4 (2009): 1064.

wish to focus here on one particular sacralized secular phenomenon that has plagued the Orthodox world: the nation. Unlike our contemporary notion of "culture"—including lingua-culturality, ethno-culturality, or even religio-culturality for that matter—"nationalisms" now carry with them politicized identity narratives and hence, produce a teleology in which any distinct collective's aim must be to create a nation-state for themselves in order for their community to fulfill its purpose within history.

Although the term "ethnic" is often used to refer to the bio-genetic relatedness of an ancestral peoples, the term "ethnos" implied a collection of people accustomed to living together and hence, implies a collective with a shared linguistic mode of communication and an inherited tradition of customs that creates a common historical narrative that serves to bind its members together in a shared sense of peoplehood. While the Latin natio refers to a place of birth and hence, originally implies a people-hood rooted in ancestral place, the "nation" has come to imply a "state," or at least an implicit desire for "statehood" by the "nation," and hence a socio-political structure to house the people. As such the "nation" has become a politicized apparatus in modernity divorced from other forms of human bonding, fellowship and communality. Despite their originally similar meanings, nation and ethnicity have come to imply distinct phenomena.

An ethnos implies an ancestry of a people united by place of origin and historical rootedness in common linguistic and cultural practices, and hence originally had as its focus the inter-relationality of persons, whereas a nation implies a collection of individuals united by a set of similarities and each one's relation to a centralized authoritative concept rather than webs of interpersonal relation. An ethnos possesses a rich affective and interpersonal dimension that is not necessary for the existence of a nation as a political entity. As the sociologist Anthony Smith has written, "When people identify with ethnies, they feel a sense of wider kinship with a fictive "super-family," one that extends outwards in space and down the generations."⁶ Smith's observation highlights the interpersonal and affective dimensions of communal bonding that takes place within ethnic communities. In such a communal bonding, a transcendence within immanence occurs whereby the self goes beyond itself in affectionate relation to a family, families to ethnies, and the ethno-cultural community's existential vitality through temporality and spatiality.

In the history of Orthodox Christianity, with the emergence of the very notion of "Christendom" came a sacralization of Empire so that a geo-politically bounded entity in the immanent frame became intimately intertwined with the population's notions of transcendence. This produced a social imaginary in which the vertical transcendence of the individual was interwoven with participation in a community committed to common convictions and practices as well as a common centralized authority figure. As Byzantium slipped away through Ottoman conquest, so did the hermeneutic significance of the geo-political entity that was once sacralized so that with time it became the linguistically and religio-culturally bounded Rum millet that was to retain the sacred hermeneutic significance that Imperial Byzantium once possessed. With the onset of modernity came a penetrating empiricism that shifted the world's social imaginary from one in which notions of transcendence were operative to one that could not see past the "immanent frame," a frame that "constitutes a "natural" order, to be contrasted to a "supernatural" one, an "immanent" world, over against a possible "transcendent" one"⁷ that de-centered persons' sense of place and purpose in history as they sought objects of devotion in the worldly order.

As ethno-linguistic differences gradually stratified the Rum millet and as each ethno-linguistic group sought liberation from the Ottoman empire, these distinct collectives, with their yearning for some form of the transcendental and the sacred began to sacralize their own ethno-linguistic ancestral collective histories

---

⁶ Anthony Smith, *Chosen Peoples: Why ethnic groups survive*, Ethnic and Racial Studies 15.3(1992): 438.
⁷ Charles Taylor, *A Secular Age*, 542.

and engage in a quasi-deification of the leaders, authorities and heroes who came to symbolize them. With the onset of the modern period, social life becomes inconceivable outside of the immanent frame, and hence politics and science became the primary avenues through which we imagine our social positioning; subsequently, *natio* becomes politicized while *ethnos* becomes biologically "racialized." Further, with modernity eroding the practice of traditional customs and displacing the transcendental understanding of reality, "political sovereignty" replaces "transcendental union with the divine" as the operative concept of salvation. Simultaneously, modernity's emphasis upon the immanent transforms the cultural aspects of ethnic ancestry so that it becomes perceived almost solely in terms of biogenetic racial markers. In the secular age the idea of ethno-nationality as a phylogenetically charged concept emerges as an object of devotion worshiped through political means.

When this occurs each individual member is imagined as relating to the nation as an individual and becomes perceived in terms of equivalence so that both the uniqueness of each particular person and the unique webs of relationality that exist amongst them are overlooked producing a demand for conformity. This will give rise to the sacralization of ethno-national groupings to the point where ecclesial forms of theological and ritualistic religiosity were placed in the service of the nation as an apparatus of group survival that became limited to a uniform collective's ability to persist "unaltered" through time. With such a narrowing of the scope of the sacred came aspirations for political sovereignty so that independence as a nation-state, and social recognition as such, became the only viable means to make the collective's existence within history meaningful; the "nation," in its most profane sense, became the sacred object of its members personal devotion as the Church was reduced to the handmaiden of its self-perpetuation. As this occurred, each group sought from the other recognition of its own collective uniqueness and the value of its cultural contributions to human history and importance in the history of the Orthodox tradition itself. As Isaiah Berlin has written,

> "Nationalism springs, as often as not, from a wounded or outraged sense of human dignity, the desire for recognition. This desire is surely one of the greatest forces that move human history. It may take hideous forms, but is not in itself either unnatural or repulsive as a feeling….the demand for recognition…is perhaps the deepest root of our social discontents…In short, they [in this case, the ethno-linguistic communities] suffer[ed] from a sense of insufficient recognition."[8]

With the springing forth of ethno-nationalist sentiments and the subsequent eruption of the warfare and violence that accompanied the decline of the Ottoman empire, we witness a series of intra-Orthodox tensions and conflicts that may be characterized as the embodiment of the Hegelian idea of a "struggle for recognition."[9] In this struggle at least two self-conscious entities not only attempt to acquire recognition and acknowledgment from the other but either attempt to subsume the other in itself hence, annihilating the unique existence of the other, or to destroy the other thereby undermining the very relationality from which consciousness as a unique self-identity emerged in the first place. From this perspective, each ethno-nationalist "Orthodox" enclave sought to affirm the significance of its existence in contradistinction to all others in a centrifugal mode of collective consciousness motivated by fear and enmity toward the other, always defining itself and the other in acts of negation—negating the worth and value of the other so that the only way the other's existence is valued, and its significance is perceived, is as something that must be subsumed in itself or destroyed in the name of a false "authenticity" as it ironically comes to loose its own communal identity by increasingly defining itself solely in terms of that which it is not.

---

[8] Isaiah Berlin, *The Sense of Reality*. (Farrar, Straus & Giroux. New York, NY, 1996), 252.
[9] Georg Wilheim Fredrick Hegel, *Phenomenology of the Spirit*.

Given the relational and interdependent nature of human self-identity on both personal and communal levels we can come to realize how such struggles and conflicts are oxymoronic and self-defeating. If group A's goal of eliminating other groups is the result of A's failure to recognize the value and relational importance of the other groups, then, if this elimination is completely achieved, group A will be left standing alone so self-absorbed and in dire need of recognition and acknowledgement that its entire purpose for existing will have come crashing to a halt. There will be no others whom can recognize the victorious self's existence, which as a result of the very struggle it has been engaged in has now been reduced and diminished to an identity that can only exist as "Not-Other," or "Other-than" and hence, would socio-ontologically cause its own self-annihilation as it eliminates the fields of otherness from which it initially arose and which it no longer has for the maintenance of the shell of an identity it is currently left with. The group as a united entity will implode upon itself as its members respectively seek other means of exclusivist recognition and fragment into sub-groups vying for dominance in a new struggle for recognition. This is precisely what we witnessed during the Balkan wars in which after an ethno-nationalist victory was achieved many nations plummeted into civil war. Although there indeed exist pre-modern roots to this "struggle for recognition," it was the secularizing tendencies of modernity that led to the formation of politicized identity constructs devoid of a genuine sense of relationality and transcendence within immanence. The politicization of collective identities that accompanies the gradual sacralization of the nation(-state) distorts our understandings of the relational dimensions of communal life by reducing the notion of solidarity to a collective's acceptance of shared political ideology and breeding purely socio-political aspirations devoid of any deeper commitments to flourishing as persons seeking forms of fellowship beyond the boundaries of citizenship.

In response to the violent ethno-nationalistic intra-Orthodox conflicts and wars that occurred during the nineteenth century, in 1872 the Patriarch of Constantinople declared "phyletism" a sin. As with the notion of symphonia, little philosophical or theological reflection and analysis on this concept has occurred. *As a sin, phyletism is not simply a love for one's ethno-cultural group. Rather, the immorality embodied in phyletism is a sense of ethno-racial, or phylogenetic, supremacy that distorts love of one's peoples from an opportunity to experience and cultivate affectionate fellowship with others into a malicious sense of superiority of one's own ethno-racial group while eschewing others.* This sin becomes worsened when an ethnic group links such a malicious sense of superiority with their membership in an Orthodox Christian ecclesial community for it undermines the very Christian ethic of love that such a community is supposed to embody. The reasons why phyletism had to be declared a sin in the first place is because of the violent, malicious and supremacist ways in which numerous ethno-nationalist groups responded to modernity and began to use their religious affiliation as an instrument of achieving their nationalistic political agendas.[10]

However, simply because phyletism is immoral it does not necessarily follow that sentimentality for one's ethno-cultural traditions and community is in and of itself a moral wrong. Just as self-conceit, or egoism, involves a form of self-concern yet is not identical to it, phyletism is not identical to ethno-affectivity. Insofar as the sin of phyletism inherently involves ethnicity, many commentators, both from within the ranks of Orthodox Christianity and observers coming from without, have criticized the ethno-religious ecclesial affiliations that have come to characterize contemporary Orthodox Christian communities, especially in the West. Yet, we must be careful not to confuse ethno-religious communal fraternity with either ethno-centric theological professions or prejudice based upon ethno-nationalist bigotry. Simply because a religious community values it's cultural and linguistic traditions does not necessarily imply it is guilty of phyletism.

---

[10] Especially guilty are the those men of the cloth—those priests & bishops—who either went along with such malicious social currents or even at times encouraged their congregants to behave maliciously.

As has already been made clear, we must remain cognizant of the differences between ethno-nationalism and ethno-culture; for culture plays an integral role in human flourishing as a necessary means of opening fields of relationality with others and does not necessarily result in bigotry. "Ethnos" as a terminological signifier of a cultural community rooted in history, customary heritage and the forbearers of tradition is linked to a person's psycho-social ability to develop affectionate bonds of fellowship as well as transmit sets of beliefs and practices. Derived from the Latin *religio*, meaning to be bound together, "religion" and "ethnicity" posses a similar social functionality of community-building and existentially orienting persons so that the two have had, and may continue to engage in, a symbiotic co-existence in the lives of a people; in a sense, an ethno-religious group may be seen as the embodiment of a symphonia between an ethno-cultural heritage and a religious faith tradition.

If we adopt a perspective of ethnos in its cultural sense we can come to understand how an initial affinity for a particular culture is not necessarily antithetical to the cultivation of a moral concern for others whom exist beyond the bounds of that particular community. Given the relational intimacy involved in community formation, as a person's sense of self begins to emerge, the person begins to empathize with others with whom s/he feels emotionally close to. This will usually initially take place within a family setting and eventually begin to expand beyond the familial circle toward the extended family and neighbors who happen to be a part of the self's ancestral, cultural and linguistic group. Here we begin to witness an expansion of one's capacity to imagine him/herself in the place of the other—an expansion of his/her horizon of empathetic engagement as s/he moves ever increasingly through the concentric circles of his/her sociality. With this empathy comes a fondness and affection for those with whom a self has empathetically engaged—a person will come to feel as though those others are inseparable from their own self-existence and come to hold a unique bond with them and affection for them. As a result of empathizing with others, our fondness for another primes us for receptiveness to the points of view and circumstances of another; in this sense, empathy and affinity become intertwined as they give rise to a self's moral sensibilities. As one develops an affinity toward other persons s/he begins to recognize the other's distinctiveness while simultaneously recognizing the other's place in his/her own self-narrative. Through this awareness emerges a person's capacity for taking the other's concerns, and concern for the other, into his/her deliberations and epistemic orientation in his/her social field of agency.

As one continually engages others in the concentric circles of sociality moving from the imagined self-in-solitude, through the family, extended family, cultural collective and then out toward the world, affinity towards the initially unknown selves immersed in one's concentric circles of sociality enables one to empathize with and develop a penchant for recognizing the value in more distant others with whom we are not yet acquainted and a moral concern for those not immediately present to us—those with whom we do not share immediate experiences or shared personal histories. Our capacity to comprehend other perspectives on a psychological level emerges from the empathetic expansion of our horizons of affinity and affection and an engagement with various forms of particularity in ever-expanding spheres of social engagement. Hence, it is from a person's tendency toward affinity that empathy emerges and from empathy that the recognition of difference and otherness can be implemented in cultivating a concern for others and an ability to perceive the value of their cultural communities as we engage in a self-reflective comprehension of the affection we feel for our own communities. Recognition of the value of particular cultural communities (first our own and then those of others) lies at the very heart of the concept of symphonia as a social ethic.

## Symphonia & multiculturalism

We must not succumb to naïve ways of conceptualizing universality, and by extension the idea of the Church's catholicity, and mistakenly believe that Orthodox Christianity's universal moral and spiritual message can only be realized through a decoupling of the ethnic and religious dimensions of Orthodox churches. Enacting symphonia as a means of combating phyletism, Orthodox Christianity must look to harmonize the particularities of ethno-cultural communities with the universalism of the Orthodox faith and find ways in which they compliment one another rather than becoming caught in a binary mode of thought that forces it to the extremes of endorsing one at the expense of the other. We live in an era of pluralism and hence, any religious tradition that is not prepared to recognize and value its own internal pluralism as a feature of lived human reality will indeed find it difficult if not impossible to flourish. As the philosopher Anthony Appiah has recognized, "A creed that disdains the partialities of kinfolk and community may have a past, but it has no future."[11]

Charles Taylor argues that by recognizing the importance of relationality in our conceptions of human nature that we ought not overlook the cultural realities that relationality produces on the communal level. Again drawing on Hegel, Taylor claims that "Due recognition is not just a courtesy we owe people. It is a vital human need."[12] Taylor explains writing,

> *"The thesis is that our identity is partly shaped by recognition or its absence, often by the misrecognition of others, and so a person or group of people can suffer real damage, real distortion, if the people or society around them mirror back to them a confining or demeaning or contemptible picture of themselves. Nonrecognition or misrecognition can inflict harm, can be a form of oppression, imprisoning someone in a false, distorted, and reduced mode of being."*[13]

---

[11] Anthony Kwame Appiah, *Cosmopolitanism: Ethics in a World of Strangers*. (New York, NY: W.W. Norton & Company, 2006), xviii.

[12] Charles Taylor, "The Politics of Recognition," in *Multiculturalism*, ed. Amy Gutmann, (Princeton, NJ: Princeton University Press, 1994), 26

[13] Ibid., 25

Consequently, to deny recognition to ethno-lingua-cultural traditions by excluding them from universal religious and moral aspirations is itself a form of harm against both communities and persons as it stifles their sense of relational meaningfulness in the social sphere. We must be able to differentiate the ethically positive aspects of ethno-culturality and lingua-culturality from the ethno-phyletic distortions (when they become self-absorbed through their failure to recognize the value in others) of such traditions. *Phyletism is immoral precisely because it involves an egoistic form of collective self-recognition coupled with either non-recognition or the misrecognition of other groups, and their members, and thus is itself a distortion of what a morally sound affinity for, and fondness of, one's own ethno-linguistic culture can be.*

As a form of racism and bigotry, phyletism involves a failure to recognize another's culture as valuable. If the Orthodox Christian Church were to fail to recognize the value in ethno-linguistic cultures it would commit the same sort of harm and moral offense that is implicit in phyletism itself—namely non-recognition. When recognition of the value of culture is denied it causes suffering upon the community of persons whom value it and from which they beget their social identity. That which spawned the violent intra-Orthodox conflicts that gave rise to the decree that phyletism is a sin was precisely the fact that various ethnic groups felt that they were not being given due recognition of their unique communal identities. If the Orthodox Church is to offer more than simple platitudes and truly engage in a robust discussion of Orthodoxy's relation to cultural pluralism it must keep in mind that, "discussions of multiculturalism are undergirded by the premises that denied recognition can be a form of oppression."[14] As Orthodox Christians continue to debate the role of ethnicity in the ecclesial organization of the Church they should take heed of Charles Taylor's words when he writes,

> "cultures that have provided the horizon of meaning for large numbers of human beings, or diverse characters

---

[14] Charles Taylor, *The Ethics of Authenticity*, 50

> and temperaments, over a long period of time—that have,
> in other words, articulated their sense of the good, the
> holy, the admirable—are almost certain to have
> something that deserves our admiration and respect,
> even if it is accompanied by much that we have to abhor
> and reject."[15]

It is logically possible to hold a deep fondness for a particular ethno-linguistic culture and an affinity toward the ways in which the Christian tradition has manifested itself in that culture while still recognizing the value in other cultures. There is much beauty to be found in the ethno-cultural and lingua-cultural dimensions of the ways in which Orthodox Christianity became manifest within the way of life of a community. On a very basic sociological level, for a local church to become actively involved in the life of a community it will necessarily become involved in and influenced by the socio-cultural customs and practices of those people. By doing so the church then becomes intertwined in the way of life of a people and arguably is better poised to achieve its mission of guiding the life of a congregation of persons. A church's celebration of an ethno-linguistic cultural community and its customs and heritage does not necessarily preclude celebrating a common faith with others. On the contrary, through such a celebration of the particular a religion is better equipped to highlight the moral commonalities that said culture shares with other cultures and, in the context of a shared faith, highlight the existence of shared beliefs, rituals and religious practices. As Aristotle made very clear, the universal must always actualize itself through the particular. Hence, a church's intertwinement with an ethno-cultural tradition does not hinder its ability to transmit universal moral and onto-metaphysical truths. A religion's fusion with an ethno-cultural tradition helps enable its manifestation as an active moral and spiritual force in the world by becoming entwined in a people's ancestral narrative and the personal identity of its members who adopt such a narrative as part of their own.

---

[15] Charles Taylor, "The Politics of Recognition," 72–73

When religion and culture intertwine in a people's history to create a braided narrative they may coalesce in a symbiosis and together form a common way of life bred by faith, custom and relation. Through this symbiosis of religion and culture, faith becomes embodied in humanity's immanence in the material world; it becomes incarnate in praxis and the material expressions of cultural custom. In this way religion both creates culture as it fuses with and creates new customs and histories of the peoples that have adopted it and is influenced by pre-existing cultures as religion adopts the languages of a people and becomes part of their historical identity narratives. Recalling and recollecting scenarios and circumstances of the past is an integral aspect of the survival and continuation of both faith traditions and ethno-linguistic cultures. Grounded in history and the experiences of temporality itself, tradition can only survive through embodiment in material expression and the re-enactment of its narrative in both ritualistic and textual forms. When religion and ethnicity combine, an ethnos is infused with an onto-metaphysical and meta-ethical paradigm as religion gains a conduit through which it can narratively ground itself in history. As the secularizing tendencies of modernity threaten religiosity, ethno-religiosity can more easily sustain a social imaginary in which the religious dimensions of its existence are capable of transcending a particular historical era and may become a more influential current in the unfolding of a community's history as a force capable of permeating the embodied realities of social life and the aesthetical and ethical features of immanent worldly existence in secularized spaces. It is through culture that faith can become incarnate in history. Given the valuable inter-relationality that exists between faith and culture, a re-conceptualized notion of symphonia recognizes the value in ethno-linguistic dimensions of culture while simultaneously seeking to de-sacralize the "nation" as it re-orients those communal gazes toward that which their common faith holds to be sacred.

Symphonia will be realized when we are able to find that balance in which valuing our cultural traditions and preserving customs is not antithetical to adopting multicultural perspectives and attitudes that can harmonize distinct ways of life as we seek to cultivate harmony and peaceability in society. A symphonic response to the social climate of the contemporary era will be one in which the nation is de-sacralized; one in which the Orthodox ethno-religious communities will be able to effectively de-couple their identity narratives from purely politico-nationalistic aims while still retaining the ethno-linguistic traditions that imbue them with a deep sense of fellowship. This will entail alternative ways of envisioning social solidarity as we come to terms with pluralism as an unavoidable social reality and persistent feature of human existence. A reinvigorated ideal of symphonia is able to cultivate a multicultural ethos of "solidarity in diversity," or "unity in plurality," amongst the various Orthodox Christian ethno-religious communities, calling for a cross-cultural common-mindedness of faith and virtue while accepting diverse cultural expressions of its manifestation in the immanent realm. In an our era of diasporas, diversity, and globalization, a religious tradition that is historically seasoned in the ways of pluralism, and fostering a symbiotic existence between faith and cultures, seems to posses a potential strength which can make it well-suited to flourish in an age committed to multiculturalism, multilingualism and religious diversity.

Phyletism may be overcome by acknowledging the other's need for cultural recognition and discovering the value in that culture as the community itself strives toward the ideal of symphonia. Instead of reifying exclusivist ethnic identities through cultural enclosure to other Orthodox communities, through symphonia ethno-religiosity has the potential to be an avenue through which members of such communities can come to recognize one another as fellow carriers of historical ethno-linguistic cultures as well as adherents to a common faith tradition. Hypostasizing the ideal of symphonia will entail transcending cultural enclosure to recognize and respect other cultural communities yet doing so without losing the unity and uniqueness of one's own cultural community. This involves transcendence within the immanent world in which the cultural communities become united in solidarity while remaining distinct social entities. Aiming toward an ideal of symphonia, members of the Orthodox communities are capable of identifying with the ways in which another relates to his or her faith through an ethno-lingua-cultural tradition—even when the ethno-linguistic culture is not shared. Such circumstances are a fertile ground for the cultivation of a type of intercultural sentiment in which an affection and affinity for one's own particular ethnic and or linguistic culture is no longer antithetical to solidarity and unity with both other ethno-religious Orthodox Christian communities and other members of global civil society.

The multicultural vision of symphonia views the existence of the bricolage of distinct autocephalous and autonomous ethno-religious Orthodox churches as a community of communities adopting a spirit of cooperative intercultural philanthropia. On the ethical plane, symphonia is related to the concept of philanthropia, or a "loving friendship" toward humanity insofar as love of humanity involves recognizing what it means to be human. In its common usage by Orthodox thinkers, philanthropia is often discussed in terms of one-to-one interpersonal encounters of loving-kindness. However, this is no prima facia reason why this concept cannot also apply to intergroup, or inter-community, relations as well. If it is true that persons always relate to humanity through the particular human cultural communities that give rise to their sense of social identity and belonging then, philanthropia, as a "love of humanity" necessarily entails the recognition of culture as an integral aspect of the human condition and a person's ability to be in relation to others. Once we come to recognize the saliency of culture to human identity, philanthropia as part of an ethic of symphonia will come to entail not simply loving-kindness amongst individual persons irrespective of their personal human uniqueness but because of it; and part of the dialogical uniqueness of each person is his/her identity as a member of a particular cultural community.

In accord with the initial ideal of symphonia, it will also include striving to achieve intercultural harmony despite group differences and reconciliation amongst communities in conflict by attempting to foster a common-mindedness on ethico-spiritual ideals. A symphonic philanthropy entails actively willing harmony in humanity while simultaneously recognizing any attempt to achieve social harmony through homogeneity is a pseudo-harmony that aims to produce a monistic order achieved through an annihilation of difference rather than a genuine concordance amongst the plurality of humanity's cultural expressions that have organically developed through history. A social telos of homogeneity does nothing but create a fertile ground for a "struggle for recognition" in that it fails to comprehend the plural nature of human sociality and fails to recognize that another's way of life is as valuable to that person as one's own way of life is to oneself.

## Conclusion

The re-conceptualized notion of symphonia I have proposed is capable of cultivating an attitude that does not eschew the ethno-cultural dimensions of the lived realities of faith but instead acknowledges the ways in which Orthodox Christianity was embraced by distinct ethno-linguistic cultures as it spread and hence, recognizes plurality as a salient aspect of the universality of the faith itself. Adopting symphonia as a social ethic will entail a conceptualization of ethno-religiosity as embodying the notion that in the pluralistic reality of human social life any universal faith will always manifest itself through the particular, thereby enabling the emergence of a religio-cultural atmosphere in which ethno-linguistic diversity is incorporated into the very moral fabric of the tradition's global and local presence itself. Within the ecclesial fold of the canonical Orthodox Christian churches, pursuing the ideal of symphonia will begin with concerted efforts to cultivate an intra-Orthodox ethos of unity in plurality that values its tradition's indigenous forms of linguistic and cultural pluralism as well as coming to realize that intra-faith harmony is not predicated upon cultural homogeneity. Ethno-religiosity must never be condemned simply because its name has been used to justify violence, hatred, division and supremacy for then we must also condemn the name of "God" and "Peace" and "Freedom," for these terms have also been used by fanatical extremists to irrationally justify warfare and segregation.

Orthodox Christianity's uniqueness as a theologically unified religious community of ethno-cultural communities, each sharing a liturgical and theological tradition and ecclesiastic structure, has primed Orthodoxy for continued survival in the coming post-secular era in which cultural assimilation and homogenization are being contested. Any religious tradition that is able to successfully balance its universalism with the realities of pluralism will be more apt to flourish and have a more prosperous future in a world that has come to be defined by cultural, linguistic and religious forms of pluralism. If Orthodoxy cannot find a way to respect and value its own internal diversity it will be less likely to be able to successfully rise to the challenges of the current era and of engaging in ecumenical as well as interfaith relations in an amicable and mutually fruitful manner. Achieving a symphonic existence whereby Orthodox Christian ethno-religious churches do not become amalgamated while engaging in dialogue and striving for common spiritual and moral ends may come to serve as an example of how to cultivate a multicultural form of common religiosity as well as the ability to feel a sense of solidarity with others despite the fact that they worship in a different language. Symphonia is capable of simultaneously cultivating an Orthodox Christian ethic of multiculturalism that may eventually enable the emergence of novel forms of engaging the world's other faiths as it seeks to preserve and celebrate its own ethno-cultural and lingua-cultural diversity.

# Bibliography

Appiah, Anthony Kwame. *Cosmopolitanism: Ethics in a World of Strangers.* New York, NY: W.W. Norton & Company, 2006.

Berlin, Isaiah. *The Sense of Reality.* Farrar, Straus & Giroux. New York, NY, 1996.

Casanova, José. *The Secular and Secularisms,* Social Research 76.4 (2009): 1049–1066.

Hegel, Georg Wilheim Fredrick. *Phenomenology of the Spirit.* Trans. A.V. Miller. Oxford: Clarendon Press, 1977(1807).

Mead, George Herbert. *Mind, Self, and Society: From the Perspective of a Social Behavioralist.* Ed. Charles W. Morris. Chicago: University of Chicago Press, 1934.

Smith, Anthony. "Chosen Peoples: Why ethnic groups survive," *Ethnic and Racial Studies* 15.3(1992): 436–456.

Taylor, Charles. *The Ethics of Authenticity.* Cambridge, Mass: Harvard University Press, 1991.

–––. "The Politics of Recognition," in *Multiculturalism*, edited by Amy Gutmann, 25–76. Princeton, NJ: Princeton University Press, 1994.

–––. *A Secular Age.* Cambridge, Mass: The Belknap Press of Harvard University, 2007.

Chapter 6

# Asceticism and creative destruction: on ontology and economic history

Dylan Pahman

## Introduction

While often admired for its theological and spiritual depth, Orthodox Christianity does not have anything comparable to Roman Catholics, Neocalvinists, and others in regards to its own unique take on Christian social thought, outside of environmental theology. Precious few scholarly sources focus on economics in particular. Notable exceptions include the following: Vladimir Solovyov's last major work, *The Justification of the Good*, contains a whole book on social morality, including a chapter on economic life.[1] Fr. Sergei Bulgakov, known principally for his controversial, sophianic theology, was a Marxist economist before becoming a politician and only later an Orthodox priest. He wrote a critique of Marx, several essays on economic issues from an Orthodox religious perspective, and a book exploring the philosophical insights of economic ideas.[2] More recently, Daniel Payne and

---

[1] See Vladimir Solovyov, *The Justification of the Good*, 2nd ed., trans. Natalie Duddington, ed. Boris Jakim (Grand Rapids, MI: Eerdmans, 2005), 282–311

[2] See Sergei Bulgakov, *Karl Marx as a Religious Type: His Relation to the Religion of Anthropotheism of L. Feuerbach*, trans. Luba Barna (Belmont, MA: Nordland, 1979); idem, "Heroism and Asceticism: Reflections on the Religious Nature of the Russian Intelligentsia," in *Vekhi: Landmarks*, trans. and ed. Marshall S. Shatz and Judith E. Zimmerman (Armonk, NY; London: M.E. Sharpe, 1994), 17–50; idem, "The National Economy and the Religious Personality (1909)," trans. Krassen Stanchev, *Journal of Markets & Morality* 11, no. 1 (Spring 2008): 157–179; idem, *Philosophy of Economy: The World as Household*, trans. and ed. Catherine Evtuhov (New Haven and London: Yale University Press, 2000). See also Krassen Stanchev, "Sergey Bulgakov and the Spirit of Capitalism," *Journal of Markets & Morality* 11, no. 1 (Spring 2008): 149–156.

Christopher Marsh have built upon Bulgakov's work to develop an Orthodox perspective on what they term Christian economics.[3] Alfred Kentigern Siewers, drawing from Bulgakov and Fr. Pavel Florensky, has argued for the importance of traditional marriage for ensuring social justice.[4] Offering his own response to Max Weber's famous thesis on the Protestant ethic, Metropolitan Irinej Dobrijević has written a positive, but not uncritical, Orthodox assessment of capitalism, drawing upon recent experience of the Serbian Orthodox Church.[5] The Moscow Patriarchate has also produced two documents that address a broad array of social-ethical questions, including economic questions.[6] Two recent monographs also pay more scholarly attention to economics: *Creation and the Heart of Man* by Fr. Michael Butler and economist Andrew Morriss and *The Cure for Consumerism* by Fr. Gregory Jensen.[7] Lastly, in my own work I have sought to develop asceticism as an Orthodox principle of social organization.[8]

---

[3] See Daniel P. Payne and Christopher Marsh, "Sergei Bulgakov's "Sophic" Economy: An Eastern Orthodox Perspective on Christian Economics," *Faith & Economics* 53 (Spring 2009): 35–51.

[4] See Alfred Kentigern Siewers, "Traditional Christian Marriage as an Expression of Social Justice: Identity and Society in the Writings of Florensky and Bulgakov," *Journal of Markets & Morality* 16, no. 2 (Fall 2013): 569–586.

[5] See Irinej Dobrijević, "The Orthodox Spirit and the Ethic of Capitalism: A Case Study on Serbia and Montenegro and the Serbian Orthodox Church," *Serbian Studies* 20, no. 1 (2006): 1–13.

[6] See Department of External Church Relations, *The Basis of the Social Concept of the Russian Orthodox Church*, 2000, https://mospat.ru/en/documents/social-concepts/; idem, *The Russian Orthodox Church's Basic Teaching on Human Dignity, Freedom and Rights*, 2008, https://mospat.ru/en/documents/dignity-freedom-rights/.

[7] See Fr. Michael Butler and Andrew Morriss, *Creation and the Heart of Man: An Orthodox Christian Perspective on Environmentalism*, Orthodox Christian Social Thought, vol. 1 (Grand Rapids, MI: Acton Institute, 2013); Fr. Gregory Jensen, *The Cure for Consumerism*, Orthodox Christian Social Thought, vol. 2 (Grand Rapids, MI: Acton Institute, 2015).

[8] See Dylan Pahman, "What Makes a Society? An Orthodox Perspective on Asceticism, Marriage, the Family, and Society," in *Love, Marriage and Family in the Eastern Orthodox Tradition*, Sophia Studies in Orthodox Theology, vol. 7 (New York, NY: Theotokos Press, 2013), 179–193; idem, "The Value of Ordered Liberty: The Orthodox View," *The City* (Summer 2014): 53–59.

This paper builds upon my past work to develop more fully the ontology of asceticism and constructively explore parallel responses to that ontology in the study of economic history and public policy.[9] This paper consists of two parts: (1) Drawing upon the Church fathers, Vladimir Solovyov, Fr. Pavel Florensky, and Christos Yannaras, et al., I outline the ontological foundations of Christian asceticism, such as the pluriformity and mutability of the world and personal identity, human mortality, and the potential for growth as well as decay, i.e. for resurrection unto life or to second death, not only at the *parousia* but daily. In particular, I highlight the practice of *memento mori* as one primary ascetic means of transfiguring the present reality of our corruption into resurrected life in the Spirit. (2) I bring this ascetic perspective to bear on the question of economic history, examining Joseph Schumpeter in particular, as well as Nassim Nicholas Taleb, to develop from that history non-predictive policy, analogous to the *memento mori* and other ascetic practices, adapted to the reality of creative destruction and what Taleb calls Black Swans—random, unforeseen shocks that so often cripple fragile systems.

## The ontology of asceticism

St. Paul offers the Church in Corinth the following epitome of the Gospel: "that Christ died for our sins according to the Scriptures, and that He was buried, and that He rose again the third day according to the Scriptures, and that He was seen by Cephas, then by the twelve" (1 Corinthians 15:3–5).[10] In fact, he makes the resurrection of Jesus Christ the sine qua non of salvation, writing that "if Christ is not risen, your faith is futile; you are still in your sins! Then also those who have fallen asleep in Christ have perished. If in this life only we have hope in Christ, we are of all men the most pitiable" (1 Corinthians 15:17–19). Furthermore, St. Paul adds an existential element. That is, while he insists on the historic resurrection of Jesus Christ and the future, bodily

---

[9] See principally Dylan Pahman, ""Alive From the Dead": Asceticism between Athens and Jerusalem, Ancient and Modern, East and West," *St. Vladimir's Theological Quarterly* 60, no. 4 (2016): forthcoming.

[10] All Scripture quotations are NKJV.

resurrection of the dead, he also believes this reality has paramount import for the present: "I affirm, by the boasting in you which I have in Christ Jesus our Lord, I die daily. If, in the manner of men, I have fought with beasts at Ephesus, what advantage is it to me? If the dead do not rise, "Let us eat and drink, for tomorrow we die!"" (1 Corinthians 15:31-32)

Here we see, even in the New Testament, something of what Perry Hamalis has termed the thanatomorphic character of Orthodox ethics, i.e. that it is "formed by death."[11] He writes,

> "Death, both spiritual and physical, impacts each of us in profound ways. Few of us have never experienced the heart-wrenching loss of a beloved parent, sibling, cousin, or friend. Similarly, few of us have never experienced a rupture in our relationship with God or an acute sense of being spiritually dead through our sinfulness. The Orthodox Church teaches that these moments of suffering—while extremely difficult—should not be minimized, quickly suppressed, or played down. Rather, these moments serve as invitations from the crucified and risen Lord to properly orient, or reorient, our existence toward our true purpose of resurrection."[12]

I wholeheartedly agree but would add to this a further dimension. Hamalis seems to limit spiritual death to the experience of sin. In one sense this is wholly correct; sin separates the soul from God just as physical death separates the body from

---

[11] See Perry Hamalis, "The Meaning and Place of Death in an Orthodox Ethical Framework," in *Thinking Through Faith: New Perspectives from Orthodox Christian Scholars*, ed. Aristotle Papanikolaou and Elizabeth H. Promodrou (Crestwood, NY: St Vladimir's Seminary Press, 2008), 183-217.

[12] Hamalis, "The Meaning and Place of Death," 215.

the soul.[13] But we actually experience another aspect of spiritual death, which may just as often prompt us *toward* temptation rather than being the effect of our downfall. That is, ontologically speaking, human persons, as created beings, are by nature mutable and changing.[14] Our whole existence, even apart from sin, is conditioned by change—a basic, phenomenological fact—and through change we undergo a continual process of death and resurrection. Yet, just as it is eschatologically, the character of that daily resurrection is conditioned by the state of our souls and the goodness of our actions (cf. Revelation 21:7–8). We either rise to new life or to second death—daily. Pregnant within St. Paul's declaration, "*I die daily*," is the corollary that I rise daily as well. And the resurrection of Jesus Christ is the source of my hope that those daily resurrections are unto new life just as much as, to quote the Creed, "*I expect the resurrection of the dead and the life of the age to come.*" In this sense, what Hamalis and others have termed "spiritual death" may more accurately be referred to as spiritual *second* death. The condition of sin breeds a life of death unto death (cf. Genesis 2:17[15]). The salvation offered to us in Christ Jesus is that "*dying ... behold we live*" (2 Corinthians 6:9)—*not* that we shall not

---

[13] See St. Augustine of Hippo, *On the Holy Trinity*, 4.3 in *NPNF*[1] 3:71–73. Especially relevant to asceticism, he writes, "*For as the soul dies when God leaves it, so the body dies when the soul leaves it; whereby the former becomes foolish, the latter lifeless. For the soul is raised up again by repentance, and the renewing of life is begun in the body still mortal by faith, by which men believe on Him who justifies the ungodly; and it is increased and strengthened by good habits from day to day, as the inner man is renewed more and more*" (71–72, emphasis added).

[14] On this in the fathers, see Nathan Jacobs, "Are Created Spirits Composed of Matter and Form? A Defense of Pneumatic Hylomorphism," *Philosphia Christi* 14, no. 1 (Summer 2012): 79–108, esp. 82–83; idem, "Created Corruptible, Raised Incorruptible: The Importance of Hylomorphic Creationism to the Free Will Defense," in *The Ashgate Research Companion to Theological Anthropology*, ed. Joshua R. Farris and Charles Taliaferro (Surrey, UK; Burlington, VT: Ashgate, 2015), 261–276, esp. 265; and idem, "On the Metaphysics of God and Creatures in the Eastern Pro-Nicenes," *Philosophy & Theology* 28, no. 1 (2016): 3–42.

[15] The Semitic idiom in this verse is literally "dying, you shall die." Though this carries the meaning of "surely you shall die," as it is commonly translated in English, it is possible that relevant theological nuance is lost that would be more apparent to readers of the Greek, Latin, or Hebrew where the idiom is preserved.

die. This is true for us spiritually as well as physically. And this daily, spiritual dying and rising is the goal of asceticism.

Pope St. Leo the Great, reflecting on how the observance of Great Lent helps us to *"feel something of the Cross,"* continues to insist that *"we must strive to be found partakers also of Christ's Resurrection."* He grounds this ascetic calling in the dynamic, changing nature of human existence:

> *"For when a man is changed by some process from one thing into another, not to be what he was is to him an ending, and to be what he was not is a beginning. But the question is, to what a man either dies or lives: because there is a death, which is the cause of living, and there is a life, which is the cause of dying."*[16]

As Fr. Pavel Florensky put it, *"The ascetic saints of the Church are alive for the living and dead for the dead."*[17] Through repentance, we die "to everything" and put to death *"evil selfhood and the lower law of identity,"*[18] by which he means a static conception of one's identity akin to the identity principle of logic (*"I = I"*[19]). The higher law of identity, to Florensky, reflects the dynamic and ever-changing reality of our lives, which we can only live in by rejecting static, essentialist understandings of our own selfhood through grace, asceticism, and love.[20]

The grace of Christ gives to us what we could not obtain ourselves: Firstly, through the incarnation, life, death, resurrection, and ascension of Jesus Christ, and the descent of the Holy Spirit at Pentecost, death is defeated and the way of salvation is opened to us. Secondly, we enter into the life in Christ through

---

[16] Pope St. Leo the Great, *Sermons*, 71, in *NPNF*² 12:182.

[17] Pavel Florensky, *The Pillar and Ground of the Truth*, trans. Boris Jakim (Princeton, NJ: Princeton University Press, 1997), 5. Henceforth, *PGT*. On Florensky's thought, see Robert Slesinski, *Pavel Florensky: A Metaphysics of Love* (Crestwood, NY: St. Vladimir's Seminary Press, 1984), esp. 169 regarding asceticism, identity, and transcendence.

[18] Florensky *PGT*, 229.

[19] Florensky *PGT*, 229. See also Siewers, "Traditional Christian Marriage," 576–577.

[20] Florensky *PGT*, 229.

the liturgical year and the sacraments of the Church,[21] where we die with Christ in baptism, are sealed with the Spirit in chrismation, and partake of Christ's shed blood in the Eucharist, that "we also should walk in newness of life" (Romans 6:4), and so on. Thirdly, and what is the primary focus of this paper, through ascetic heuristics and practices we deny ourselves, take up our cross daily, and follow Jesus Christ (cf. Luke 9:23; Matthew 16:24), actualizing the grace given to us in the sacraments, continually striving for the acquisition of the Holy Spirit,[22] and martyrically carrying divine grace with us into every aspect of our lives in the world.[23] We cannot live a resurrected life without first dying to ourselves, confronting and even encouraging the sacrificial destruction of our souls. *"Whoever desires to save his soul will lose it,"* says Christ, *"but whoever loses his soul for My sake will find it. For what profit is it to a man if he gains the whole world, and forfeits his own soul?"* (Matthew 16:25–26[24])

As our lives are multifarious and every aspect is constantly subject to change, the ascetic life includes a wide variety of

---

[21] On this, see St. Nicholas Cabasilas, *The Life in Christ*, trans. Carmino J. de Catanzaro (Crestwood, NY: St Vladimir's Seminary Press, 1974); Fr. Alexander Schmemann, *For the Life of the World: Sacraments and Orthodoxy* (Crestwood, NY: St. Vladimir's Seminary Press, 1973).

[22] I here refer to that phrase of St. Seraphim. See "The Acquisition of the Holy Spirit," in *Little Russian Philokalia, Vol. 1: St. Seraphim of Sarov* (Ouzinkie, AK: New Valaam Monastery, 1991), 109–119.

[23] On the connection between martyrdom, asceticism, and witness, see Dylan Pahman, "The Sweat of Christians is the Seed of Martyrdom: A Paradigm for Modern Orthodox Christian Witness," *International Journal of Orthodox Theology* 6, no. 2 (2015): 99–115. On the connection between asceticism and social engagement, see idem, "What Makes a Society?"

[24] I have here slightly amended the NKJV to better reflect the Greek, which does not say "life" (*bios, zoe*) but "soul" (*psyche*) and not, in v. 26, "lose" (*apolesei*) but "forfeit" (*zemiothe*). I would add, but cannot easily convey in translation, that *apolesei*, which is used in v. 25, carries the connotation not simply of misplacing something but of it being destroyed.

practices, even to the point of redundancy.²⁵ Orthodox Christians, to the extent they are able, pray, fast, give alms, practice solitude and hesychasm, attend vigils, and live chastely—whether by complete abstinence from sexual activity or sexual moderation through the faithfulness between a husband and a wife in the sacrament of marriage. As Vladimir Solovyov put it, *"True asceticism ... has two forms—monasticism and marriage."* Indeed, Fr. Alexander Schmemann insisted, *"A marriage which does not constantly crucify its own selfishness and self-sufficiency, which does not "die to itself" that it may point beyond itself, is not a Christian marriage."*²⁶ From an Orthodox perspective, no Christian is free from the demands of asceticism; the difference between monks and those in the world is more one of degree than of kind.²⁷ Ascetic practices take many forms to help us confront the many deaths we experience every day, when our earthly conceptions, ideals, hopes, dreams, and desires come to naught or, perhaps more insidiously, when they seem to be confirmed. In both cases, the problem is being deceived by Florensky's "lower law of identity": we imagine that the things of this life, including our own selves, will persist as

---

²⁵ I cannot expand on this at length here, but similar redundancies also can be found in the first two aspects listed above (i.e. the life and work of Christ and the sacramental life of the Church). Nearly every feast of the Church year, we sing about how through *this* event—Nativity, Theophany, Annunciation, Pascha, Pentecost, and so on—we and all the world are saved. Again, we *"confess one baptism for the forgiveness of sins"* (Nicene Creed) but also that the Eucharist is the *"blood of the new covenant, which is shed for many for the remission of sins"* (Matthew 26:28) and *also* that through the sacrament of confession our sins are forgiven and even that through holy unction we receive the grace not only of physical healing but also of spiritual healing, which again includes the forgiveness of sins. I am reminded of one hymn from the Jewish Passover in which all that God has done for the Jewish people is recounted, and they repeat after each one, "Dayenu!"—"It would have been enough!" So also, our liturgies are full of redundancies—there is something about who we are that needs multiple layers and facets of care in order to properly heal. One method or means might be enough, but through Jesus Christ we receive far more than enough: *"grace upon grace"* (John 1:16).

²⁶ Schmemann, *For the Life of the World*, 90.

²⁷ See Fr. Georges Florovsky, "Christianity and Civilization," in *Christianity and Culture*, The Collected Words of Georges Florovsky, vol. 2 (Belmont, MA: Nordland, 1974), 125-126; Pahman, "What Makes a Society?" 183-188.

we conceive them to be when, in fact, they are constantly in flux, even when they do not appear to be. Or else, we are aware that they will not persist and fear it, unwilling to accept their transience and desperately clinging to them as they run like water through our hands, an existential embrace of, rather than victory over, death. So our passions push us toward selfishness and sin.

Evagrios describes how the three most basic ascetic practices combat our most basic passions and psychological faculties: "*the Physician of souls*," he writes, "*corrects our incensive power through acts of compassion [i.e., almsgiving], purifies the intellect through prayer, and through fasting withers desire.*"[28] And St. Maximus describes the cycle of passions common to our lives apart from salvation: "*Man's will, out of cowardice, tends away from suffering, and man, against his own will, remains utterly dominated by the fear of death, and, in his desire to live, clings to his slavery to pleasure.*"[29] Christ conquers pleasure and desire through his fasting and solitude in the wilderness. He conquers fear in Gethsemane and suffering through Golgotha.[30] The way in which we who are in Christ experience victory over death in these and other areas of our lives is not through avoidance, ignorance, or delusion—that is Florensky's lower law of identity, a denial of the reality of death and thus a denial of the hope of resurrection. Rather, just as Christ tramples down death by death, we pattern our whole lives around dying and rising to new life, year after year, week after week, day after day, breath after breath. "*Every voluntary mortification of the egocentricity which is "contrary to nature,"*" wrote Christos Yannaras, "*is a dynamic destruction of death and a triumph for the life of the person.*"[31] In

---

[28] Evagrios the Solitary, "Texts on Discrimination in Respect of Passions and Thoughts," in St. Nikodimos of the Holy Mountain and St. Makarios of Corinth, *The Philokalia: The Complete Text*, vol. 1, trans. and ed. G.E.H. Palmer, Philip Sherrard, and Kallistos Ware (London: Faber and Faber, 1979), 40.

[29] St. Maximus the Confessor, Ad Thalassium 21: On Christ's Conquest of the Human Passions in On the Cosmic Mystery of Jesus Christ: Select Writings from St Maximus the Confessor, trans. Paul M. Blowers and Robert Louis Wilken (New York, NY: St Vladimir's Seminary Press, 2003), 112.

[30] See St. Maximus, Ad Thalassium 21, 113.

[31] Christos Yannaras, The Freedom of Morality (Crestwood, NY: St Vladimir's Seminary Press, 1996), 116.

denying ourselves through ascetic disciplines, we are able to cling more strongly to God, and the love and virtue that come from him, who alone is without change and who is our only true source of life, identity, and stability. It is *"through glory and virtue"* that we *"become partakers of the divine nature, having escaped the corruption that is in the world through lust* [epithemia*]"* (2 Peter 1:3–4). Through ascetic practices and heuristics, we create a virtuous cycle that prepares us for even unpredictable temptations, disappointments, and tragedy. *"[W]hoever hears these sayings of Mine, and does them,"* says Christ,[32] *"I will liken him to a wise man who built his house on the rock: and the rain descended, the floods came, and the winds blew and beat on that house; and it did not fall, for it was founded on the rock"* (Matthew 7:24–25[33]).

While all ascetic practices work toward this end, one practice in particular serves to focus our attention on our ever-present mortality: *memento mori*, the remembrance of death. This practice, like many others,[34] receives the highest endorsement from Evagrios and other desert fathers, *"If you always remember your*

---

[32] The phrase "these sayings of Mine," in context, refers to the rest of the Sermon on the Mount, in which Christ details ethical ideals (the Beatitudes), moral instruction ("you have heard it was said…"), and spiritual/ascetic practices (e.g. private and corporate prayer, solitude, almsgiving, and fasting). See Matthew 5–7.

[33] In our present era of modern meteorology, we may miss how unpredictable such storms were—more akin to earthquakes for us today. Similarly, on the need to prepare for the unpredictable, compare Matthew 24:43–44: "[I]f the master of the house had known what hour the thief would come, he would have watched and not allowed his house to be broken into. Therefore you also be ready, for the Son of Man is coming at an hour you do not expect."

[34] Hence, there is again a natural tendency to redundancy in practice. Many practices are said by the fathers to be a sure way to salvation, but they recommend all of them, not just one. We could see this as an inconsistency in their teaching, but I think a more charitable reading is that they were not content with only one practice, no matter how effective. Relying on just one or two disciplines would be to embrace spiritual fragility and leave oneself vulnerable to temptation in times of laxity or exhaustion in that one habit. In other words, with only one or two disciplines one may still be like the house without a solid foundation: "the rain descended, the floods came, and the winds blew and beat on that house; and it fell. And great was its fall" (Matthew 7:27).

*death,"* Evagrios taught, *"and do not forget the eternal judgement, there will be no sin in your soul."*[35] The constant remembrance of one's mortality is the sharpest reminder that our existence is ever-changing and that we are constantly subject to death and in need of salvation. Our existence here can become anchored in Christ, the Logos, and in the moral law rooted in him, if we enter into Christ through faith and grace and if we ascetically imitate his humility (cf. Philippians 2:1–16), confessing with the patriarch Abraham that apart from him, we are, after all, *"but dust and ashes"* (Genesis 18:27). In this way, despite the ever-changing nature of created existence, *"the word [logos] of God ... lives and abides forever"* (1 Peter 1:23; cf. Isaiah 40:8), and we, through it, can abide in eternal life, even now in each passing moment of the present.

## Economic history and creative destruction

The foregoing can be summarized as follows: In our spiritual lives, we need a Savior to deliver us from the tyranny of our mortality, daily present to us in a plurality of forms in the inescapable reality of change. Not only do we need a Savoir, but we need some way of receiving the deliverance he wins for us, which is where the Church comes in. Lastly, we need not only to receive deliverance, but then to embody it through asceticism. Asceticism involves a plurality of practices that help us holistically fulfill the exhortation of St. Paul: *"Set your mind on things above, not on things on the earth. For you died, and your life is hidden with Christ in God"* (Colossians 3:2). In this way we do not reject earthly life but find it transfigured in the kingdom of heaven, just as we do not hope to escape our bodies but rather that they would be raised as spiritual bodies (cf. 1 Corinthians 15:44). Through an ascetic way of life, particularly *memento mori*, we prepare ourselves for unexpected trials that might otherwise mean our spiritual ruin.

The economic historian Joseph Schumpeter helps us see how economic progress in the midst of our ever-changing created

---

[35] Sayings of the Desert Fathers, 11.10 in Western Asceticism, Library of Christian Classics, vol. 12, trans. and ed. Owen Chadwick (Philadelphia, PA: Westminster Press, 1958), 132.

reality does, in fact, follow the pattern of asceticism and practices akin to it. By way of disclaimer, however, I would like to acknowledge that, of course, economic and material progress is not more important than spiritual and moral progress. But, at the same time, it is not an unspiritual matter to care for the economically disadvantaged. Vladimir Solovyov made this point well: "*It is written that man does not live by bread alone [Deuteronomy 8:3], but it is not written that he lives without bread.*"[36] So what insight does Schumpeter offer regarding how standards of living have historically been improved?—Creative destruction.

"[T]he contents of the laborer's budget," he wrote (originally in 1942),

> *"say from 1760 to 1940, did not simply grow on unchanging lines but they underwent a process of qualitative change. Similarly, the history of the productive apparatus of a typical farm, from the beginnings of the rationalization of crop rotation, plowing and fattening to the mechanized thing of today—linking up with elevators and railroads—is a history of revolutions. So is the history of the productive apparatus of the iron and steel industry from the charcoal furnace to our own type of furnace, or the history of the apparatus of power production from the overshot water wheel to the modern power plant, or the history of transportation from the mail-coach to the airplane. The opening up of new markets, foreign or domestic, and the organizational development from the craft shop and factory to such concerns as U. S. Steel illustrate the same process of industrial mutation—if I may use that biological term—that incessantly revolutionizes the economic structure from within, incessantly destroying the old one, incessantly creating a new one. This process of Creative Destruction is the essential fact about*

---

[36] Solovyov, The Justification of the Good, 394–395.

*capitalism. It is what capitalism consists in and what every capitalist concern has got to live in."*[37]

Thus, economies have historically advanced due to a process of dying and rising—one company or market displaces another. For Schumpeter creative destruction is important because it mitigates the concentration of power in a monopoly.[38] That is, even when a market is monopolized, the monopoly must still fear the possibility that the whole market will be circumvented by something new, unexpected, and unknown. This displacement, to Schumpeter, is *"the essential fact about capitalism,"* which we may still regard as the economic system of most developed and even many developing countries today, though degrees of state intervention and specific forms vary widely. Thus, Schumpeter's observation of how the general welfare, and not just that of the rich, has historically been improved under capitalism—albeit of various forms—ought still to be instructive for us today.

For example, the automotive industry displaced the market for blacksmiths but brought with it a massive rise in the well-being of nearly everyone in and beyond the industry, not just Henry Ford. Even if the state had sought to protect blacksmiths and they had improved their craft to the highest level of efficiency and quality,

---

[37] Joseph A. Schumpeter, *Capitalism, Socialism, Democracy*, 3rd ed. (New York; Hagerstown; San Francisco; London: Harper & Row, 1950), 83. For more on Schumpeter's conception of the entrepreneur, see Joseph A. Schumpeter, *The Theory of Economic Development*, trans. Redvers Opie (New Brunswick; London: Transaction Publishers, 1934, 1983). For secondary material on Schumpeter on the entrepreneur and creative destruction, see, e.g. Israel M. Kirzner, *Competition and Entrepreneurship* (Chicago; London: University of Chicago Press, 1973), 72–74, 79–81; Michael Perelman, "Retrospectives: Schumpeter, David Wells, and Creative Destruction," *Journal of Economic Perspectives* 9, no. 3 (Summer 1995): 189–197; Aron S. Spencer and Bruce A. Kirchhoff, "Schumpeter and New Technology Based Firms: Towards a Framework for how NTBFs Cause Creative Destruction," *International Entrepreneurship and Management Journal* 2, no. 2 (June 2006): 145–156; J. Hanns Pichler, "Innovation and Creative Destruction: At the Centennial of Schumpeter's Theory and Its Dialectics," *Nase Gospodarstvo* 56, no. 5/6 (2010): 52–58; Paul Nightingale, "Schumpeter's Theological Roots? Harnack and the Origins of Creative Destruction," *Journal of Evolutionary Economics* 25, no. 1 (January 2015): 69–75.

[38] See Schumpeter, *Capitalism, Socialism, Democracy*, 89.

they could never bring about the advances that came from their destruction without transforming themselves into something else entirely. With the advent of the assembly line, not only could cars be made cheaply, they could be bought by the people who made them. Increased mobility changed other markets as well (e.g. mail and pizza delivery, not to mention the widespread effect of trucking).

Since that time the U.S. auto industry has taken serious losses as it has struggled to innovate and adjust to competition from Japan, South Korea, and elsewhere. The American auto industry has proved to be as mortal as the rest of life, but its destruction has meant the significant improvement of the lives of many new autoworkers in other countries as well as many Americans, since cheaper options for reliable cars became available through Toyota, Honda, and others (many of whom have factories in the United States). If protectionism had prevailed, there would still have been an opportunity cost to American consumers, who would have had to spend far more for transportation or settle for lower quality and less reliable used cars.

Other notable instances of creative destruction include the displacement of print newspapers by online media. Many have lost their jobs in this process, but many others—web developers, IT experts, social media marketers, et al.—have gained. Turmoil in one sector is not always a bad thing for an economy as a whole. Protecting firms—such as General Motors—from destruction can cause an economy to miss out on this benefit and postpone inevitable destruction without the benefit of parallel and greater creation. As economist Matthew Mitchell writes,

> *"As protected firms become less innovative, a country's overall economic growth may suffer. This is because, as Schumpeter emphasized nearly a century ago, economic growth thrives on "creative destruction." In a healthy economy, new firms constantly arise to challenge older, less-innovative behemoths. One of the leading experts on entrepreneurship, Amar Bhidé of the Columbia Business School, has argued that big firms, encumbered by larger*

> internal bureaucracies, are virtually incapable of capitalizing on radical ideas. Indeed, research finds that new firms are more likely than existing firms to license novel technology. And compared with larger firms, smaller firms are about twice as likely to file "high-impact" patents.
>
> For these reasons, turnover among a nation's largest firms is a sign of vitality. The list of U.S. Fortune 500 companies is illustrative: Only 13.4 percent of those companies on the Fortune 500 list in 1955 were still there in 2010. But not all nations experience the same sort of "churn" among their top firms. To test Schumpeter's theory, Kathy Fogel, Randall Morck, and Bernard Yeung recently examined the link between turnover among nations' top firms and economic growth. They looked at the lists of top firms in 44 countries in 1975 and again in 1996. After controlling for other factors, they found that those nations with more turnover among their top firms tended to experience faster per capita economic growth, greater productivity growth, and faster capital growth. Looking at the factors that correlate with faster firm turnover, they found that "big business turnover also correlates with smaller government, common law, less bank-dependence, stronger shareholder rights, and greater openness [to trade]." Thus, turnover is less likely when firms are privileged."[39]

We may compare the privileged company to the unascetic person. Comfortably sheltered from the reality of her mortality, she views herself statically, according to Florensky's "lower law of identity," despite the dynamic nature of reality. As a consequence, she fails to develop spiritually—and in fact degenerates—due to the fear of death. As St. Maximus notes, her fear enslaves her to

---

[39] Matthew Mitchell, The Pathology of Privilege: The Economic Consequences of Government Favoritism (Arlington, VA: Mercatus Center, 2012), 21–22.

fleeting pleasures. But death cannot be stopped by ignoring it. It always comes eventually, and like the house built on sand, that person's fall will be great and unexpected. So too, we may think of companies like Solyndra, which despite its desire to manufacture innovative "clean" energy in the form of solar power, went bankrupt just a year and a half after receiving a half-billion dollar loan from the U.S. federal government. Insulated from the reality of the market, in which private banks may not have granted such high-risk loans, Solyndra spent too much time pursuing favors and protection than actually producing viable products. Their fear of death ironically led them more speedily to it.[40]

The factors that make for healthy businesses, markets, and economies, however, respond to the realities of change, death, and pluriformity with practices and policies akin to those that adorn the ascetic life. Like the *memento mori*, healthy companies must always be open to innovation and change, or they will be unprepared when it comes. If possible, a diversity of products is preferable, just as a redundancy of spiritual practices makes one robust to short periods of laxity.

A great example of this would be the Japanese company Nintendo. Known today for video games and consoles, the company began in 1889 making Japanese playing cards. In 1959, they benefitted from the growing popularity of Disney by manufacturing the first cards to feature Disney characters, *"opening up a new market in children's playing cards and resulting in a boom in the card department."*[41] In 1963 they expanded beyond cards to producing other games. In 1970 Nintendo *"began selling the Beam Gun series ... introducing electronic technology into the toy industry for*

---

[40] See Joe Stephens and Carol D. Leonnig, "Solyndra: Politics infused Obama energy programs," Washington Post, December 25, 2011, http://www.washingtonpost.com/solyndra-politics-infused-obama-energy-programs/2011/12/14/gIQA4HllHP_story.html; "Greenlighting Solyndra," Washington Post, December 2011, http://www.washingtonpost.com/wp-srv/special/politics/solyndra-key-players/; and "Solyndra scandal timeline," Washington Post, December 2011, http://www.washingtonpost.com/wp-srv/special/politics/solyndra-scandal-timeline/.

[41] "Nintendo History," https://www.nintendo.co.uk/Corporate/Nintendo-History/Nintendo-History-625945.html.

*the first time in Japan.*"⁴² In 1973, the company developed "a laser clay shooting system."⁴³ It was not until 1975, nearly a century after its start and right at the dawn of the new industry, that Nintendo made its first videogame system. Not all of its videogame consoles have been a success. The Virtual Boy flopped, and the Wii U is in trouble.⁴⁴ But Nintendo has been a strong company through diversifying its products as well as establishing staple franchises to fall back on, which enable it to take innovative risks. Mario, Pokémon, and Zelda are household names for many Gen-Xers and Millennials, and these franchises and others will continue to profit the company through various venues, whether home or handheld systems or—continuing their past legacy in a very different form— card games. When times changed, Nintendo changed with them and more than once even acted as a catalyst for change. The video game market is very open, diverse, and competitive, and while the gaming system market has less diversity, it also has proven open in the past to newcomers (e.g. Microsoft, Sony) as well as able to bear the losses of those who couldn't compete (e.g. Sega, Atari). Nintendo may not last forever—it too is mortal—but it offers an excellent model for what an analogue to various ascetic practices in business looks like.

For markets in general, benefiting from creative destruction means the more open, diverse, and competitive the market, the better.⁴⁵ Closed and monopolized markets are especially vulnerable to being on the receiving end of—rather than benefiting from— creative destruction. On a more macro level, whole economies are in a better position for the good of creative destruction when they are diverse and open as well. Marx and Engels are right to point to

---

⁴² "Nintendo History," https://www.nintendo.co.uk/Corporate/Nintendo-History/Nintendo-History-625945.html.

⁴³ "Nintendo History," https://www.nintendo.co.uk/Corporate/Nintendo-History/Nintendo-History-625945.html.

⁴⁴ See Alex Fitzpatrick, "Nintendo's New Game Could Save the Wii U," *Time*, May 8, 2015, http://time.com/3849388/splatoon-wii-u-nintendo/.

⁴⁵ On the various forms of markets, as well as on the difference between open and closed supply and demand, see Walter Eucken, *The Foundations of Economics: History and Theory in the Analysis of Economic Reality*, trans. T. W. Hutchison (Chicago, IL: University of Chicago Press, 1951), 129–158.

the varied nature of social life, even if they are wrong in rejecting the value of religion and advocating for violent revolution instead of peaceful reform.[46] Furthermore, despite their and Schumpeter's optimism for the state, historically innovation that sparks creative destruction comes much easier to the private sector than to nationalized industries and corporations. Probabilist Nassim Nicholas Taleb argues that *"a reading of Schumpeter shows that he did not think in terms of uncertainty and opacity; he was completely smoked by interventionism, under the illusion that governments could innovate by fiat.... Nor did he grasp the notion of layering of evolutionary tensions."*[47]

With Gregory Treverton, Taleb outlines five sources of economic fragility: *"a centralized governing system, an undiversified economy, excessive debt and leverage, a lack of political variability, and no history of surviving past shocks."*[48] The fewer of these factors that an economy has, the better. Some can be changed through better policy: Governments can be decentralized, distributing more power from central to local bodies; debt can be paid down through increased revenue; leverage can be staved off by decreasing spending and increasing privatization; deficits can be avoided with balanced budget amendments and more responsible fiscal practices; and political variability can be ensured through term limits and minimizing restrictions that limit freedom of association, in this case especially for political parties. Like the ascetic life, the more such practices the better—redundancy is a good thing. And like ascetic practices, most all of these involve limiting oneself—in this case the state—for the sake of a greater good. Governments cannot

---

[46] See, e.g. Karl Marx, "Society and Economy in History," in *The Marx-Engels Reader*, 2nd ed., ed. Robert C. Tucker (New York, NY; London: Norton & Company, 1978), 136–142; Friedrich Engels, "Letters on Historical Materialism," in *The Marx-Engels Reader*, 760–768.

[47] Nassim Nicholas Taleb, *Antifragile* (New York, NY: Random House, 2012), 193.

[48] Nassim Nicholas Taleb and Gregory F. Treverton, "The Calm Before the Storm: Why Volatility Signals Stability, and Vice Versa," *Foreign Affairs* (January/February 2015), https://www.foreignaffairs.com/articles/africa/calm-storm.

diversify their economies by fiat, but they can regulate in favor of entrepreneurship, open markets, and sound antitrust measures.[49]

As for *"surviving past shocks,"* the only way to create such a history is to enter the future prepared for the shocks that will surely come, just as the true ascetic lives each day before God ready for it to be her last. This does not mean being able to predict those shocks beforehand, just as Christians do not know the day or the hour that Christ will return, but they can be prepared for him to come. Taleb calls these shocks Black Swans and defines them as an event characterized by "rarity, extreme impact, and retrospective (though not prospective) predictability."[50] The more people, communities, and nations learn successfully to recover and even benefit from these shocks and to resist retroactively explaining away their unpredictability, the healthier an economy becomes and the more opportunity there will be for better employment and upward mobility. Orthodox Christians, who confess the risen Christ as Lord and in their ascetic disciplines imitate him in conquering death by death, ought to welcome and encourage such realism in the face of our economic mortality for the sake of the historic economic benefits it brings to all classes of people, as Schumpeter pointed out.

So we can see both macro- and microeconomic policies and practices that resemble asceticism and respond to the same ontological realities as asceticism. But it would be uncritical and

---

[49] As Eucken put it, "State planning of [market] forms—Yes; state planning and control of the economic process—No!" Walter Eucken, This Unsuccessful Age: Or the Pains of Economic Progress (New York, NY: Oxford University Press, 1952). Eucken's subtitle, notably, is directed at those who believed economic progress was inevitable and obscured concrete economic details due to this conviction. The ascetic paradigm presented in this paper is decidedly an open dialectic—one either rises to new life or to second death. The only inevitability is death; one's response is a matter of freedom. Thus, progress is not inevitable.

[50] Nassim Nicholas Taleb, The Black Swan: The Impact of the Highly Improbable, 1st ed. (New York, NY: Random House, 2007), xviii.

overly monumentalist, to use Nietzsche's term,[51] to highlight only the benefits of creative destruction without also addressing the real losses that come with it. I have already noted Solovyov's point that material benefit for the poor is a spiritual task, but one may yet ask, for example: granted that the auto industry lifted many to higher standards of living, yet what about the blacksmith? To be sure, creative destruction shows that economic gain is not the result of a zero-sum game, where wealth is merely redistributed from losers to winners. The economic gains since 1760 highlighted by Schumpeter are important precisely because they show real and substantial increases in total wealth *as well as* a broad distribution of that wealth not only to the rich but also to the middle classes and the poor through more and better opportunities for employment and cheaper and better consumer goods. In some cases, however, people are not able to switch careers, gain new training, or otherwise recover when they are on the destruction side of economic creative destruction. This, however, is where the spiritual practices of asceticism come into direct contact with its economic analogue. A society in which people in their personal lives make a regular habit of self-limitation for the sake of better loving God and their neighbors would be one in which the generosity and hospitality needed by those left behind as economies advance would be present. And, I would add, such people have an advantage over others in already practicing in their everyday lives the sort of disciplines needed for economic health, knowing by personal experience their great potential for good.[52]

---

[51] See Friedrich Nietzsche, "The Use and Abuse of History," trans. Adrian Collins, in idem, The Complete Works of Friedrich Nietzsche, ed. Oscar Levy, vol. 2: Thoughts out of Season, part 2 (Edinburgh; London: T.N. Foulis, 1909), 1–100.

[52] On a particularly striking example of this regarding risk management, see Rupert Read and Nassim Nicholas Taleb, "Religion, Heuristics, and Intergenerational Risk Management," Econ Journal Watch 11, no. 2 (May 2014): 219–226, http://econjwatch.org/articles/religion-heuristics-and-intergenerational-risk-management.

## Conclusion

There is far more to economic history and public policy than what has been briefly covered herein. We may note, in passing, sound monetary policy, the ethics of taxation, the use and misuse of safety nets, the optimal extent and character of regulation, and so on. However, this paper makes advances on the state of scholarship by expounding the underlying ontological presumptions of Orthodox asceticism and using that Orthodox paradigm as a way of approaching economic history and public policy. This analysis is grounded both upon philosophical and historical-empirical grounds; they are not mere abstractions. Indeed, even the ontological and theological foundation of asceticism is rooted in the undeniable, existential facts of change, diversity, death, and resurrection, either to new life or to second death. Future research could apply this paradigm to other areas of social and economic life as well as expand it to accommodate realities that it may be inadequate to assess in its current form, adjusting it to concrete realities and improving upon it rather than falling into a dialectical monism. After all, it would quickly become just another ideology if it were not itself open to its own death and resurrection.

## Bibliography

Augustine of Hippo. *On the Holy Trinity*. In *A Select Library of the Nicene and Post-Nicene Fathers of the Christian Church*. First Series. Vol. 3, 17–228. Edited by Philip Schaff and Henry Wace. Grand Rapids, MI: Eerdmans, 1889.

Bulgakov, Sergei. "Heroism and Asceticism: Reflections on the Religious Nature of the Russian Intelligentsia." In *Vekhi: Landmarks*, 17–50. Translated and edited by Marshall S. Shatz and Judith E. Zimmerman. Armonk, NY; London: M.E. Sharpe, 1994.

———. *Karl Marx as a Religious Type: His Relation to the Religion of Anthropotheism of L. Feuerbach*. Translated by Luba Barna. Belmont, MA: Nordland, 1979.

———. "The National Economy and the Religious Personality (1909)." Translated by Krassen Stanchev. *Journal of Markets & Morality* 11, no. 1 (Spring 2008): 157–179.

———. *Philosophy of Economy: The World as Household*. Translated and edited by Catherine Evtuhov. New Haven and London: Yale University Press, 2000.

Butler, Michael and Andrew Morriss. *Creation and the Heart of Man: An Orthodox Christian Perspective on Environmentalism*. Orthodox Christian Social Thought, vol. 1. Grand Rapids, MI: Acton Institute, 2013.

Cabasilas, Nicholas. *The Life in Christ*. Translated by Carmino J. de Catanzaro. Crestwood, NY: St Vladimir's Seminary Press, 1974.

Department of External Church Relations. *The Basis of the Social Concept of the Russian Orthodox Church*. Moscow, 2000. https://mospat.ru/en/documents/social-concepts/.

———. *The Russian Orthodox Church's Basic Teaching on Human Dignity, Freedom and Rights*. Moscow, 2008. https://mospat.ru/en/documents/dignity-freedom-rights/.

Dobrijević, Irinej. "The Orthodox Spirit and the Ethic of Capitalism: A Case Study on Serbia and Montenegro and the Serbian Orthodox Church." *Serbian Studies* 20, no. 1 (2006): 1–13.

Engels, Friedrich. "Letters on Historical Materialism." In *The Marx-Engels Reader*, 760–768. 2nd ed. Edited by Robert C. Tucker. New York, NY; London: Norton & Company, 1978.

Eucken, Walter. *This Unsuccessful Age: Or the Pains of Economic Progress*. New York, NY: Oxford University Press, 1952.

———. *The Foundations of Economics: History and Theory in the Analysis of Economic Reality*. Translated by T. W. Hutchison. Chicago, IL: University of Chicago Press, 1951.

Florensky, Pavel. *The Pillar and Ground of the Truth*. Translated by Boris Jakim. Princeton, NJ: Princeton University Press, 1997.

Florovsky, Georges. *Christianity and Culture*. The Collected Words of Georges Florovsky, vol. 2. Belmont, MA: Nordland, 1974.

Fitzpatrick, Alex. "Nintendo's New Game Could Save the Wii U." *Time*. May 8, 2015. http://time.com/3849388/splatoon-wii-u-nintendo/.

"Greenlighting Solyndra." *Washington Post*. December 2011. http://www.washingtonpost.com/wp-srv/special/politics/solyndra-key-players/

Hamalis, Perry. "The Meaning and Place of Death in an Orthodox Ethical Framework." In *Thinking Through Faith: New Perspectives from Orthodox Christian Scholars*, 183–217. Edited by Aristotle Papanikolaou and Elizabeth H. Promodrou. Crestwood, NY: St Vladimir's Seminary Press, 2008.

Jacobs, Nathan. "Are Created Spirits Composed of Matter and Form? A Defense of Pneumatic Hylomorphism." *Philosphia Christi* 14, no. 1 (Summer 2012): 79–108.

—————. "Created Corruptible, Raised Incorruptible: The Importance of Hylomorphic Creationism to the Free Will Defense." In *The Ashgate Research Companion to Theological Anthropology*, 261–276. Edited by Joshua R. Farris and Charles Taliaferro. Surrey, UK; Burlington, VT: Ashgate, 2015.

—————. "On the Metaphysics of God and Creatures in the Eastern Pro-Nicenes." *Philosophy & Theology* 28, no. 1 (2016): 3–42.

Jensen, Gregory. *The Cure for Consumerism*. Orthodox Christian Social Thought, vol. 2. Grand Rapids, MI: Acton Institute, 2015.

Kirzner, Israel M. *Competition and Entrepreneurship*. Chicago; London: University of Chicago Press, 1973.

Leo the Great. *Sermons*, 71. In *A Select Library of the Nicene and Post-Nicene Fathers of the Christian Church*. Second Series. Vol. 12, 181–184. Edited by Philip Schaff and Henry Wace. Grand Rapids, MI: Eerdmans, 1890.

Marx, Karl. "Society and Economy in History." In *The Marx-Engels Reader*, 136–142. 2nd ed. Edited by Robert C. Tucker. New York, NY; London: Norton & Company, 1978.

Maximus the Confessor. *On the Cosmic Mystery of Jesus Christ: Select Writings from St Maximus the Confessor*. Translated by Paul M. Blowers and Robert Louis Wilken. New York, NY: St Vladimir's Seminary Press, 2003.

Mitchell, Matthew. *The Pathology of Privilege: The Economic Consequences of Government Favoritism*. Arlington, VA: Mercatus Center, 2012.

Nietzsche, Friedrich. "The Use and Abuse of History." Translated by Adrian Collins. In *The Complete Works of Friedrich Nietzsche*. Edited by Oscar Levy. Vol. 2: *Thoughts out of Season*. Part 2, 1–100. Edinburgh; London: T.N. Foulis, 1909.

Nightingale, Paul. "Schumpeter's Theological Roots? Harnack and the Origins of Creative Destruction." *Journal of Evolutionary Economics* 25, no. 1 (January 2015): 69–75.

Nikodimos of the Holy Mountain and Makarios of Corinth. *The Philokalia: The Complete Text*, vol. 1. Translated and edited by G.E.H. Palmer, Philip Sherrard, and Kallistos Ware. London: Faber and Faber, 1979.

"Nintendo History." https://www.nintendo.co.uk/Corporate/Nintendo-History/Nintendo-History-625945.html.

Pahman, Dylan. ""Alive From the Dead": Asceticism between Athens and Jerusalem, Ancient and Modern, East and West." *St. Vladimir's Theological Quarterly* 60, no. 4 (2016): forthcoming.

——————. "The Sweat of Christians is the Seed of Martyrdom: A Paradigm for Modern Orthodox Christian Witness." *International Journal of Orthodox Theology* 6, no. 2 (2015): 99–115.

——————. "The Value of Ordered Liberty: The Orthodox View." *The City* (Summer 2014): 53–59.

——————. "What Makes a Society? An Orthodox Perspective on Asceticism, Marriage, the Family, and Society." In *Love, Marriage and Family in the Eastern Orthodox Tradition*, 179–193. Sophia Studies in Orthodox Theology, vol. 7. New York, NY: Theotokos Press, 2013.

Payne, Daniel P. and Christopher Marsh. "Sergei Bulgakov's "sophic" Economy: An Eastern Orthodox Perspective on Christian Economics." *Faith & Economics* 53 (Spring 2009): 35–51.

Perelman, Michael. "Retrospectives: Schumpeter, David Wells, and Creative Destruction." *Journal of Economic Perspectives* 9, no. 3 (Summer 1995): 189–197.

Pichler, J. Hanns. "Innovation and Creative Destruction: At the Centennial of Schumpeter's Theory and Its Dialectics." *Nase Gospodarstvo* 56, no. 5/6 (2010): 52–58.

Read, Rupert and Nassim Nicholas Taleb. "Religion, Heuristics, and Intergenerational Risk Management." *Econ Journal Watch* 11, no. 2 (May 2014): 219–226. http://econjwatch.org/articles/religion-heuristics-and-intergenerational-risk-management.

*Sayings of the Desert Fathers*. In *Western Asceticism*. Library of Christian Classics, vol. 12. Translated and edited by Owen Chadwick. Philadelphia, PA: Westminster Press, 1958.

Schmemann, Alexander. *For the Life of the World: Sacraments and Orthodoxy*. Crestwood, NY: St. Vladimir's Seminary Press, 1973.

Schumpeter, Joseph A. *Capitalism, Socialism, Democracy*. 3$^{rd}$ ed. New York; Hagerstown; San Francisco; London: Harper & Row, 1950.

——————. *The Theory of Economic Development*. Translated by Redvers Opie. New Brunswick; London: Transaction Publishers, 1934, 1983.

Seraphim of Sarov, *Little Russian Philokalia, Vol. 1: St. Seraphim of Sarov*. Ouzinkie, AK: New Valaam Monastery, 1991.

Siewers, Alfred Kentigern. "Traditional Christian Marriage as an Expression of Social Justice: Identity and Society in the Writings of Florensky and Bulgakov." *Journal of Markets & Morality* 16, no. 2 (Fall 2013): 569–586.

Slesinski, Robert. *Pavel Florensky: A Metaphysics of Love*. Crestwood, NY: St. Vladimir's Seminary Press, 1984.

Solovyov, Vladimir. *The Justification of the Good*. 2$^{nd}$ ed. Translated by Natalie Duddington. Edited by Boris Jakim. Grand Rapids, MI: Eerdmans, 2005.

"Solyndra scandal timeline." *Washington Post*. December 2011. http://www.washingtonpost.com/wp-srv/special/politics/solyndra-scandal-timeline/.

Spencer, Aron S. and Bruce A. Kirchhoff. "Schumpeter and New Technology Based Firms: Towards a Framework for how NTBFs Cause Creative Destruction." *International Entrepreneurship and Management Journal* 2, no. 2 (June 2006): 145–156.

Stanchev, Krassen. "Sergey Bulgakov and the Spirit of Capitalism." *Journal of Markets & Morality* 11, no. 1 (Spring 2008): 149–156.

Stephens, Joe and Carol D. Leonnig. "Solyndra: Politics infused Obama energy programs." *Washington Post*. December 25, 2011. http://www.washingtonpost.com/solyndra-politics-infused-obama-energy-programs/2011/12/14/gIQA4HllHP_story.html

Taleb, Nassim Nicholas. *Antifragile*. New York, NY: Random House, 2012.

—————. *The Black Swan: The Impact of the Highly Improbable*. 1st ed. New York, NY: Random House, 2007.

Taleb, Nassim Nicholas and Gregory F. Treverton. "The Calm Before the Storm: Why Volatility Signals Stability, and Vice Versa." *Foreign Affairs*. January/February 2015. https://www.foreignaffairs.com/articles/africa/calm-storm.

Yannaras, Christos. *The Freedom of Morality*. Crestwood, NY: St Vladimir's Seminary Press, 1996.

Chapter 7

# The common path of ontology and history: Orthodoxy and theology of liberation in dialogue

Angelos Gounopoulos

## Ontology and history

Ontology and History have not always maintained a good relationship with each other in the context of philosophical and theological thought. Father George Florovsky used to argue that "there is a tendency to stress the "otherworldliness" of the "Life Eternal" to such an extent that human personality is in danger of being rent in twain."[1] Greek philosopher and Eastern Orthodox theologian Christos Yannaras detects a more wide-ranging problem of western thought, namely *"the polarization between the transcendental and the worldly, between abstract idealism ... and the recognition of the value of material goods in life."*[2] This is a problem of dualism. Therefore, this bifurcated logic suggests a division between eschatology and secularism, which leads to a problematic understanding of incarnation.

Gustavo Gutiérrez, a Peruvian Dominican priest and professor of theology, considered one of the main founders of Theology of Liberation, rejected any problem of dualism and added that the *"natural and the supernatural orders are therefore intimately unified."*[3]

---

[1] George Florovsky, *Christianity and Culture* (Belmont Massachusetts: Nordland Publishing Company, 1974), 20.

[2] Christos Yannaras, Κεφάλαια Πολιτικῆς Θεολογίας [Chapters in Political Theology] (Athens: Grigoris, 1983), 9-10.

[3] Gustavo Gutiérrez, *A Theology of Liberation. History, Politics, and Salvation*, ed. and trans. Sister Caridad Inda and John Eagleson (Maryknoll, New York: Orbis Books, 1973), 70.

The person of faith (*prosopo*) lives on the fringes of historical context, on the limits of historical life, at the time/no time of the freedom of Christ's love. Pope Francis points out that,

> "There is always the lurking danger of living in a laboratory. Ours is not a "lab faith," but a "journey faith," a historical faith. God has revealed himself as history, not as a compendium of abstract truths. I am afraid of laboratories because in the laboratory you take the problems and then you bring them home to tame them, to paint them artificially, out of their context. You cannot bring home the frontier, but you have to live on the border and be audacious."⁴

Ontology usually tries to reveal the hidden and unalterable essence of a stable and eternal Being (*Einai*). This paper moves away from this approach and, by following Yannaras, deals with the question of *how* God or a human person *acts*, and not with the question of *what* God's or a person's substance or essence *is*.⁵ The question of *what* the Being *is* in its essence cannot be answered by human thought (*noesis*). But what it *does* or how it *acts*, this can be an object of knowledge. As Basil of Caesarea remarks, *"we know the greatness of God, his power, his wisdom, his goodness, his providence over us and the justness of his judgments; but not his essence ... We know our God from his operations, but do not undertake to approach near his essence. His operations come down to us, but his essence remains beyond our reach."*⁶ In this sense, Gustavo Gutiérrez points out that *"from an abstract, essentialist approach, we moved to an existential, historical, and*

---

⁴ "Interview with Pope Francis by Fr Antonio Spadaro," accessed October 14, 2016. https://w2.vatican.va/content/francesco/en/speeches/2013/september/documents/papa-francesco_20130921_intervista-spadaro.html.

⁵ Christos Yannaras, "Χριστούγεννα: τὸ Πῶς καὶ τὸ Τί" [Christmas: the *How* and the *What*], *Kathimerini*, December 22, 2013, 21. See also Christos Yannaras, Ὀρθὸς Λόγος καὶ Κοινωνικὴ Πρακτικὴ [Rationality and Social Practice] (Athens: Domos, 2006), 142.

⁶ Basil of Caesarea, *Letter* 234, 1, in *Saint Basil: The Letters*, volume III, Loeb Classical Library, ed. and trans. Ray J. Deferreri (Cambridge MA: Harvard University Press, 1986), 372.

*concrete view which holds that the only man we know has been efficaciously called to a gratuitous communion with God."*[7] In addition, for Maximus the Confessor the attributes of God's Energies define the *way* in which the Being exists and through lived experience reveals its reason (Logos).[8]

In the Bible, God was revealed to Moses saying *"Ehyeh asher ehyeh,"* (Exodus, 3:14). According to the author Savvas Michael this phrase stands for *"I am that I am."* As Michael mentions, the untranslated *asher,* stands for *relation* and the verb *ehyeh* means *"this is who I became through the relation."*[9] So the literal translation of God's phrase is *"I Am, what I Will Be."*[10] Moreover, the Christian theology, ontology and anthropology argue that human nature (*physis*) bears a similarity with the way God exist. A human person transforms her own personal nature via historical and social relations during her lifetime. At the *end of time* we shall know what a human person became, what her life was, and which will be the way her whole nature appeared inside history. In the same vein, Greek poet Andreas Empirikos declares: *"We are within our future."*[11]

Every person is a possibility, a hope.[12] Especially for theology, the human person is made in God's own image which means that every person is born free, even if not totally free like God. But a human person is also made in God's likeness through love, which means that she can resemble God as she lives and act her freedom

---

[7] Gutiérrez, *Theology of Liberation*, 153. See also Enrique Dussel, *History and the Theology of Liberation. A Latin American Perspective,* trans. John Drury (Maryknoll, New York: Orbis Books, 1976).

[8] Maximos the Confessor, *Ambigua* 22 (Patrologia Graeca, 91:1257 AB), as cited in Kallistos Ware, Οἰκολογικὴ Κρίση καὶ Ἐλπίδα [Ecological Crisis and Hope] (Athens: Akritas, 2008), 151.

[9] Savvas Michael, Μορφὲς τοῦ Μεσσιανικοῦ [Forms of the Messianic] (Athens: Agra, 1999), 49.

[10] Ibid.

[11] Andreas Embirikos, Ὑψικάμινος, [Blast Furnace] (Athens: Agra, 1980), 71.

[12] Rubem Azevedo Alves, *A Theology of Human Hope* (Washington and Cleveland: Corpus Books, 1969). See also Ernst Bloch, *The Principle of Hope,* trans. Neville Plaice, Stephen Plaice and Paul Knight (London: MIT Press, 1995). See also Jürgen Moltmann, *A Theology of Hope: On the Ground and the Implications of a Christian Eschatology*, trans. James W. Leitch (New York: Harper & Row, 1967).

through loving. The human being becomes a person (*prosopo*), which means something unrepeatable, something that constitutes a singularity because of the person's unique relation to others and to God. Therefore, we talk about the ontology of relation where the Being *is not*, but *becomes*.[13] A human person is one who is becoming, as a creation of the history and the acts that she performs through her relationship with the world, fellow man, and God. This is a critical ontology of presence, rather than the ontology of essence.

Theology expresses the presence of God's love in the context of historical relations; theology expresses the ontology of love. Yannaras argues: *"Every moment of historical time reveals the particular quality of time, that is, man's experience of eternity when he loves,"*[14] and the human person *"struggles in every moment of time, to dig up a potentiality for love."*[15] Martyr Archbishop Oscar Romero adds that *"close to the end of your life, you shall be judged on whether you loved."*[16]

Therefore, according to Metropolitan John Zizioulas *"the only exercise of freedom in an ontological manner is love ... Love is identified with ontological freedom."*[17] In the same vein Father Florovsky adds that *"the sole foundation of the world consists in God's freedom, in the freedom of Love."*[18] The Christian Logos of life is the *truth* of the Christian *way* of love; love to God, to human person and to nature as a whole. Love is an empirical matter of historical relations and not a question of human intellect. As an empirical matter, it is also historical and practical. As Brazilian Roman Catholic priest Frei Betto argues, *"in reality, we only know what we know empirically ... thus spirituality is a way of life, it is life according to the Spirit ... the best way*

---

[13] Christos Yannaras, *Relational Ontology*, trans. Norman Russell (Brookline-Massachusetts: Holy Cross Orthodox Press, 2011).

[14] Yannaras, *Κεφάλαια Πολιτικῆς Θεολογίας* [Chapters in Political Theology], 137.

[15] Ibid., 138.

[16] Oscar Romero, "'Ἕνας Μάρτυρας Ἀρχιεπίσκοπος" [A Martyr Archbishop], *Synaxis* 26 (1988): 65. See also Oscar Romero, *The Church is All of You: Thoughts of Archbishop Oscar Romero* (London: Collins-Fount Paperback, 1985).

[17] John D. Zizioulas, *Being as Communion: Studies in Personhood and the Church* (Crestwood, New York: St. Vladimir's Seminary Press, 1997), 46.

[18] Georges Florovsky, *Creation and Redemption* (Belmont Massachusetts: Nordland Publishing Company, 1976), 71.

*for a Christian to believe, is to live."*[19] A Dutch theologian Carlos Mesters correctly remarks that *"the Bible is useful as the critical mirror of life."*[20]

Faith is not a belief about the correctness of certain values but an event of trust and confidence between the human person and God. In such a context it is impossible for someone to have faith while material and empirical proof are absent. A human person who believes does not embrace an ideology, but rather experiences a living relationship with God. Moreover, a human person baptizes all reality in the meaning of love and the Logos of this relation and through that she draws significance from its spirituality. Faith is trust, lived historical reality. Faith in the freedom of God's love expresses the experience of its truth. Experience composes faith, the existential trust of the human person in God's truth. Christianity is a historical apocalypse, because it is eschatological. Greek theologian Athanasios Papathanasiou comments that *"the Eschaton does not render historical facts valueless, it gives them meaning and perspective."*[21]

According to relational ontology an ahistorical understanding of human nature and society cannot exist. Moreover, we should not forget that the interpretation of historical incidents that seeks to replace the laws of nature or God's laws cannot ignore the ontology of relation and love. Such an approach to history substitute's classical ontology or offers an alternative to it, while the historical framework relativizes actions and meanings. For Karl Marx, *"men make their own history, but they do not make it just as they please; they do not make it under circumstances chosen by themselves, but under circumstances directly encountered, given and transmitted from the past. The tradition of all dead generations weighs like a nightmare on the*

---

[19] Frei Betto and Fidel Castro, Ὁ Φιντὲλ καὶ ἡ Θρησκεία [Fidel & Religion] (Athens: Gnosi, 1987), 68–9.

[20] Carlos Mesters, *Defenseless Flower. A New Reading of the Bible* (Maryknoll, New York: Orbis Books, 1989), 80.

[21] Athanasios Papathanasiou, Ἡ Ἐκκλησία Γίνεται Ὅταν Ἀνοίγεται [The Church is Being Realized as Long as It Opens Itself Up] (Athens: En Plo, 2009), 107.

*brains of the living.*"²² Thus, history is the field of social experience and knowledge. For Marxism, human nature is a *social nature*, which means a historically formed nature. For Christianity, it is a *deified nature* that still remains social and historical. Deified nature is not distinct from history and society, but when it is realized, history gains a new meaning through its *metamorphosis*.

Returning to Yannaras, he states:

> *"The language of ecclesial experience appears to maintain complete awareness of the epistemological impasse presented by any nonhistorical metaphysics. That is why it marks the boundaries of its own theology with the givens arising from the event of the incarnation of God in the historical person of Jesus Christ. That which the Church Knows about God, it infers from the experience of the historical testimony of Jesus Christ as recorded by those who were eyewitnesses."*²³

Therefore, the theological, ontological and eschatological perspective is also historical. According to Frei Betto *"if the God of Christians is absent from historical evolution, it is because Christians have not yet met the God of Jesus Christ."*²⁴ The experience of this meeting is historical and we describe it using human and socially formed means, like language, even though it is impossible to understand God only with them. History, society and Christology are thus interconnected.

---

[22] Karl Marx, "The Eighteenth Brumaire of Louis Bonaparte," in *Karl Marx and Friedrich Engels, Collected Works*, Vol.11, "1851–1853" (New York: International Publishers, 1979), 103.

[23] Yannaras, *Relational Ontology*, 58.

[24] As cited in Stelios Papathemelis, Τὸ Ἅλας τῆς Γῆς [The Salt of Earth] (Athens: Parousia, 1999), 50. Also cited in Andreas Argiropoulos, Ἡ Θεολογία τῆς Ἀπελευθέρωσης στὸ Μάθημα τῶν Θρησκευτικῶν [The Theology of Liberation in Religion Courses] (Athens: manifesto, 2011), 16.

## The great history of God

The empirical relationship between the human person and God takes place inside history and contributes to its metamorphosis. The Church often disregards this truth. As Christian philosopher and political activist Cornel West argues,

> *"For Marx and Engels, religion often overlooks the socioeconomic circumstances that condition its expression, principally because the religious preoccupation with cosmic vision, ontological pronouncements on human nature and personal morality hold at arm's length social and historical analysis. Hence religion at its worst serves as an ideological means of preserving and perpetuating prevailing social and historical realities and at its best yields moralistic condemnations of and utopian visions beyond present social and historical realities—with few insights regarding what these realities are and how to change them."*[25]

This is why the German-Jesuit priest and theologian Karl Rahner, one of the most influential Catholic theologians of the 20th century, perceives the theology of his time as a "winter," even though he admits that *"some parts of the Church exist, in which life is holy and charismatic, such as the Churches of Latin America, with their practice, their theology and moreover with their martyrs."*[26] But how can one explain the historical and theological phenomenon of the Latin American Theology of Liberation as a Political Theology?

According to German Catholic theologian, Johann Baptist Metz, the emergence of the Theology of Liberation is *"a symptom, a specimen of how Latin American Theology experiences the social and historical conditions of the continent and tries to activate theological*

---

[25] Cornel West, *The Cornel West Reader* (New York: Civitas Books, 1999), 373. See also Cornel West, *Prophetic Fragments: Illuminations of the Crisis in American Religion and Culture* (Grand Rapids, Michigan: William B. Eerdmans, 1988), 14.

[26] Sobrino, "Karl Rahner and Liberation Theology," 54.

*consciousness."*²⁷ As Gutiérrez put it, it is an effort to answer the basic question of *"how can we speak about God who is revealed as love, when we live in a reality which is characterized by poverty, abjection and oppression."*²⁸ That is why the Theology of Liberation connects personal liberation with the social and political situation.

The Church can neither be independent and autonomous from the world nor can she ignore the world. Of course, liberation as a social and political procedure is not complete salvation.²⁹ Furthermore, humanity's inability to achieve the absolute inside history does not despair the human person, instead it mobilizes her. This mobilization happens because human life is not sacrificed in expectation for a reward in the Eschaton, but this sacrifice becomes a reality of salvation inside history, *here* and *now*. Precisely because the saved human person is motivated by love and not by the expectation of reward, sacrifice itself loses its meaning. The human person does not sacrifice anything with her offering, but on the contrary she fulfills her existence.

It is very important to clarify that for Christianity the human person's action in history (*praxis*) cannot be disconnected from the history of *salvation*.³⁰ As Betto argues, *"the persons who want to become Christians do not ask what to believe in instead they ask what they have to do."*³¹ Creation (*cosmos*) continues to be created in every

---

²⁷ Argiropoulos, Ἡ Θεολογία τῆς Ἀπελευθέρωσης στὸ Μάθημα τῶν Θρησκευτικῶν [The Theology of Liberation in Religion Courses], 14–15. See also Dorothee Sölle, *Stations of the Cross: A Latin American Pilgrimage* (Minneapolis: Fortress Press, 1993).

²⁸ Gustavo Gutiérrez, *Hablar de Dios Desde el Sufrimiento del Inocente* [On Job: God-Talk and the Suffering of the Innocent] (Salamanca: Sigueme, 1988), 14. See also Dom Helder Camara, *Spiral of Violence*, (London: Sheed and Ward Ltd, 1971).

²⁹ Gutirérez, *Theology of Liberation*, 172–78.

³⁰ Clodovis Boff, *Theology and Praxis: Epistemological Foundations*, trans. Robert R. Barr (Maryknoll, New York: Orbis Books, 1987).

³¹ Betto and Castro, Ὁ Φιντὲλ καὶ ἡ Θρησκεία [Fidel & Religion], 347. See also Gustavo Gutiérrez, "Liberation Praxis and Christian Faith," in *Frontiers of Theology in Latin America*, ed. Rosino Gibellini, (Maryknoll, New York: Orbis Books, 1979), 1–33. See also Maria Pineda, "Liberation Theology: Practice of a People Hungering for Human Dignity," *The Way* 38 (1998): 231–239. See also Howland T. Sanks and Brian H. Smith, "Liberation Ecclesiology: Praxis, Theory, Praxis," *Theological Studies* 38 (1977): 3–38.

minute and human person is its co-creator. Orthodox bishop Kallistos Ware summarizes:

> "Cosmos is not only a gift, but also an opus ... the work of the human person, as Saint John Chrysostom said, is to be the bridge of divine Creation. Uniting heaven and earth, making earth heavenly, and heaven earthly, we render the holy presence obvious, in the heart of all creation. Precisely this duty was assigned to the first Adam in Paradise, and this duty after the fall is the work that was fulfilled by the Second Adam, Christ, through his Incarnation, Transfiguration, Crucifixion and Resurrection."[32]

In addition, it is also crucial to emphasize the unity between history and salvation. Specifically, the Theology of Liberation distinguishes between political liberation and the whole of salvation. Referring to the synergy between God and the human person, Gutiérrez wrote that *"we can say that the historical, political liberating event is the growth of the Kingdom and is a salvific event; but it is not the coming of the Kingdom, not all of salvation. It is the historical realization of the Kingdom and, therefore, it also proclaims its fullness. This is where the difference lies."*[33] Moreover, it is also important to add that it is impossible for the theology to provide a specific political program for the transformation of society even though it has a very important social role and interest with many political consequences.

The union between history of the human person and history of salvation in the Theology of Liberation is the *"great history of God."* The two worlds, created and uncreated, are directly related *here* and *now*. Father Sobrino argues that *"transcendence here is not something beyond history but within it. The history of God and of humanity becomes one single great history of God."*[34] The common sharing of the *"great history of God"* is to participate in Christ's life.

---

[32] Ware, Οἰκολογικὴ Κρίση καὶ Ἐλπίδα [Ecological Crisis and Hope], 71, 77.

[33] Gutiérrez, *Theology of Liberation*, 177.

[34] Sobrino, "Karl Rahner and Liberation Theology," 61.

Salvation inside history does not become the means to the end of God's Kingdom, but the means and the end are unified into a way of life, *here* and *now*. The human person either experiences the Gospel's joyful message through practising love within history, or ignores it. Theological thought distinguishes the *times* of the people who live within the freedom of God's love and the *times* of those who ignore it. As these *times* are different from each other, so are the stories/histories. The common ways and reasons of life are the common histories of human beings. The presence (*parousia*) is an intertwining of the past leaving its trace, with the possibilities for the future, that acts *here* and *now*. This is the *"great history of God"*; the history of the freedom of God's love and also the catholic history of the Creation's salvation. Eschatology is understood in a way that brings it at the forefront again, not in a superior position from history but in a balance and in a common course with it.

The element that differentiates *histories* and *times* is the meaning of time. The meaning of time is the Logos of historical life and it is not the same for all the people. Just as we perceive the meaning of historical life in different ways, in the same manner we occupy different dimensions of time and history. The merging of the time of history with the *time of Christ* reveals the *"great history of God."* Father Sobrino argues that

> "History expresses God, is sacramentally charged with God … The history of God and of humanity becomes one single "great history of God" … Liberation theology insists that there is only one history, with two dimensions that we need to see as a history of grace and a history of sin —abstract distinctions like "nature and grace" or "sacred and secular" will not do."[35]

The *"great history of God"* concerns the history of Creation in which the un-created acts and not some supposed sum of the two. The un-created exists in no time at all, nor history. Therefore, it is erroneous to characterize it either as the history of the un-created

---
[35] Ibid.

or as the history of Grace. On the contrary the created constantly changes, have a beginning and an end, time and history. The *"great history of God"* is the history of synergy between the created and the un-created and thus as Kallistos Ware argues *"we enter into the dimensions of holy space and holy time."*[36] Sin and Grace exist as discrete situations *here* and *now* inside history. Sin and Grace emerge as distinct historical experiences.

The history of salvation is the history of incarnated Logos. Gustavo Gutiérrez summarizes:

> *There are not two histories, one profane and one sacred, "juxtaposed" or "closely linked." Rather there is only one human destiny, irreversibly assumed by Christ, the Lord of history. His redemptive work embraces all the dimensions of existence and brings them to their fullness. The history of salvation is the very heart of human history.*[37]

## History and ontology of the Incarnation

According to Father Basil Thermos, "the Incarnation of the Logos of Creation reveals the deeper reason of Creation. Incarnated Logos means union and incorporation of Creator and creature."[38] When this union fails, the Logos of Creation is ignored, and sacramental life becomes occultism; this is the experience of the Fall. As Father Basil Gontikakis puts it "this separation is sin itself, this is evil."[39] Consequently, a human person possesses the existential will to be unified with God and her fellow humans, and the existential will to be saved from the sinful situation of separation. Love is the meaning of incarnated Creation, which connects not only the Creator with the creation, but also ontology with history into the "great history of God." This "great history of God" is the life of

---

[36] Ware, Οἰκολογικὴ Κρίση καὶ Ἐλπίδα [Ecological Crisis and Hope], 54.

[37] Gutiérrez, *Theology of Liberation*, 153.

[38] Basil Thermos, Ὁ Ἔρωτας τοῦ Ἀπολύτου [Love of the Absolute] (Athens: Armos, 2010), 54–55.

[39] Basil Gontikakis, Ἡ Παραβολὴ τοῦ Ἀσώτου Υἱοῦ [The Parable of the Prodigal Son] (Athens: Domos, 1995), 11.

possibility for the human person and nature which can be fulfilled through the freedom offered by love and which can be saved from oblivion and death in a false, meaningless life.

Incarnation has an ontological criterion, which is disclosed empirically in the person (prosopo) of Jesus Christ. The Creator and the creation in Christ are bridged and connected inside history, interrupting the time and the history of sin and revealing the time and the history of salvation. Through incarnation, the way of the human person becomes similar to the way of God, as Protopresbyter Nikolaos Loudovikos writes.[40] The mystery somehow becomes transparent (Epiphany) and the Eschaton ceases to be a metaphysical horizon and intangible concept. The incarnated Christ, and not the transcendent God, creates Christianity. With this incarnation, mystery is empirically revealed inside history.

The notion of flesh in theological thought implies the human being of history, which is the person separated from Christ and the freedom that His love provides; whereas the notion of spirit implies the human person of the "great history of God," which is unified with Christ and the freedom that His love provides. Christ as an incarnation of Logos and historical event (presence/parousia), brings about a transcendence of time and of the history of the Fall but also brings about the experience of incarnated salvation within time and history. Moreover, Apostle Paul distinguishes between body and flesh, as he also distinguishes between soul and spirit. The human person is a psychosomatic unity, which means that soul and body are not different substances unified in an inseparable unity, but different expressions of a single existence. This wholeness is either fleshly or spiritual. This should not be taken to mean that this wholeness is sometimes material and sometimes immaterial, as Kallistos Ware explains, "flesh in the Epistles means the whole man in the condition of the Fall, while spirit means the whole man in the condition of

---

[40] Nikolaos Loudovikos, Ψυχανάλυση καὶ Ὀρθόδοξη Θεολογία. Περὶ Ἐπιθυμίας, Καθολικότητας καὶ Ἐσχατολογίας [Psychoanalysis and Orthodox Theology: About Desire, Catholicity and Eschatology] (Athens: Armos, 2003), 95.

Salvation; consequently, the soul and the body, can be corporeal, and the body, as well as the soul, can be spiritual."[41] Frei Betto clarifies these notions by asking "what does it mean theologically to obtain spirituality? It means to acquire a way to follow Jesus."[42] Jesus' spirituality was not a denial of earthly reality, but a metamorphosis thereof.

Spirituality does not mean withdrawal from Creation and history. It is the experience of freedom of love within Creation and history. According to Oscar Romero,

> *"Flesh is the specific person ... humans whose scars of time are visible: the child who just began to live, the vigorous adolescent, the old man who gets close to the end. Flesh is the real human condition ... which has a beginning and an end, which gets sick and dies, which sins, which has grief or happiness, depending on its obedience to God; this thing became Logos. Logos has become flesh."*[43]

Incarnation is the baptizing of Logos in the history of the world. This is what Gutiérrez means when he writes that Theology of Liberation is *"the theology of salvation into the structural, historical, and political conditions of our days."*[44] Chilean priest Segundo Galilea adds that under diverse cultural and social conditions, many different human relationships and experiences arise and grow; therefore the Logos is expressed in different ways.[45] As theologian Leonardo Boff stresses, *"every generation brings a new presence of Christ because the*

---

[41] Ware, Οἰκολογικὴ Κρίση καὶ Ἐλπίδα [Ecological Crisis and Hope], 125–26.

[42] Betto and Castro, Ὁ Φιντέλ καὶ ἡ Θρησκεία [Fidel & Religion], 65-6.

[43] Romero, "'Ένας Μάρτυρας Ἀρχιεπίσκοπος" [A Martyr Archbishop], 65.

[44] Gustavo Gutiérrez, *The Power of the Poor in History*, trans. Robert R. Barr (Maryknoll, New York: Orbis Books, 1983), 63. See also José Miguez Bonino, *Doing Theology in a Revolutionary Situation*, ed. William H. Lazareth, (Philadelphia: Fortress Press, 1975). See also Enrique Dussel, *A History of the Church in Latin America: Colonialism to Liberation (1492-1979)*, trans. Alan Neely, (Grand Rapids: Wílliam B. Eerdmans, 1981).

[45] Segundo Galilea, "The Spirituality of Liberation," *The Way* 25, (1985): 190–91.

*Savior gives to every era a new composition of life and faith.*"⁴⁶ In addition, Papathanasiou recalls that the liturgical texts of the Church *"are broods of specific cultural affinities, in the unremitting effort of incarnation of ecclesiastical truth, in space and time."*⁴⁷ For Jesuit priest, philosopher, and theologian Ignacio Ellacuria, the truth of Holy Scripture did not occur in history as a one-off event that has since remained unchangeable; scriptures are instead interpreted constantly within the context of particular historical conditions. It is only within these conditions that the meaning of scriptures unfolds. This is why professor of social theology Apostolos Nicolaidis explains that *"Orthodoxy has not systematically articulated a Christian social teaching, which can be valid in all historical periods and frameworks, because whenever this happened, the Christian teaching was transformed into an ideology."*⁴⁸

The particular history of the Theology of Liberation was born *"in the context of the Basic Ecclesial Communities of Latin America."*⁴⁹ According to Roman Catholic priest and author Phillip Berryman *"base communities have developed only where priests or sisters have worked to set them up,"*⁵⁰ where *"the emphasis was on dialogue. Pastoral agents sought not only to listen to the words, but to try to tap into people's*

---

⁴⁶ Leonardo Boff, "Salvation in Jesus Christ and the Process of Liberation," *Concilium* 96 (1974): 78. See also Leonardo Boff, *Jesus Christ Liberator: a Critical Christology for our Time*, trans. Patrick Hughes (MaryKnoll, New York: Orbis Books, 1978).

⁴⁷ Papathanasiou, Ἡ Ἐκκλησία Γίνεται Ὅταν Ἀνοίγεται [The Church is Being Realized as Long as It Opens Itself Up], 63. See also John Meyendorff, *Living Tradition: Orthodox Witness in the Contemporary World* (Crestwood, New York: St. Vladimir's Seminary Press, 1978), 15.

⁴⁸ Apostolos Nikolaidis, Κοινωνικοπολιτικὴ Ἐπανάσταση καὶ Πολιτικὴ Θεολογία [Sociopolitical Revolution and Political Theology] (Katerini: Tetrios, 1987), 181.

⁴⁹ Betto and Castro, Ὁ Φιντὲλ καὶ ἡ Θρησκεία [Fidel & Religion], 67. See also Leonardo Boff, *Ecclesiogenesis. The Base Communities Reinvent the Church*, trans. Robert R. Barr (Maryknoll, New York: Orbis Books, 1986). See also William T. Cavanaugh, "The Ecclesiologies of Medellín and the Lessons of the Base Communities," *Cross Currents* 44, (1994), 74–81. See also Warren Edward Hewitt, *Base Christian Communities and Social Change in Brazil* (Nebraska: Lincoln University of Nebraska Press, 1991).

⁵⁰ Phillip Berryman, *Liberation Theology: The Essential Facts About the Revolutionary Movement in Latin America and Beyond* (New York: Random House, Inc., 1987), 5.

*experience and learn from them—to be evangelized by the people."*[51] Jesuit Father Juan Luis Segundo stresses that the Church exists for the human person rather than the human person for the Church.[52] Therefore, Incarnation influences the secular space. Similarly, Father Sobrino considers that the single most important contribution of the Christology of Liberation[53] is its understanding of the historical dimension of God's Kingdom as a march together with the poor towards the Eschaton.

## Secularization and religiosity

The antagonistic relation between secularization and religiosity is historically shaped in cultural terms within the framework of the western world at the end of the 18th and the beginning of the 19th century. The term secularization, according to professor of theology Rosino Gibellini, means *"the emancipation of cultural life (politics, sciences, economy, literature, philosophy, art and ethics) from ecclesiastical custody."*[54] This evolution expressed the desire of civil society to be liberated from the embrace of religious authority and the ideological hegemony of the Church.

Lutheran theologian Friedrich Gogarten disagrees with this definition. According to him, secularization is not opposed to

---

[51] Phillip Berryman, "Basic Christian Communities and the Future of Latin America," *Monthly Review* 36 (1984): 30.

[52] Juan Luis Segundo, *The Community Called Church,* trans. John Drury (Maryknoll, New York: Orbis Books, 1973), 6.

[53] Jon Sobrino, "La Centralidad del "Reino de Dios" en la Teología de la Libaracion," *Revista Latinoamericana de Teologia* 3, (1986): 247-281. See also Leonardo Boff, *Jesucristo y la Liberacion del Hobre, Christiandad* (Madrid: *Cristiandad,* 1981), 26-28 and 83-109. See also Jon Sobrino, *Christology at the Crossroads: A Latin American Approach,* trans. John Drury (Mary knoll, New York: Orbis Books, 1978). See also Jon Sobrino, *Jesus the Liberator: A Historical-Theological Reading of Jesus of Nazareth,* trans. Paul Burns and Francis McDonagh (Maryknoll, New York: Orbis Books, 1991).

[54] Rosino Gibellini, Ἡ Θεολογία τοῦ Εἰκοστοῦ Αἰῶνα [Twentieth Century Theology] (Athens: Artos Zois, 2009), 153. On the other hand, according to Karl Löwith, the primal church saw its mission in the world as an attempt to overcome it and to prepare it for the Eschaton (the end), to which it was solely concentrated (Karl Löwith, *Meaning in History* (Chicago and London: The University of Chicago Press, 1949), 195-98.

Christianity. On the contrary, it is its historical consequence. Christianity for the first time places the human person at the center of the world and gives her the responsibility of her own freedom.[55] The human being, recognized in the pagan universe as the victim of natural necessity, becomes with Christianity God's free co-creator of Creation (the cosmos). The human person and God act inside history, and their relationship becomes a secularized relationship.

Secularization understood as a radical anthropocentrism started with Christianity, when human civilization transcended the mythical symbolic world with nature at its epicenter, and established the world of the historically conscious and self-reliant person. With Christianity, the human person is able to distance herself from the world and contemplate it free from the necessities that the world imposed upon her. Now, the new epicenter of the world is the human person and her free will. While the human person engenders this new conception of the world, at the same time humanity is not separated from the world. In this way the human person is able to make decisions about the world, thus constituting her moral existence by taking responsibility for it. The human person does not passively submit to a cosmic destiny, but instead creates her world actively. As Michael says, *"resurrection, with which comes the restoration of everything, can be seen not as a disembodiment, but as Disenchantment: the spells are broken, the myths are blown up. The sleeping beauty awakens at last."*[56] This move signifies the human person's disenchantment in two ways: first, it signifies the human person's disenchantment from the magical pagan universe, and her rejection of mysticism in favor of the mystery of love; second, this move disabuses the person from historical cynicism and nihilism and restores the meaning of life. Incarnated Logos restores the truth of the Creation, into the cosmos.

The Theology of Liberation advocates for faith to be secularized, a proposition which does not stand for the denial of religious doctrines and the abandonment of the eschatological dimension of

---

[55] Gibellini, Ἡ Θεολογία τοῦ Εἰκοστοῦ Αἰῶνα [Twentieth Century Theology], 153–88.
[56] Michael, Μορφὲς τοῦ Μεσσιανικοῦ [Forms of the Messianic], 301–02.

history, but rather for an Incarnation of the Logos into the contemporary cultural, social and political conditions. Therefore secularization, understood in its connection with scientific *ratio*, is not antithetical to eschatology and faith; on the contrary, according to Gutiérrez, *"it also favours a more complete fulfilment of the Christian life insofar as it offers man the possibility of being more fully human."*[57]

## History and eschatology

Greek philosopher Kostas Papaioannou traces historical consciousness as an eschatological march of progress in time back to the Jewish religion. In the Bible, God creates the world and intervenes in it, in order to guarantee the salvation of his chosen people. With Christianity, the New Testament concerns all mankind. Christianity has an ecumenical core and interest, fulfilling the prophecy and the promise for the end of the history of the *Fall*. Therefore, for Christian theology, eschatology does not promise salvation at the end of time and only then. Salvation is a reality here and now within the Grace of God, because the meaning and the Logos of existence have already been revealed and incarnated. Resurrection has already taken place. It is not just a promise, but it is also a lived experience.

Christ is not anticipated at the end of history or at some moment in the future, as it happens in other eschatologies, but His paradigm is experienced everyday, *here* and *now*. The way is already given and the path has already been trodden. This is why professor of theology George Mantzaridis mentions Gregory Palamas' assertion, that *"the granting of God is not anticipated in the historical future, but was already offered one-off in the past, and was therefore made communicable in every historical present and is expected to be revealed in its completeness beyond history and time."*[58] Moreover, Lutheran theologian Oscar Cullmann focuses on this strain between *already* on one hand, and *not yet* on the other.[59] It is

---

[57] Gutiérrez, *Theology of Liberation*, 67.
[58] George Mantzaridis, Παλαμικά, [On Palamas] (Thessaloniki: Pournaras, 1998), 66.
[59] Oscar Cullmann, *Christ and Time: The Primitive Christian Conception of Time*, trans. Floyd V. Filson (London: SCM, 1962), 202.

impossible to believe in a promise for the future, if this promise has not already taken place. No hope of Second Coming would be possible, had the First Coming not have happened. The presence of love is the event that convinces us of the ascetic of love, the event through which faith is strengthened.

The main characteristic of the Theology of Liberation is its prejudice in favour of the *poor*.[60] Poverty is a historical and social situation and not an ontological necessity. But the question of dealing with the poor and the *sinful* social structures which create poverty is an ontological matter, because it is pertinent to the history of salvation, which means the freedom of love that we can experience. Poverty is a sinful situation, because its existence is a symptom of the absence of love and grace in the world. Poverty is the testimony of the presence of sinful egoism. Thus, the existential relation between the Theology of Liberation and the poor is historical, as well as ontological.

This relation between Christians and the poor does not only express their common fights and efforts to change the *sinful* social structures and gain their liberation from social and political oppression. This relation also manifests a specific life worldview, according to which we can see the social and political structures through their (the poor's) eyes, from their point of view.[61] This preference for the poor, establishes the Church of the poor.[62] Emphasis on the poor becomes the main distinctive characteristic of the Theology of Liberation. According to Frei Betto *"when the poor invaded the Church, priests and bishops began to turn to Christianity."*[63] The main characteristic of the Church of the poor is

---

[60] See Leonardo Boff, *Cry of the Earth, Cry of the Poor*, trans. Phillip Berryman (Maryknoll, New York: Orbis Books, 1997). See also Leonardo Boff, *When Theology Listens to the Poor*, trans. Robert R. Barr (San Francisco: Harper & Row, 1988). See Also James H. Cone, *God of the Oppressed* (Maryknoll, New York: Orbis Books, 1997).

[61] Jon Sobrino, *The True Church and the Poor*, trans. Matthew J. O'Connell (Maryknoll, New York: Orbis Books, 1981). See also Jon Sobrino, *Christ the Liberator: A View from the Victims*, trans. Paul Burns (Maryknoll, New York: Orbis Books, 1999).

[62] Jon Sobrino, *No Salvation Outside the Poor: Prophetic-Utopian Essays* (Maryknoll, New York: Orbis Books, 2008).

[63] Betto and Castro, Ὁ Φιντὲλ καὶ ἡ Θρησκεία [Fidel & Religion], 302.

that priests live with the poor, think like them, and fight with them. Their common will is for their liberation from the personal sin of egoism and against the oppression of the *sinful* social and political structures. Consequently, God's people are liberated in two ways: the first one is liberation *from* something (egoism, injustice, oppression, etc.); the second one is liberation *because of* something (love and community). For Christians subscribing to the Theology of Liberation, this ascetic of the freedom of love takes place in the context of history of human being which is the *"great history of God,"* from the beginning until the end of time.

Orthodox tradition is established on the ecclesial and eucharistic event. This event reveals the eschatological dimension of history. The eucharistic event reveals the dialectic between *already* and *not yet*. Moreover, it would not be far from the truth to point out that according to Orthodox tradition the *not yet* dimension is not as important as the dimension of *already*. In contrast to Orthodox tradition, Western theology emphasizes eschatology over the eucharistic event. As Paul McPartlan argues,

> "To the Western mind, eschatology as orientation appears to be common sense. How can the end be other than simply our eventual destination? The Orthodox would say that there is a paradox here that confounds common sense, namely the truth that the end is present and formative of the earthly pilgrim Church in the regular celebration of the eucharist."[64]

With the eucharistic life, the person becomes accepted in the Church, with all its sinfulness. There is an *economy*, a realistic

---

[64] Paul McPartlan, "The Local and the Universal Church: Zizioulas and the Ratzinger-Kasper Debate's," in *Theology of John Zizioulas: Personhood and the Church*, ed. Douglas Knight (Aldershot: Ashgate, 2007), 173. See also Paul McPartlan, *The Eucharist Makes the Church. Henri de Lubac and John Zizioulas in Dialogue* (Edinburgh: T&T. Clark, 1993; new edition, Fairfax, VA: Eastern Christian Publications, 2006), 256–64.

acceptance of the world and of the reality of daily life.⁶⁵ The ecclesiastical *economy* is expressing the way in which God's love relates with the world as it is, *here* and *now*.

In Theology of Liberation the dialectic between *already* and *not yet* is present also. But according to some critical perspectives, the eschatological dimension is absolutely absent or very underrated because the historical praxis is more important.⁶⁶ But this praxis mostly has to do with the transformation of the political and social structures and does not emphasize the eucharistic event so much. The Orthodox context places stronger emphasis on the person's relations, whereas the Theology of Liberation context places stronger emphasis on structural social and political relations.⁶⁷ Nevertheless, the primary interest for both of them is the metamorphosis of historical human beings and their social relations within the *"great history of God."* Christology is historical and anthropocentric; because of this event it is also community-centered. In conclusion, the *ascesis* of the freedom of love takes place in the context of society as a social event and not as an individual achievement.

The Eschaton exists in a sacramental way, *here* and *now*. As Luke the Evangelist declared: *"The kingdom of God is not coming with signs to be observed; nor will they say, "Lo, here it is!" or "There!" for behold, the kingdom of God is in the midst of you."* (Luke 17:20–21). For Father Sobrino, Christ is a *liberator* because he is neither a mystic, nor a political activist, but the true paradigm of the freedom of love through history.⁶⁸ In approaching this concept, the Theology of Liberation follows the tracks of Christ with agony and hope. As Theology of Liberation treads with its own feet, it leaves its own

---

⁶⁵ Nikos Kokosalakis, "'Ελληνικὴ 'Ορθοδοξία, Νεωτερικότητα καὶ Πολιτική" [Greek Orthodoxy, Modernity and Politics], in *'Ορθοδοξία καὶ Νεωτερικότητα* [Orthodoxy and Modernity], ed. Pantelis Kalaitzidis and Nikos Ntontos. (Athens: Indiktos, 2007), 376.

⁶⁶ Arthur McGovern, *Liberation Theology and Its Critics. Toward an Assessment* (Maryknoll, New York: Orbis Books, 1989).

⁶⁷ Christian Smith, *The Emergence of Liberation Theology: Radical Religion and Social Movement Theory* (Chicago: The University of Chicago Press, 1991).

⁶⁸ Gibellini, *Ἡ Θεολογία τοῦ Εἰκοστοῦ Αἰῶνα* [Twentieth Century Theology], 457.

tracks. Following the history of Jesus, it has transformed the history of sin into a history of ascetic love.

Love is the motivation of Theology of Liberation and also the foundation of the Orthodox tradition. In summary, Orthodox Archbishop of Tirana, Durrës and all Albania, Anastasios Yannoulatos, argues that love for an Orthodox believer, as revealed in the person (*prosopo*) of Jesus Christ and his acts, is the core of life and fulfils life's experiences. This love grows and embraces everything, fulfilling the metamorphosis of the world's history.[69] Love gives to everything a new meaning and a new purpose; the freedom of love develops a new logic of understanding the whole existence and also a new way for action inside history. The power of love, and the power of love's freedom, accomplish the metamorphosis of political and social structures and moreover the metamorphosis of political and social life as a whole.

## Epilogue

Kallistos Ware quotes a narration from the ecological manifesto of the American Benedictine Abbesses:

> "During World War II, a German widow was hiding some Jewish refugees in her house. When her friends found out, they were terrified. "You are in a big danger," they told her. "I know," was her answer. "Then why do you insist on this madness?" The answer was immediate. "I do it," she said, "because the time is now and I am here.""[70]

Theologians, priests, nuns and Christian laymen took up this fight, this madness, along with the poor, because at that certain moment, they were there. Because they were motivated by love, to them everything looked as though it had already been fulfilled. They exemplify the struggling, crucified and resurrected human person walking through history and realizing her presence in it.

---

[69] Anastasios of Androussa (Yannoulatos), Ἱστορία Ἐπιζόντων Θρησκευμάτων [History of Active Religuous] (Athens: Vima, 2016), 423.

[70] Ware, Οἰκολογικὴ Κρίση καὶ Ἐλπίδα [Ecological Crisis and Hope], 44.

## Bibliography

Alves, Rubem Azevedo. *A Theology of Human Hope*. Washington and Cleveland: Corpus Books, 1969.

Anastasios of Androussa (Yannoulatos), Ἱστορία Ἐπιζόντων Θρησκευμάτων [History of Active Religions]. Athens: Vima, 2016.

Argiropoulos, Andreas. Η Θεολογία της Απελευθέρωσης στο Μάθημα των Θρησκευτικών [The Theology of Liberation at the Lesson of Religious]. Athens: manifesto, 2011.

Basil of Caesarea. *Saint Basil: The Letters*. Edited and Translated by Ray J. Deferreri. Loeb Classical Library. Cambridge MA: Harvard University Press, 1986.

Berryman, Phillip. "Basic Christian Communities and the Future of Latin America." *Monthly Review* 36 (1984): 27–40.

———. *Liberation Theology: The Essential Facts About the Revolutionary Movement in Latin America and Beyond*. New York: Random House, Inc., 1987.

Betto, Frei, and Fidel Castro. Ὁ Φιντὲλ καὶ ἡ Θρησκεία [Fidel & Religion]. Athens: Gnosi, 1987.

Bloch, Ernst. *The Principle of Hope*. Translated by Neville Plaice, Stephen Plaice and Paul Knight. London: MIT Press, 1995.

Boff, Clodovis. *Theology and Praxis: Epistemological Foundations*. Translated by Robert R. Barr. Maryknoll, New York: Orbis Books, 1987.

Boff, Leonardo. "Salvation in Jesus Christ and the Process of Liberation." *Concilium* 96 (1974): 78–91.

———. *Jesus Christ Liberator: a Critical Christology for our Time*. Translated by Patrick Hughes. MaryKnoll, New York: Orbis Books, 1978.

———. *Jesucristo y la Liberacion del Hobre*, Christiandad. Madrid: Cristiandad, 1981.

———. *Ecclesiogenesis. The Base Communities Reinvent the Church*. Translated by Robert R. Barr. Maryknoll, New York: Orbis Books, 1986.

———. *When Theology Listens to the Poor*. Translated by Robert R. Barr. San Francisco: Harper & Row, 1988.

———. *Cry of the Earth, Cry of the Poor*. Translated by Phillip Berryman. Maryknoll, New York: Orbis Books, 1997.

Bonino, José Miguez, *Doing Theology in a Revolutionary Situation*. Edited by William H. Lazareth. Philadelphia: Fortress Press, 1975.

Camara, Dom Helder. *Spiral of Violence* (London: Sheed and Ward Ltd, 1971).

Cavanaugh, T. William. "The Ecclesiologies of Medellín and the Lessons of the Base Communities." *Cross Currents* 44 (1994), 74–81.

Cone, James H. *God of the Oppressed*. Maryknoll, New York: Orbis Books, 1997.

Cullmann, Oscar. *Christ and Time: The Primitive Christian Conception of Time*. Translated Floyd V. Filson. London: SCM, 1962.

Dussel, Enrique, *History and the Theology of Liberation. A Latin American Perspective.* Translated by John Drury. Maryknoll, New York: Orbis Books, 1976.

———. *A History of the Church in Latin America: Colonialism to Liberation (1492-1979).* Translation by Alan Neely. Grand Rapids: Willliam B. Eerdmans, 1981.

Empirikos, Andreas. Ὑψικάμινος [Blast Furnace]. Athens: Agra, 1980.

Florovsky, Georges. *Christianity and* Culture. Belmont Massachusetts: Nordland Publishing Company, 1974.

———. Creation and Redemption. Belmont Massachusetts: Nordland Publishing Company, 1976.

Pope Francis. Γιὰ μιὰ Ἐκκλησία Φτωχὴ καὶ τῶν Φτωχῶν [For a Poor Church and for a Church of the Poor]. Athens: Polis, 2014.

Galilea, Segundo. "The Spirituality of Liberation." *The Way* 25 (1985): 186-94.

Gibellini, Rosino. Ἡ Θεολογία τοῦ Εἰκοστοῦ Αἰῶνα [Twentieth Century Theology] Athens: Artos Zois, 2009.

Gontikakis, Basil. Ἡ Παραβολὴ τοῦ Ἀσώτου Υἱοῦ [The Parable of the Prodigal Son]. Athens: Domos, 1995.

Gutierrez, Gustavo. *A Theology of Liberation. History, Politics, and Salvation.* Translated and Edited by Sister Caridad Inda and John Eagleson. Maryknoll, New York: Orbis Books, 1973.

———. *The Power of the Poor in History.* Translated by Robert R.Barr. Maryknoll, New York: Orbis Books, 1983.

———. "Liberation Praxis and Christian Faith." In *Frontiers of Theology in Latin America*, edited by Rosino Gibellini, 1-33. Maryknoll, New York: Orbis Books, 1979.

———. *Hablar de Dios Desde el Sufrimiento del Inocente.* Salamanca: Sigueme, 1988.

Hewitt, Warren Edward. *Base Christian Communities and Social Change in Brazil.* Nebraska: Lincoln University of Nebraska Press, 1991.

Kokosalakis, Nikos. "'Ελληνικὴ Ὀρθοδοξία, Νεωτερικότητα καὶ Πολιτική" [Greek Orthodoxy, Modernity and Politics]. In Ὀρθοδοξία καὶ Νεωτερικότητα [Orthodoxy and Modernity], edited by Pantelis Kalaitzidis and Nikos Ntontos, 371-406. Athens: Indiktos, 2007.

Loudovikos, Nikolaos. Ψυχανάλυση καὶ Ὀρθόδοξη Θεολογία: Περὶ Ἐπιθυμίας, Καθολικότητας καὶ Ἐσχατολογίας [Psychoanalysis and Orthodox Theology: About Desire, Catholicity and Eschatology]. Athens: Armos, 2003.

Löwith, Karl, *Meaning in History.* Chicago and London: The University of Chicago Press, 1949.

Mantzaridis, George. Παλαμικά [On Palamas]. Thessaloniki: Pournaras, 1998.

Marx, Karl. "The Eighteenth Brumaire of Louis Bonaparte." In *Karl Marx and Friedrich Engels, Collected Works.* Vol.11, "1851-1853," 99-197. New York: International Publishers, 1979.

McGovern, Arthur. *Liberation Theology and Its Critics. Toward an Assessment.* Maryknoll, New York: Orbis Books, 1989.

McPartlan, Paul. "The Local and the Universal Church: Zizioulas and the Ratzinger-Kasper Debate's." In *Theology of John Zizioulas: Personhood and the Church*, edited by Douglas Knight, 171-182. Aldershot: Ashgate, 2007.

———. *The Eucharist Makes the Church. Henri de Lubac and John Zizioulas in Dialogue.* Edinburgh: T&T. Clark, 1993; new edition, Fairfax, VA: Eastern Christian Publications, 2006.

Mesters, Carlos. *Defenseless Flower. A New Reading of the Bible.* Maryknoll, New York: Orbis Books, 1989.

Meyendorff, John. *Living Tradition: Orthodox Witness in the Contemporary World.* Crestwood, New York: St.Vladimir's Seminary Press, 1978.

Michael, Savvas. *Μορφές του Μεσσιανικού* [Forms of the Messianic]. Athens: Agra, 1999.

Moltmann, Jürgen. *A Theology of Hope: On the Ground and the Implications of a Christian Eschatology.* Translated by James W. Leitch. New York: Harper & Row, 1967.

Nikolaidis, Apostolos. *Κοινωνικοπολιτικὴ Ἐπανάσταση καὶ Πολιτικὴ Θεολογία.* [Socio-political Revolution and Political Theology]. Katerini: Tetrios, 1987.

Papathanasiou, Athanasios. *Ἡ Ἐκκλησία Γίνεται Ὅταν Ἀνοίγεται* [The Church is Being Realized as Long as It Opens Itself Up]. Athens: En Plo, 2009.

Papathemelis, Stelios. *Τὸ Ἅλας τῆς Γῆς* [The Salt of Earth]. Athens: Parousia, 1999.

Pineda, Maria, "Liberation Theology: Practice of a People Hungering for Human Dignity." *The Way* 38 (1998): 231-239.

Romero, Oscar. *The Church is All of You: Thoughts of Archbishop Oscar Romero.* London: Collins-Fount Paperback, 1985.

———. "'Ἕνας Μάρτυρας Ἀρχιεπίσκοπος" [A Martyr Archbishop]. *Synaxis* 26 (1988): 65-67.

Sanks, Howland T. and Brian H. Smith, "Liberation Ecclesiology: Praxis, Theory, Praxis." Theological Studies 38 (1977): 3-38.

Segundo, Juan Luis. *The Community Called Church.* Translated by John Drury. Maryknoll, New York: Orbis Books, 1973.

Smith, Christian. *The Emergence of Liberation Theology: Radical Religion and Social Movement Theory.* Chicago: The University of Chicago Press, 1991.

Sobrino, Jon. *Christology at the Crossroads: A Latin American Approach.* Translated by John Drury. Mary knoll, New York: Orbis Books, 1978.

———. *The True Church and the Poor.* Translated by Matthew J. O'Connell. Maryknoll, New York: Orbis Books, 1981.

———. "La Centralidad del "Reino de Dios" en la Teología de la Libaracion." *Revista Latinoamericana de Teologia* 3 (1986): 247-81.

———. *Jesus the Liberator: A Historical-Theological Reading of Jesus of Nazareth.* Translated by Paul Burns and Francis McDonagh. Maryknoll, New York: Orbis Books, 1991.

———. *Christ the Liberator: A View from the Victims*. Translated by Paul Burns. Maryknoll, New York: Orbis Books, 1999.

———. "Karl Rahner and Liberation Theology." *The Way* 43/4, (2004): 53–66.

———. *No Salvation Outside the Poor: Prophetic-Utopian Essays*. Maryknoll, New York: Orbis Books, 2008.

Sölle, Dorothee. *Stations of the Cross: A Latin American Pilgrimage*. Minneapolis: Fortress Press, 1993.

Thermos, Basil. *Ὁ Ἔρωτας τοῦ Ἀπολύτου* [Love of the Absolute]. Athens: Armos, 2010.

Ware, Kallistos. *Οἰκολογικὴ Κρίση καὶ Ἐλπίδα* [Ecological Crisis and Hope]. Athens: Akritas, 2008.

West, Cornel. *The Cornel West Reader*. New York: Civitas Books, 1999.

———. *Prophetic Fragments: Illuminations of the Crisis in American Religion and Culture*. Grand Rapids, Michigan: William B. Eerdmans, 1988.

Yannaras, Christos. *Κεφάλαια Πολιτικῆς Θεολογίας* [Chapters of Political Theology]. Athens: Grigoris, 1983.

———. "Χριστούγεννα: τὸ *Πῶς* καὶ τὸ *Τί*." [Christmas: the *How* and the *What*]. *Kathimerini*, December 22, 2013.

———. *Ὀρθὸς Λόγος καὶ Κοινωνικὴ Πρακτική* [Rationality and Social Practice]. Athens: Domos, 2006.

———. *Relational Ontology*. Translated by Norman Russell. Brookline-Massachusetts: Holy Cross Orthodox Press, 2011.

Zizioulas, John D. *Being as Communion: Studies in Personhood and the Church*. Crestwood, New York: St. Vladimir's Seminary Press, 1997.

Chapter 8

# Mustard seeds and the *Eschaton*: how an Aristotelian metaphysics solves the paradox between history and Eschatology[1]

Marc W. Cole

## I. Introduction and methodology

This paper attempts to make progress on the apparent paradox between history and the *Eschaton* through a neo-Aristotelian account of hylomorphism and causal pluralism. Ultimately, I am going to argue that Christ is the formal, efficient, and final causes of humanity. The *Imago Dei*, the Living Christ, is the formal cause of humanity, instantiated in the dust of the earth. It is also Christ who set creation in motion (efficient cause). And it is for Christ and unity with him that is the aim of history (final cause). This latter does not sound like Christ Himself is the final cause, but the discussion of the *Imago Dei* later will make it clear what I have in view.

This paper proceeds in the following way: first, I discuss the paradox between the *Eschaton* and history in greater detail, motivating it, and showing why it is problematic. I also point to key questions the paradox generates. After that, I draw on one illustration from the Gospel—Jesus' mustard seed parable—that both embraces the paradox and gives clues to its resolution. In particular, I argue, the parable points to what is called, in Aristotelian terms, a formal cause. Following this, I introduce a neo-Aristotelian theory of hylomorphism and causal pluralism.

---

[1] I would like to thank Joe Vukov for extensive comments on and discussion about this paper.

After that, I take the Aristotelian tools in play, combine them with the theological doctrines of the Holy Trinity and *Imago Dei*, and show how the apparent paradox is ameliorated by the Aristotelian metaphysic. Finally, I show how the view on offer handles the difficult questions posed by the paradox.

A few notes on methodology. First, I am taking Catholic (and Orthodox) teachings on the Holy Trinity, the *Imago Dei*, history, and the *Eschaton* at face value and without argument. Certainly, these doctrines as I present them are disputed across the Catholic, Orthodox, and Protestant spectrums. But it is beyond the scope of this paper to act as arbiter across the various views. On the other hand, the views I present here are also held by many across the Catholic, Orthodox, and Protestant spectrums too, historically and currently. Rather, I take a dominate historical strand of Christian thought and see what work an Aristotelian metaphysic can accomplish. Second, my interpretive moves of Aristotle are disputed in the literature of Aristotelian exegesis. Again, it is beyond the scope of this paper to settle these debates. However, the line of thought I follow is recognizably Aristotelian in flavour; it is at least neo-Aristotelian. Third, this paper is providing a framework within which to work out the finer details; it gives the shape of the solution to the paradox. More detailed work and more detailed testing is required in the usual empirical, philosophical, and theological ways. Finally, all Scripture citations are from the Revised Standard Version—Catholic Edition. With these points in view, let's get started. The first thing to do is get clear about the nature and motivation of the paradox.

## II. The paradox between *Eschaton* and history: its contours and motivations

The tension stems from two claims that appear to be jointly inconsistent. First, the fullness of heaven was present in Christ. Second, the fullness of heaven is comes with Christ's second coming and the inauguration of the *Eschaton*. Which is it? Is heaven fully present with the person of Christ, or is the fullness yet to come? Notice that denying either one resolves the paradox. One could deny that the fullness of heaven was present in Christ, and is yet to come. Or, one could deny that there is any more work yet to do, and that Christ's kingdom was fully and is fully present. However, the Church has staunchly held to both claims being true and this is the source of the paradox. But the Church has good reasons for keeping both claims.

### II.A *The fullness of heaven...*

As to the fullness of heaven in the Incarnation, here are some claims from the Scriptures and the Catechism of the Catholic Church (CCC).

"*For in him* [Jesus Christ] *the whole fulness of deity dwells bodily...*" (Colossians 2.9).

Here are some quotes from the CCC:

> "..."*The time is fulfilled, and the Kingdom of God is at hand*"..."*To carry out the will of the Father Christ inaugurated the kingdom of heaven on earth.*" *Now the Father's will is* "*to raise up* [humans] *to share in his own divine life.*" *He does this by gathering* [people] *around his Son Jesus Christ. This gathering is the Church...Christ stands at the heart of this gathering of men into the* "*family of God*"...*Into this union with Christ all* [people] *are called.*"[2]

Also:

> "*Christ is Lord of the cosmos and of history. In him human history and indeed all creation are* "*set forth*" *and transcendently fulfilled.*"[3]

---

[2] *Catechism of the Catholic Church*, Popular and Definitive Edition ed. (London and New York: Burns & Oates, 2012), n. 541–42.
[3] CCC, n. 668.

And:

> "Since the Ascension God's plan has entered into its fulfilment..."[4]

There are several important points to draw from this. While heaven can refer to the place of God, in eschatological terms, it has much more to do with the union of the Church to Christ. Thus, it is helpful to think of the *Eschaton* as the fulfilment of our union with God through Christ. It is Christ's completed work through his life, death, resurrection and ascension that effected the fullness of the union. Thus, denying the fullness of heaven on earth is tantamount to saying that Christ's work was not complete.

Moreover, the union of heaven and earth was perfected in Christ Himself. That is, in Christ's very person is the union of Heaven and Earth, since he is both True Man and True God. He is not half man and half god; nor is there any quantifiable distinction to be made between His Divinity and His Humanity. He is fully God and fully Man. Here is a quote from the Catechism:

> "The unique and altogether singular event of the Incarnation of the Son of God does not mean that Jesus Christ is part God and part man, nor does it imply that he is the result of a confused mixture of the divine and the human. He became truly man while remaining truly God. Jesus Christ is true God and true man" (CCC, 464).

In this way, the life of Christ effects the *Eschaton* insofar as Christ is himself the living union of Heaven and Earth.

In summary, because the fullness of God was revealed in Christ, and because Christ's work was complete, the Church has held that the fullness of Heaven both in terms of revelation, and familial unity was effected in Christ. Not only this, but Christ Himself is the union of heaven and earth.

---

[4] CCC, n. 670.

## II.B The fullness of heaven comes with the second coming of Christ...

But if we look at the world around us, it seems quite clear that heaven and earth are not unified. There are at least two fronts we can see. First, the world contains vast quantities of injustice. Untold millions suffer in poverty and starvation, while relatively few live comfortable, well-fed lives. People are exploited; even whole nations are exploited for labor. Second, even in my own life, I see how I frequently choose to treat others poorly, or how I treat God poorly in various ways. Through these and a myriad of other ways, it appears that the union of heaven and earth is incomplete. And, in fact, Church teaching upholds this:

> *"I consider that the sufferings of this present time are not worth comparing with the glory that is to be revealed to us. For the creation waits with eager longing for the revealing of the sons of God..." (Romans 8.18-19).*

And:

> *"...Already the final age of the world is with us, and the renewal of the world is irrevocably under way; it is even now anticipated in a certain real way, for the Church on earth is endowed already with a sanctity that is real but imperfect."*[5]

Whatever "sanctity" is referring to, it is intimately connected with our union with Christ. If our union was perfect, our sanctity would also be perfect. Notice also the "present time" contains sufferings. Moreover, the family of God has yet to be (fully?) revealed. Nevertheless, the renewal of the world is underway. It is clear that there is a process underway that will end in the renewal of the world. For my purposes in this paper, we can identify history with this incomplete process by which the world moves toward renewal. Caught up in this process are our individual lives, which,

---

[5] CCC, n. 670.

through our own choices, we can align ourselves with the Divine Will, or move away from it. By our choices, we move closer to that perfect union with heaven, or further from it.

Denying that the world is undergoing renewal and that we are undergoing a purifying and sanctifying process would yield bizarre results. Suppose one maintained that Christ's completed work perfectly effected the union of heaven and earth, but denied this process. It would seem that one would have to be committed to the idea that God intends all the apparent evil we see and experience (and commit), or that all of the evil in the world is actually illusory somehow.

There is another interesting consequence of taking history seriously. When the *Eschaton* is complete, it will be shaped by history. This is so in two ways. Again, if we think of the *Eschaton* as the fullness of God revealed and as the perfected union between God and humans, we get the following consequences. First, God in Christ acted in history. If history is moving us toward union, then the culminating series of events that effected this were found in the Incarnation when God entered human history. These historical acts by Christ shaped our end.

But it is also true to say that the *Eschaton*, the fully revealed God and our completed union with him, also impacts human history. So history both shapes the end, *Eschaton*, and the *Eschaton* also shapes history. This is just a more specific way of spelling out what it means for heaven and earth to be in interaction. Heaven is our aim, and on earth, we move toward (or away from) heaven.

## II.C The paradox revisited

As we have seen, the Church has good reasons for maintaining both that fullness of the Kingdom of Heaven was present in Christ, and that we are undergoing a process of increasing union and sanctification with Christ. But good reasons notwithstanding, there is a paradox at hand, and we can see it even more sharply if we put it thus:

(1) We affirm the full and unmitigated reality and presence of the *Eschaton*, which is the fullness of God on earth, and the fullness of our union with God.

(2) We affirm the full and unmitigated reality of history, the process by which we move toward the *Eschaton*.

The paradoxical tension between (1) and (2) generates a number of questions that are very hard to answer:

(A) Most obviously, how is *Eschaton* fully present, but not fully present?

(B) Relatedly, if the *Eschaton* has already been effected, why does evil still occur?

(C) Finally, the *Eschaton* is partially shaped by history. In particular, Christ's life, death, resurrection, and ascension are historical events. However, the Church also teaches the *Eschaton*, also shapes history, helping to make history what it is. How should we understand this relation?

A good starting place to find a way forward is found in Jesus' parable of the mustard seed. I turn now to this.

## III. How the mustard seed parable highlights the paradox and points toward resolution

In one of his parables about the Kingdom of Heaven, Jesus himself highlights the paradox. It is the parable in which Christ compares the Kingdom of Heaven to a mustard seed. In this section, I explain the parable, and the metaphysic it implies.

All three synoptic Gospels record the parable of the mustard seed in which Jesus compares the Kingdom of Heaven to a mustard seed. Here is the version from Matthew 13.31–32:

*"Another parable he put before them, saying, "The kingdom of heaven is like a grain of mustard seed which a man took and sowed in his field; it is the smallest of all seeds but when it has grown it is the greatest of shrubs*

*and becomes a tree, so that the birds of the air come and make nests in its branches."*[6]

Jesus is comparing the kingdom of heaven to a mustard seed. A man, presumably the Father, plants the seed in a field. The field is plausibly the Earth, and history. Over time, and through a process, the seeds grow to maturity, offering a home to the birds of the air. This final state of maturity can be compared to the *Eschaton* when the seed finishes and its process and ends in a final state of maturity, and is home to the saints. So far, so straight-forward. But I have not yet explained the central focus of the parable, which is in what way the seed itself is like the kingdom of heaven.

In the second section, I gave two ways to understand the kingdom of heaven.[7]

(1) The kingdom of heaven is the final state when heaven and earth are fully united.

(2) The union of the kingdom of heaven and earth is perfectly united in the person of Jesus Christ.

From what I have said so far, the final mature state of the tree maps onto (1). Once the seed grows to its final state, the kingdom of heaven is made perfect. For this reason, many interpreters through the ages have taken Jesus' parable to express the already-but-not-yet nature of the kingdom of heaven. The kingdom of heaven is already present, but not fully mature. However, I think interpretation misses some very important details on the one hand, and fails to explain anything on the other. The reason it explains nothing is because the paradox is after how the kingdom of heaven is fully present, and not yet mature. Taken at face value, the already-but-not-yet view glosses over what needs explaining. How is it already here but not yet? And, worse, it could be read as implying that it's here, but in an incomplete form, awaiting fulfilment. But this is problematic for the reasons given in section

---

[6] See also: Mark 4.30–32 and Luke 13.18–19.
[7] The Kingdom of Heaven can also be identified as the "place" of God's abode. But, insofar as the subject matter deals with the Eschaton, the focus should be on the aspects of the Kingdom that essentially involve the union of God's abode and the earth.

two: it could imply that Christ's work was not complete, or it could imply that Christ's has not fully unified earth and heaven, which is also problematic given his very nature. This parable has another dimension, however.

If we think heaven and earth are completely united in the Incarnation, (2) requires more interpretive work. Let's identify the seed with the incarnate Jesus Christ. But how could this possibly work? Well, remember we are explaining the union of heaven and earth. So, the seed should also represent the total unity of two different components. On the one hand, the seed is composed of the stuff of earth, of matter.[8] But on the other, there is also the way the seed is structured or organized. That is, everything the mustard seed will become is contained in this exceedingly small seed. Under the right conditions, the mustard seed will direct its own growth, assimilating surrounding matter into itself, become a large and shady tree in time. Although, the seed is barely visible with the unaided eye, it nevertheless will become (if conditions are right) a large tree; but nothing new is added to the biological directives within the seed. As such, although the tree is *fully present* within the seed, it is not yet a tall tree with many branches. Far from supporting the already-but-not-yet interpretation, this parable highlights the great mystery of the fullness of *Eschaton* being entirely present, but not yet fully grown. If we compare the *Eschaton* with the Incarnation, we can helpfully compare Jesus to the mustard seed. Although Heaven is fully present in Christ, there is still an assimilation process by which Christ "takes up" creation into Himself, transforming the matter of it into the fully grown tree of heaven. And this matter is in complete union with the structure of the tree.

The metaphor breaks down in some illuminating places. Let's look at two places where the metaphor breaks down. As the mustard tree grows, it transforms other matter into itself; presumably this results in the destruction of key nutrients, say, as they are turned into the matter of the tree. The Kingdom of

---

[8] I am not here taking a stance on just what matter amounts to. The critical point is that whatever matters turns out to be, it is of this world/universe.

Heaven will transform the world into what God intended before the Fall. Rather than a pure destruction via transformation, Christ *restores* the created order through Himself. Secondly, whereas a tree can "force" matter to become itself, the Kingdom of Heaven is freely chosen by those who will participate in grace, and freely rejected by those who will not. Notice that the metaphor does not break down at the sharp point of the paradox in contradistinction to the already-but-not-yet interpretation. With the mustard seed, we at once have both the fullness of the mustard tree present in seed form, but also there is still the historical process of growth required in order to come to maturation.

Notice, too, that the final form of the tree essentially requires the matter it takes up. Although the structure of the seed, which includes the biological information, full and complete, it still requires the historical process of maturation, which essentially involves the stuff of earth. So there is the beginning of an answer to question (C). We begin to see how the *Eschaton* is both what shapes the historical process, and how the historical process also shapes it. I revisit this theme in due course.

To summarize. If we think of the mustard seed parable as, in part, a parable about how the unity of heaven and earth can be fully complete in the Incarnation, and yet require a process toward the *Eschaton*, we get the beginnings of a resolution of the paradox of the *Eschaton* and history. Just as the seed is a singular substance with two distinct components, structure and matter, so Christ is a singular substance composed of two distinct components of heaven and earth. Moreover, although the tree is fully present within the seed, it still requires a process of growth by which it assimilates and organizes other material into itself. Similarly, although Christ is the perfect union of heaven and earth, there is still a process by which Christ assimilates humanity into himself.

But how can the mustard seed be one substance with two distinct components? This is the subject of the next section wherein I introduce a neo-Aristotelian metaphysic.

## IV. Aristotle, hylomorphism, and causal pluralism

Hylomorphic theories are first and foremost theories about the nature of substances. And typically, they also versions of causal pluralism. I discuss each in turn.

Aristotle is well-known for founding hylomorphism. The thesis of hylomorphism, most basically, is that any substance has two constituent parts, matter and form. In fact, the matter and form are what make the substance the sort of thing it is. Christopher Shields puts the basics of hylomorphism this way:

> *"Hylomorphism =$_{df}$ ordinary objects are composites of matter and form.*
>
> *The appeal in this definition to "ordinary objects" requires reflection, but as a first approximation, it serves to rely on the sorts of examples Aristotle himself employs when motivating hylomorphism: statues and houses, horses and humans. In general, we may focus on artefacts and familiar living beings. Hylomorphism holds that no such object is metaphysically simple, but rather comprises two distinct metaphysical elements, one formal and one material."*[9]

Any object or substance is what it is because of matter and form. To appreciate what is unique about hylomorphism, let's briefly look at two kinds of substance dualism: Platonic and Cartesian. In Platonic dualism, it is the forms (sometimes identified with universals) that confer forms onto matter. Notice, though, that whether or not the forms confer properties or not, they still are their own substance. That is, they are what they are apart from matter. Matter does not constitute the forms in any way.

---

[9] Christopher Shields, "Aristotle," ed. Edward N. Zalta, Spring 2014 Edition ed., *The Stanford Encyclopedia of Philosophy* (2014), http://plato.stanford.edu/archives/spr2014/entries/aristotle/. 44. I set to one side concerns about non-ordinary objects. Humans, my focus, are paradigmatically hylomorphic on Aristotle's account. Also, I have already conceded that there are likely more causes than four. This already implies discussion is required on these fronts.

Cartesian dualism posits two substances—mind and matter. When isolating mind as substance, Descartes used a methodology of doubt. Even if the whole of the phenomenal world could be doubted away, or the product of some evil demon's machinations, it is impossible to doubt that *I* exist. This *I* is the mental substance. And it is what it is apart from matter or a material body. The material world operates in a law-like, mechanistic fashion and is distinct from mind. Even though there is an intimate connection between my mind and my body, both mind and body can be defined as substances apart from one another.[10]

Aristotle is on about something quite different for ordinary objects and living organisms. For Aristotle objects, and especially living organisms, are *essentially* constituted by form and matter. To properly answer the question "What is it?," one must specify both the matter and form. In both dualisms discussed, what can ask "What is it?" about forms and mind and not need to appeal to matter at all. Moreover, Aristotle's view does not allow for "free-floating" forms; that is, Aristotle does not think there are uninstantiated forms.[11] But forms are what make a thing the sort of thing it is; it is just that when a thing essentially has matter too.

Let's get a bit clearer on what matter and form are for Aristotle. Now, as the Shields quote pointed out, Aristotle holds that form and matter are metaphysically distinct. How are they distinct? John Haldane says that matter *"is the possibility or potentiality for the reception of structure [form]"* and that form *"stands to it as an actualising principle"* (263).[12] So matter is possibly structured, and the structure, or form, makes some thing the sort of thing it is.

---

[10] For an excellent paper on how Cartesian and Platonic dualisms are similar and different, see: Sarah Broadie, "Soul and Body in Plato and Descartes," *Proceedings of the Aristotelian Society, New Series* 101 (2001).

[11] Except for possibly the Unmoved Mover.

[12] John Haldane, "A Return to Form in the Philosophy of Mind," *Ratio: An International Journal of Analytic Philosophy* 11, no. 3 (1998): 263. Haldane also discusses "Aquinas's potency/act distinction" (Ibid, 263). See also footnote in Haldane (1998, 263fn14). But this distinction, or something like it, is also in Aristotle's *De Anima* 2.1 412a9–10: "*Matter is potentiality, while form is realization or actuality...*" (W.S. Hett's translation). Greek: "*esti d' hai men hule dunamis, to d' eidos entelecheia...*"

Structure here can be thought of as the organization of something. For example, a house has particular features, or powers (or capacities) in virtue of its organization (keeps out the wind, rain, etc.) that a pile of nails, wood, bricks, and mortar would not.[13] Later, I discuss kind of organization or structure possessed by living organisms.

But how are forms gained and lost? Answering this question requires discussion of Aristotle's causal pluralism. For Aristotle, physics (as applied to the sublunary world) is all about change. And change is all about the gaining and losing of forms, whether at the most basic constituents of the world, to the most complex entities (such as persons). And how does change occur?[14] Aristotle gives these four kinds of cause (*aitia*) in *Physics* 2.3[15] and *Metaphysics* 5.2:[16]

---

[13] For excellent discussions on Aristotelian powers, powers generally, and dispositions, see: John Greco and Ruth Groff, eds., *Powers and Capacities in Philosophy: The New Aristotelianism* (New York and Abingdon, UK: Taylor & Francis Ltd, 2013); Anna Marmodoro, ed. *The Metaphysics of Powers: Their Grounding and Their Manifestations*, Routledge Studies in Metaphysics (New York and London: Routledge Taylor & Francis Group, 2010).

[14] Aristotle employs two kinds of changes or processes, which I adapt from David Charles, "Aristotle's Psychological Theory," in *Proceedings of the Boston Area Colloquium in Ancient Philosophy*, ed. John J. Cleary and Gary M. Gurtler (Leiden; Boston: Brill, 2009), 21–26.

A. Some ..."*processes involve a specific type of transition from one contrary to another, involving the destruction of the first contrary.*" (See Physics V for Aristotle's description of this.) For example, a transitions from white to black, from naked to clothed, from toothless to toothed. (See Physics V, Part I).

B. But there are also changes that occur that are not transitions from one contrary to another. For example, a house. A transition from a not-house to a house is not a contrary. A change from a lump of bronze to a statue is not a transition of contraries. David Charles calls these changes "completions" not unplausibly from the Greek: *epiteleioseis*. Completions are changes/processes that occur that do not involve transitioning from one contrary to another, yet nevertheless are changes of some sort.

[15] Aristotle, *The Physics Books I-Iv*, ed. Jeffrey Henderson, trans. Philip H. Wicksteed and Francis M. Cornford, vol. Aristotle IV, Loeb Classical Library (Cambridge, Massachusetts; London, England: Harvard University Press, 1957).

[16] *Metaphysics Books I-Ix*, ed. Jeffrey Henderson, trans. Hugh Tredennick, vol. Aristotle XVII, Loeb Classical Library (Cambridge, Massachusetts; London, England: Harvard University Press, 1933).

*Material Cause:* "*that from which something is generated and out of which it is made, e.g. the bronze of a statue.*"[17]

*Formal Cause:* "*the structure which the matter realizes and in terms of which it comes to be something determinate, e.g., the shape of the president, in virtue of which this quantity of bronze is said to be a statue of a president.*"[18]

*Teleological Cause:* "*the purpose or goal of the compound of form and matter, e.g. the statue was created for the purpose of honoring the president.*"[19]

*Efficient Cause:* "*the primary source of the change...,*" *e.g., the artisan, the art of bronze-casting the statue, the man who gives advice, the father of the child.*"[20]

We have already discussed the material and formal causes. Matter, such as the bronze of a statue say, is potentially a statue of the President. But it is the form, the shape and contours of the President that determine the bronze as a statue. Similarly, the form, or soul, of a living organism determines and arranges the biological matter into a living being. More needs saying about efficient and teleological causes.

The efficient cause is that which is the primary, or main, initiator of change. And change, recall, is about the gaining or losing of form. There are three things to note about efficient causes, two of which are found in Shield's definition. First, Aristotle thought efficient causes could explain how forms were imposed. Suppose I am looking at a stove. There is nothing in the properties of metal that would cause it, of itself, to be a stove. The structure of stove had to imposed on it. And whoever or whatever imposed the structure is the efficient cause. So the second thing to note about efficient causes is that a conscious agent can set change in motion, such as when the artisan is making the statue. But, third, efficient causes can also be non-conscious, such as the "art" of bronze-

---

[17] Shields, 41.
[18] Ibid., 41.
[19] Ibid., 41.
[20] Andrea Falcon, "Aristotle on Causality," in *The Stanford Encyclopedia of Philosophy*, ed. Edward N. Zalta (2015), 3.

casting the statue. There are other processes in nature or elsewhere that initiate changes too, and these would also be non-conscious efficient causes.

What I would like to focus on momentarily is how the "art" of something can be an efficient cause, as it plays a critical role later. As seen, Falcon's definition of efficient cause included "the art of bronze-casting." The word "art" is translated from the Greek word *techne*. According to Preus, *techne* can be translated as "art," "craft," "skill," and even "science."[21] The concept of *techne*, says Nussbaum, is *"closely associated with practical judgment or wisdom...with forethought, planning, and prediction."*[22] It also has a specified aim, or *telos*. Some examples of *technai* include dancing, guitar playing, farming, beer brewing and mathematics.[23] So there are many kinds of *techne*. An individual can learn a *techne*, but to properly employ a *techne*, the user has to employ wisdom, judgment, and foresight. A *techne*, therefore, requires skill and deliberation.

Perhaps surprisingly, it is the *techne*, when present, that is the more accurate specification of the efficient cause, according to Aristotle. Andrea Falcon says, using the bronze-casting *techne* as an example:

> *"There is no doubt that the art of bronze-casting resides in an individual artisan who is responsible for the production of the statue. But, according to Aristotle, all the artisan does in the production of the statue is the manifestation of specific knowledge. This knowledge, not the artisan who has mastered it, is the salient explanatory factor that one should pick as the most*

---

[21] Anthony Preus, *Historical Dictionary of Ancient Greek Philosophy*, ed. Jon Woronoff, vol. 78, Historical Dictionaries of Religions, Philosophies, and Movements (Lanham, Maryland: The Scarecrow Press, Inc., 2007), 258–59. See also: Martha Nussbaum, "The Protagoras: A Science of Practical Reasoning," in *Varieties of Practical Reasoning*, ed. Elijah Millgram (Cambridge, Massachusetts: The MIT Press, 2001), 155–56.

[22] Nussbaum, 160.

[23] See a similar list in: Ibid., p. 159.

*accurate specification of the efficient cause (Phys. 195 b 21-25)."*[24]

This point invites and important consideration. Notice that when explaining how statues come to be, the *most accurate* specification of efficient cause is the *techne*. However, this does not mean the only efficient cause in play here is the *techne*. The artisan is also an efficient cause. By implication, then, any given event might have many, many contributing factors in play. But it seems that Aristotle thinks the multiplicity of causes can be further organized under the four kinds of cause.[25] The event of the statue-making has two efficient causes in this case, with the most accurate specification being the *techne*. So much for the efficient cause.

Finally (pun intended), there is the oft-misunderstood teleological, or final, cause. The teleological cause is the "that for the sake of which" cause. Here is an example of how it works. The builder (efficient cause) organizes the wood (material cause) into a house (formal cause) for the sake of a dwelling. The end goal of the efficient cause is that for the sake of which the process is initiated. And, if there is a *techne* involved, the end is what the *techne* is for, and determines the content of the *techne*.

This is where the oft-misunderstandings of the teleological cause come in. Many have thought that Aristotle "psychologized" nature in some way. But this is not at all what Aristotle was doing. Rather, Aristotle was trying to account for regularity in nature. His most complete defense of the teleological cause is found in Physics 2.8. He sets up the discussion by introducing an opponent of the teleological cause. This opponent might press Aristotle this way. The rain cycle has no determinant goal or purpose, but rather is the result of necessity, of water vapor rising and condensing. When

---

[24] Falcon, 4.
[25] Lurking nearby are questions about explanatory completeness and the relationship between causation and explanation more generally. These are beyond the scope of this paper. However, for interesting discussion on hylomorphism (not necessarily Aristotle's) and causal pluralism, see: William Jaworski, *Structure and the Metaphysics of Mind: How Hylomorphism Solves the Mind-Body Problem* (New York: Oxford University Press, 2016), 201–05.

the rain falls, it only incidentally ruins crops, or nourishes the earth. But it does not rain for the sake of these things. Why not suppose the rest of nature is this way? Perhaps teeth formation can be understood by chance and/or necessity in the same way. Teeth grow in animals, in the ways they do, as the result of necessity, but not for the sake of anything. The incidental effects of nutrition and chewing are incidental.

Aristotle's answer is that this does not explain the regular occurrence of the specific way teeth grow in a given animal on the one hand, and, on the other, it does not explain the constant connection between the needs of the animal and the pattern of teeth formation. This latter point is made the more sharp by thinking about not just teeth, but the constant regularity between the needs of the animal, and its various parts—eyes, ears, livers, etc. Necessity or chance cannot explain the regular connections between needs of the animal and its corresponding parts. Falcon says:

> *"In other words, to say that the teeth grow as they do by material necessity and this is good for the animal by coincidence is to leave unexplained the regular connection between the growth of the teeth and the needs of the animal. Aristotle offers final causality as his explanation for this regular connection: the teeth grow in the way they do for biting and chewing food and this is good for the animal."*[26]

But saying that there is purposiveness does not mean for Aristotle that nature is *consciously* aiming at certain ends. The end of a clock is to tell time, and what it does is directed toward this purpose, each of its parts directed at this end. But the clock is not consciously aiming at this. Similarly, teeth do not grow in an

---

[26] Falcon, 9.

organism the way they do because they "want" to, but teeth are placed the way they are for the sake of nutrition/survival.[27]

I am going to stick with Aristotle's four causes in discussing causal pluralism and hylomorphism for the sake of simplicity. There is discussion on whether or not there are other kinds of causes.[28] But, I think that even if this turns out to be true, they would be *in addition to* these four kinds. And it is these four kinds only that I need to make my point.

In summary, we have discussed the relevant notion of hylomorphic substance, as well as Aristotle's version of causal pluralism. The next step is to apply this framework to the paradox of history and *Eschaton*.

## V. The *Imago Dei*, blessed Trinity, and the four causes of humanity

What is yet to be done is to apply hylomorphism to problem of history and *Eschaton*. But before I do this, I need to explain two bits of doctrine: the *Imago Dei* and the Blessed Trinity. This is done to establish the efficient causes of humanity, which play a role in the rest of hylomorphic causal pluralist framework on offer. As shall be seen, getting the story straight here will help in resolving the tension between *Eschaton* and history. This section also specifies the other causes of humanity—formal, material, and teleological.

Following my pattern so far, I will hold as fixed what Church teaching gives us. The CCC says: ..".*It is in Christ, "the image of the invisible God," that man has been created "in the image and likeness" of*

---

[27] However, not everything has a teleological cause. For example, coincidences. Coincidences, on Aristotle's account, would not have teleological causes. See: Ibid., 7–10. See also Aristotle's Physics II.8.

[28] Aristotle himself in Physics 2.3 and Metaphysics 5.2 discusses various modes and manner in which the causes can operate. There are those who think, though, that there could be more than four kinds of cause. See: John Haldane "Privative Causality," *Analysis* 67, no. 3 (2007); "Identifying Privative Causes," *Analysis* 71, no. 4 (2011); William Jaworski, *Philosophy of Mind: A Comprehensive Introduction* (Chichester, United Kingdom: Wiley-Blackwell, 2011); *Structure and the Metaphysics of Mind: How Hylomorphism Solves the Mind-Body Problem.*

*the Creator."*²⁹ A few points here. First, the Image and Likeness of God is Jesus Christ. Second, humans are created in the Image and Likeness of God.

From these two points, we can identify two candidates for the efficient cause of humans: the Blessed Trinity and *Imago Dei* as *techne* or blueprint that informed the crafting of humans. The first candidate seems obvious: we hold that God created the world and set it in motion. The second candidate is the *techne* of humanity. The basic idea is that God *knows how* to make a person created in his image and likeness. This *know how* requires application of a specific sort of knowledge. For this reason, human-making is a *techne*, but a really interesting kind, as we shall see.

What is the content of knowledge employed in the *techne* of humanity? Knowledge of both God and humanity.

### V.1 Knowledge of God and the "living techne" of humanity—efficient and final causes

Being made in the image and likeness of God means being made in the image and likeness of the Blessed Trinity. One of the tenets of the Trinity is one God and three divine persons: the Father, the Son, and the Holy Spirit. Although we confess three Divine persons, we do not confess three Gods. The CCC says: "*We do not confess three Gods, but one God in three persons, the "consubstantial Trinity." The divine persons do not share the one divinity among themselves but each of them is God whole and entire...*"³⁰ If this is right, then there is an interesting consequence. If each person of the Trinity is God whole and entire, that means each of them reveals God whole and entire. In other words, where any one person of the Trinity is, the other two are fully revealed.

For us, the fullness of the revelation of God is Jesus Christ. Colossians 2.9 says: "*For in him* [Jesus Christ] *the whole fullness of deity dwells bodily...*" And Colossians 1.15 says that Jesus "*...is the image of the invisible God...*" If the "whole fullness" of deity dwells

---

²⁹ CCC, n. 1701.
³⁰ CCC, n. 253.

bodily, then Jesus must also reveal the Father and the Holy Spirit.[31] And if Jesus is the image of the invisible God, this must also mean he is the image of the Father and Spirit in some real sense. God's nature is such that there are three divine persons who are God whole and entire, and yet we only worship one God.

If we were made in the image and likeness of God our own natures must correspond to this. If we are made in the image and likeness of God, then we must also reveal God.

In fact, we so embodied the Godhead, that Henri de Lubac says that we could not have spoken of billions of people any more than we can speak of three gods.[32] We were intended as being inseparably one person. However, simultaneously, each member of the Trinity is a distinct person, as is each one of us.

At the fall, continues de Lubac, an individuation process occurred by which the one being that is man, was shattered like glass.[33] William Cavanaugh argues that *"the effect of sin is the very creation of individuals as such, that is, the creation of an ontological distinction between individual and group."*[34] This individuation process was compared to a piece of glass shattering by St. Augustine. The one

---

[31] Although Jesus reveals Father and Spirit in his very existence, we also see Jesus revealing them through his words too. Matthew 11.27: *"All things have been delivered to me by my Father; and no one knows the Father except the Son and any one to whom the Son chooses to reveal him."* And John 16.13–15: *"When the Spirit of truth comes, he will guide you into all the truth; for he will not speak on his own authority, but whatever he hears he will speak, and he will declare to you the things that are to come. He will glorify me, for he will take what is mine and declare it to you. All that the Father has is mine; therefore I said that he will take what is mine and declare it to you."*

[32] Henri de Lubac, *Catholicism: Christ and the Common Destiny of Man*, trans. Lancelot C. Sheppard and OCD Sister Elizabeth Englund (San Francisco, CA: Ignatius Press, 1988), 28–30.

[33] Ibid., 28–30.

[34] William T. Cavanaugh, *Theopolitical Imagination* (New York: T & T Clark Ltd., 2002), 13.

person that was human was shattered like glass creating billions of individuals.[35]

Christ, de Lubac continues, (still quoting and paraphrasing St. Augustine), melted the shards of glass, reuniting and re-stamping the Imago Dei and thus returned the primal unity.[36] It was the life, death, resurrection, and ascension of Jesus Christ that returned this unity, drawing humanity in the very life of God Himself.

At this point, enough has been said to specify the efficient and final causes of humanity. If we follow Aristotle's set-up for efficient cause, we get these two candidates: the specific knowledge God employed in making humans. The knowledge employed is not only knowledge about how to en-form the material world, but the very knowledge of God Himself. And the revelation of this God is Christ Jesus. The other candidate for efficient cause is the artisan himself, in this case the Blessed Trinity. If we followed Aristotle further, we would say that most accurate specification of the efficient cause is the specific knowledge employed in the creation of people. I do not think we need to follow Aristotle this far. On the one hand, it is dangerous to put epistemology ahead of ontology when it comes to God's nature. But on the other, the relevant sense of knowledge is specifically about God and person-making. And it is a complete knowledge. This could make a different in settling the debate. However, I think for my purposes that it is enough to specify the two efficient causes in play without making a final decision as to which is the more accurate, if there is one. I turn now to the final cause of humanity.

The teleological cause of humanity is full union with God. We were created for the sake of union with God through Christ. As previously discussed, the fullness of this unity came in the Incarnation on the one hand, and will be fully effected later on the other. Adam and Eve were created for this end; it was disrupted by

---

[35] Importantly, notice that the view discussed by de Lubac and St. Augustine is not concerned about apparent separation across both space *and* time. Wherever the Image and Likeness of God appears, the fullness of God is manifested seems to be the governing idea.

[36] Lubac, 28–30. This section can be helpfully compared with the CCC, n. 253–255.

the Fall. One purpose of the Incarnation was to re-forge and effect the end for which we were made. Another purpose was, to use St. Augustine's language, to re-stamp the *Imago Dei* that was almost worn away. What remains to be discussed is the hylomorphic nature, or substance, of humanity. As we shall see, just as Christ fully reveals God, he also fully reveals humanity.

*V.2 The hylomorphic substance of heaven and earth—formal and material causes*

In the last section, we saw that there are two efficient causes of humanity. First, we saw the specific knowledge employed by God to make humans is that of Jesus Christ, the *Imago Dei* Himself. In this sense, the *Imago Dei* (Christ) is something like the Living Blueprint, or the Living *Techne* of humanity. So just as a house-builder has a deep knowledge of the *techne* of house-building, so God has a deep (and even complete) knowledge of the Living *Techne* of humanity, who is the *Imago Dei*. Second, God through Christ could be thought of as the specific artisan who set the creation in motion. We also saw that the purpose of this creative act was to bring humanity to full union with God.

But it is also the case that the fullness of heaven was made complete in the Incarnation despite the fact that we are also moving toward the fullness of unity. I also discussed how the hylomorphic notion of form helps to resolve this seeming paradox and how this lesson seems present in Christ's parable of heaven and the mustard seed. The last piece of the puzzle before looking at the tensions of the paradox is to explain the hylomorphic substance of humanity.

Let's get clear on the formal cause of humanity first. Recall Shields definition of Aristotle's formal cause: "*the structure which the matter realizes and in terms of which it comes to be something determinate, e.g., the shape of the president, in virtue of which this quantity of bronze is said to be a statue of a president.*" The matter of the statue, bronze, become something determinate in virtue of the structure, in this case the shape of the president. And we can also cast this in terms of the potency/act distinction too. The bronze was potentially a statue, while the structure actualized the statue. Importantly, the form of the statue does not exist in Aristotle's view until actualized in material. And, if there is no material to instantiate the structure, there is no realization of the structure. The statue of the president only exists when instantiated, and instantiation requires a determinate structure and matter capable of receiving the form.

Living organisms are also structured on Aristotle's view. The structures of living organisms are "souls" (*psuche*). But "soul" here does not mean something like a ghost in the bodily machine. Victor Caston puts Aristotle's view this way: *"the soul is not itself a certain kind of body (as the Atomists think), but neither can it exist without a body (as the Platonists think)."*[37] Part of the reason Aristotle holds this view is the commitment to no uninstantiated forms. If the soul is the formal cause of a living organism, then it must be instantiated in matter. Thus, one cannot give a full account of the substance, in this case a living organism, without reference to the kind of soul it has, and the kind of matter in which it is instantiated.[38]

Substances also have the powers they do in virtue of their structure or form. The formal cause makes things the sorts of things they are, and we can learn of what they are by attending to their powers. Living organisms have certain interesting powers, such as self-sustenance, growth, and decay. Aristotle says: *"But of natural bodies some have life and some have not; by life we mean the capacity for self-sustenance, growth, and decay"* (*De Anima* 2.1 412a13–

---

[37] Victor Caston, "Aristotle's Psychology," in *A Companion to Ancient Philosophy*, ed. Mary Louise Gill and Pierre Pellegrin, Blackwell Companions to Philosophy (Oxford: John Wiley and Sons Ltd, 2006), 318.

[38] A critical question is lurking hereabouts. Just what is the relation between form and matter that should hold on hylomorphism? As Caston further says says that this is one of Aristotle's big concerns in *De Anima* (see Caston, 317). This is a critical component to the hylomorphic project, and getting straight on this has been an exegetical concern with the Aristotelian texts themselves, and an ongoing concern across the varieties of hylomorphism. For an example of a contemporary hylomorphist view, see: Kathrin Koslicki *The Structure of Objects* (Oxford: Oxford University Press, 2008). At any rate, my project in this paper is to simply to present a hylomorphic framework.

15; Hett's translation).³⁹ Let's return to the mustard seed. The mustard seed indeed has a principle that, if left uninhibited, self-sustains the organism through a process of growth, which includes the assimilation of other materials into itself on its way to maturation.⁴⁰

What we are looking for as the formal cause of humanity, then, is something that is instantiated in matter and explains the self-sustenance and growth of human beings, that also explains certain key powers of human beings, such as intellection, reason, etc. And I think the proper candidate for this is the Living *Techne* of Humanity, Jesus Christ. Now, it might appear we are running into trouble. Jesus Christ is the union of heaven and earth and embodies the future state of the Church; thus, Christ is in an important sense our aim and goal. And God through Christ set things in motion. So it looks as if Christ is the efficient, final, and now formal cause.

But Aristotle would not find the coinciding of these three causes as strange and explicitly discusses how they often coincide. Aristotle says this in Physics 2.7: "*But in many cases three of these...[causes]...coincide; for the essential nature of a thing and the purpose for which it is produced are often identical (so that the final cause coincides with the formal), and moreover the efficient cause must bear some resemblance in "form" to the effect (so that the efficient cause too must, so far, coincide with the formal); for instance, man is begotten by man*" (198a25–28).

Living things, such as people, typically have these causes coinciding. The key here is Aristotle's oft-repeated sentiment that "man is begotten by man."⁴¹ The end (final cause) of human

---

[39] By "decay," Aristotle has in view what we might term "aging." Just as organisms grow and flourish, so too they also age. For more on Aristotle's views here, see: *On Youth and Old Age; On Life and Death* in Aristotle and Hett, VIII.

[40] Aristotle posits a hierarchy of souls: vegetative, animal, and human. For more discussion on this, see *De Anima*. But also: St. Thomas Aquinas' *Summa Theologiae* Ia, q. 79, aa. 2 &3. See also part III of Thomas Aquinas and Timothy McDermott, *Thomas Aquinas Selected Philosophical Writings*, trans. Timothy McDermott, Oxford World's Classics (Oxford: Oxford University Press, 2008).

[41] Andrea Falcon helpfully gives this list of where this phrase occurs: *Physics* 194b13 198a23–26; *Metaphysics* 1032a25, 1033b32, 1049b25, 1070a8, 1092a16 (see: Falcon, 7.)

generation is the fully-developed human, say a man. But, as Falcon points out, "*what a fully developed man is is specified in terms of the form of a man, and this form is realized in its full development at the end of generation.*"[42] So the fully developed form of man is also the aim of the development. So here we have a close link between final and formal causes. And as Falcon rightly notes, "*...a fully developed man is not only the end of generation; it is also what initiates the process.*"[43] The act of sexual intercourse sets in motion a series of events that produce a human child, say a boy, whose process of growth and development is directed at being a fully developed man.

Similarly with the mustard seed. The aim of the mustard seed is a fully mature mustard tree. The form of mustard tree is instantiated in the relevant material and directs a process of growth and self-sustenance that results in this end. The "parent" of the mustard seed, a grown, mature mustard tree, is the efficient cause of this seed.

And similarly for humanity. The end (final cause) of humanity is full union with God. But due to the temporal constraints imposed by our material nature, there is a process of maturation we undergo until we reach this, not unlike the process undergone by a child developing into a man. But the final cause in this case, the full union of heaven and earth, is a person, Christ Jesus. Thus, the formal cause of humanity has to be identified with Christ as well. And, of course, it was Christ that set the creation of humanity in motion (efficient cause) by both applying a specific body of knowledge, and by being the artisan.

It might appear there are tensions here. For example, if we identify the *Eschaton* with the full union of heaven and earth, it might be difficult to think of this as being pretty much synonymous with Christ's incarnation. I take it that this due to thinking of heaven and earth as primarily places, rather than persons. Indeed, the Tradition holds that God resides in heaven while humans reside on earth. There is a sense in which heaven and earth are places. But when discussing the *Eschaton* and the nature of heaven and earth, we are not thinking of locations, but

---

[42] Ibid., 7.
[43] Ibid., 7.

people. A marriage is not about putting together two households, as much as it is about the union of two people. There could be a putting together of two households, but this is the result of a personal union, not its cause. The aim of human life is full union with God. Our formal cause, therefore must be the full union of heaven and earth, and we see this in Christ Jesus.

There is another difficulty nearby.[44] While Aristotle is a realist about form and matter, he thinks we can only think of them in the abstract. If we ask *"what is pure matter?"* or *"what is pure form?,"* we have already committed an error. The question of "what" is about a substance. And substance necessarily has matter and form already. There is no sense in which we can ask about the so-called substances of matter and form, because they are not substances properly speaking. All substances have matter and form. As I said, though, he is a realist about matter and form, and in the abstract, we can think of them as actualization and potency. The problem for Christian theology is that we can explain earth apart from heaven,[45] and certainly we can explain heaven without any reference to earth since the Holy Trinity preceded creation. Thus, it might seem that Christianity is committed to a kind of substance dualism between earth and heaven. But if we are committed to substance dualism, we cannot be hylomorphists because a substance is only a substance when it has matter and form. Two comments are in order.

First, hylomorphism is about substantial unity and change. The aim is to understand when and how a substance comes to be and passes away. Such a theory could only apply to mutable things. God is immutable, so hylomorphism as a theory would not relate to

---

[44] The interpretive moves of Aristotle in this paragraph are inspired by a discussion with Anna Marmodoro.

[45] This is certainly debatable. One might think we must reference heaven in discussing earth, since God made the earth. On the other hand, though, we might think we can discuss earth without reference to God on the grounds that matter is not part of the substance of God. This is just part of what creation ex nihilo means. Whatever the outcome of this debate, I do not need to settle it here. Interestingly, and in contradistinction to Church theology, Aristotle thinks that matter is co-eternal with the Unmoved Mover. Change is eternally occurring as forms are gained and lost.

heaven. Moreover, hylomorphism, in contradistinction to Platonic and Cartesian dualism argues that many of capacities cannot be understood properly apart from their material causes. So it is a theory that requires a particular intimacy between structure and matter. As seen, Aristotle agrees that forms in some confer powers insofar as they are responsible for making something the sort of thing it is. It is just that these powers are not understandable apart from matter. So even if one is a substance dualist about form and matter, one could still hold that is impossible to understand uninstantiated forms.

The second comment is this. I think we can certainly discuss God without reference to earth. And we could explain the divine economy of Father, Son, and Holy Spirit without any reference to earth. But we could *not* explain Jesus Christ. Jesus Christ is the name of the union between God the Son and humanity (heaven and earth). And this union is a person. If we must make appeal to earth to explain Jesus Christ, I think hylomorphism offers the best tools to explain how this might work without falling into heresy.

What remain is to show how the view on offer answers the questions we started with.

## VI: Dissolving the paradox

This section dissolves the paradox with the neo-Aristotelian resources on offer. Here again is the sharp point of the paradox as well as the associated questions:

(1) We affirm the full and unmitigated reality and presence of the *Eschaton*, which is the fullness of God on earth, and the fullness of our union with God.

(2) We affirm the full and unmitigated reality of history, the process by which we move toward the *Eschaton*.

The paradoxical tension between (1) and (2) generates a number of questions that are very hard to answer:

(A) Most obviously, how is *Eschaton* fully present, but not fully present?

(B) Relatedly, if the *Eschaton* has already been effected, why does evil still occur?

(C) Finally, the *Eschaton* is partially shaped by history. In particular, Christ's life, death, resurrection, and ascension are historical events. However, the Church also teaches the *Eschaton*, also shapes history, helping to make history what it is. How should we understand this relation?

So how do we hold both (1) and (2)? Jesus Christ is the Incarnate *Eschaton*. In his person he fully reveals the Triune God, but he also restores our corporate unity with God and one another via his nature.[46] Thus, while we have Jesus fully in the Incarnation, and in the Blessed Sacrament too, there is still the process by which he assimilates us into himself. This is like the mustard seed. The end of the mustard seed is a fully grown mustard tree and form of the mustard is present in the seed. The end of humanity is full union with Jesus. And this union of heaven and earth is the formal cause of humanity. We can see here too how we hold (2). Although the form is fully present in the seed, there is a process of maturation, growth, and self-sustenance. Similarly, although the union of heaven and earth is fully present in Christ, there is still a process of assimilation, growth, and self-sustenance.

We have already answered (A). Just as the mustard tree is fully present in the seed, so the *Eschaton* is fully present with Christ. Both require a process of assimilation.

The answer to (B) is similar. Evil has occasion to occur for two reasons. First, people have a choice to conform to the household of God or not. Second, although the *Eschaton* is fully present, there is still the maturation and assimilation process under way.

The answer to (C) has been hinted at. How do we understand that the *Eschaton* both shapes and is shaped by history? The mustard seed, as it grows, takes into self and changes portions of the surrounding environment. The surrounding environment thus

---

[46] But the process by which he assimilates others into the form requires acts of will on their part. But it also requires a process, often called sanctification, by which the believer draws closer to God via the path established by Christ. Cross-reference with Hebrews 12.2.

constitutes the end result of the mustard tree. What Christ takes into himself through the historical process of growth and assimilation are persons through his Church. The form of the mustard tree is not in itself fundamentally altered, although the end, mature state of the mustard is what it is because of the surrounding environment. Similarly, the form of the Eschaton, the union of Christ and humanity, is not fundamentally altered in the Eschaton, but the end state of this full union would not be what it is without the persons who are part of the structure.

Interestingly, the metaphor breaks down in an interesting way. The mustard seed transforms the surrounding environment into itself. Christ also transforms us into himself. But whereas the surrounding materials lose their identity when they become part of the mustard tree, we do not lose ours in Christ. Part of the Triune Mystery is that not one of the persons of the Holy Trinity lose their identity *even though* there is one God. Being made in the image and likeness of God means we embody the same mystery, and this mystery is made perfect in Christ.

## VII: Conclusion

This paper has looked at how a hylomorphic and causal pluralist view of the world can resolve the paradox between the here and now being real, but the *Eschaton* being the really real, and the questions this paradox generates.

The view was merely sketched, however. Having a hylomorphic and causal pluralist view of the world goes against many of the ways we are accustomed to understanding the world. To this end, further study and development is required to test the view for viability.

# Bibliography

Aquinas, Thomas. *The Summa Theologica*. Translated by Fathers of the English Dominican Province. New York: Benziger Brothers, 1947.

Aquinas, Thomas, and Timothy McDermott. *Thomas Aquinas Selected Philosophical Writings*. Translated by Timothy McDermott. Oxford World's Classics. Oxford: Oxford University Press, 2008.

Aristotle. *Metaphysics Books I-Ix*. Translated by Hugh Tredennick. Loeb Classical Library. Edited by Jeffrey Henderson Vol. Aristotle XVII, Cambridge, Massachusetts; London, England: Harvard University Press, 1933.

———. *The Physics Books I-Iv*. Translated by Philip H. Wicksteed and Francis M. Cornford. Loeb Classical Library. Edited by Jeffrey Henderson Vol. Aristotle IV, Cambridge, Massachusetts; London, England: Harvard University Press, 1957.

Aristotle, and W. S. Hett. *On the Soul Parva Naturalia on Breath with an English Translation by W. S. Hett*. Translated by W. S. Hett. The Loeb Classical Library. Edited by G. P. Goold Vol. VIII, Cambridge, Massachusetts; London, England: Harvard University Press, 1995.

Broadie, Sarah. "Soul and Body in Plato and Descartes." *Proceedings of the Aristotelian Society, New Series* 101 (2001): 295-308.

Caston, Victor. "Aristotle's Psychology." Chap. 17 In *A Companion to Ancient Philosophy*, edited by Mary Louise Gill and Pierre Pellegrin. Blackwell Companions to Philosophy, 316-46. Oxford: John Wiley and Sons Ltd, 2006.

*Catechism of the Catholic Church*. Popular and Definitive Edition ed. London and New York: Burns & Oates, 2012.

Cavanaugh, William T. *Theopolitical Imagination*. New York: T & T Clark Ltd., 2002.

Charles, David. "Aristotle's Psychological Theory." Chap. 1 In *Proceedings of the Boston Area Colloquium in Ancient Philosophy*, edited by John J. Cleary and Gary M. Gurtler, 1-29. Leiden; Boston: Brill, 2009.

Falcon, Andrea. "Aristotle on Causality." In *The Stanford Encyclopedia of Philosophy*, edited by Edward N. Zalta, 2015.

Greco, John, and Ruth Groff, eds. *Powers and Capacities in Philosophy: The New Aristotelianism*. New York and Abingdon, UK: Taylor & Francis Ltd, 2013.

Haldane, John. "Identifying Privative Causes." *Analysis* 71, no. 4 (2011): 611-19.

———. "Privative Causality." *Analysis* 67, no. 3 (2007): 180-86.

———. "A Return to Form in the Philosophy of Mind." *Ratio: An International Journal of Analytic Philosophy* 11, no. 3 (1998): 253-77.

*The Holy Bible: Revised Standard Version Catholic Edition*. Charlotte, North Carolina: Saint Benedict Press, 2010.

Jaworski, William. *Philosophy of Mind: A Comprehensive Introduction*. Chichester, United Kingdom: Wiley-Blackwell, 2011.

———. *Structure and the Metaphysics of Mind: How Hylomorphism Solves the Mind-Body Problem*. New York: Oxford University Press, 2016.

Koslicki, Kathrin. *The Structure of Objects*. Oxford: Oxford University Press, 2008.

Lubac, Henri de. *Catholicism: Christ and the Common Destiny of Man*. Translated by Lancelot C. Sheppard and OCD Sister Elizabeth Englund. San Francisco, CA: Ignatius Press, 1988. 1947.

Marmodoro, Anna, ed. *The Metaphysics of Powers: Their Grounding and Their Manifestations*, Routledge Studies in Metaphysics. New York and London: Routledge Taylor & Francis Group, 2010.

Nussbaum, Martha. "The Protagoras: A Science of Practical Reasoning." Chap. 8 In *Varieties of Practical Reasoning*, edited by Elijah Millgram. Cambridge, Massachusetts: The MIT Press, 2001.

Preus, Anthony. *Historical Dictionary of Ancient Greek Philosophy*. Historical Dictionaries of Religions, Philosophies, and Movements. Edited by Jon Woronoff Vol. 78, Lanham, Maryland: The Scarecrow Press, Inc., 2007.

Shields, Christopher. "Aristotle." In *The Stanford Encyclopedia of Philosophy*, edited by Edward N. Zalta2014.
http://plato.stanford.edu/archives/spr2014/entries/aristotle/.

Chapter 9

# The Incarnation as a saturated phenomenon: Between ontology, phenomenology and theology

Daniel Isai

## 1. Introduction

Heidegger and Husserl form the main sources for the emergence of phenomenology. In the case of the former, we find a very conclusive definition of the notion of phenomenon. In Heidegger's main work, we can read the following:

> "the Greek word φαινόμενον, *to* which the term *"phenomenon,"* derives from the verb φαίνεσθαι that means: *to manifest itself; hence,* φαινόμενον *has the following meaning:* what is shown, *what is being* manifested. φαινόμενον itself is *the* average form *of* φαίνω—*"to bring* to light" ... *namely* that thing in which something can become manifest, visible in itself ... *the* meaning of the word "phenomenon" *is:* what-is-being-manifest-in-itself ... "the *phenomena* are *therefore the* sum of all things *that are* in the full light of *the* day ... what the Greeks sometimes simply *identify as* τὰ ὄντα (the act of being)."[1]

What phenomenology attempts is an invitation to return to the things themselves through the donor intuition that gives a shape to all those received in one's own consciousness and is different

---

[1] Martin Heidegger, *Being and Time,* trans. Gabriel Liiceanu and Cătălin Cioabă (Bucharest: Humanitas, 2006), 38.

from empiricism that resorts to senses and touch. Edmund Husserl states that he resorts *"to what we can highlight, according to its essence, based on consciousness itself and remaining on the plan of pure immanence."*[2]

Phenomenology seeks to achieve revealing that is related to truth. It uses the method of the reduction to what is simply given and rules out the transcendent. Discussing the method of reduction, J.L. Marion maintains:

> "*Reduction rules out*, even from its emergence, everything that is not given/*donated* without restrictions: appearances and confusion, imaginary *things about and the* memories of what is given, *all things related to* transcendences *that mistake what is lived for the* object concerned are recovered, *filtered*, and finally removed from what is given/*the gift* that remains."[3]

In phenomenology, *ousia*, otherwise as cause, loses its privileges, simply because they do not appear at all, or rather, when they occur, they do so partially.[4] What is being given in phenomenology is not being given in concept, but is being given in intuition, which is to be conceptualized afterwards. In the field of phenomenology, there are at least three types of phenomena: those poor in intuition (of technical character); those rich in intuition and hence, the concept comes into play and clarifies; this also defines the third type of phenomena overabounding in intuition that cannot be displayed in concept anymore, but saturate it. The saturated phenomenon exceeds and floods the gaze so that it goes beyond the categories of the intellect and avoids objectification. We could say that the transcendent may be relevant as long as it manifests

---

[2] Edmund Husserl, *Ideas Pertaining to a Pure Phenomenology and to a Phenomenological Philosophy. First Book: General Introduction to a Pure Phenomenology*, trans. Christian Ferencz-Flatz (Bucharest: Humaniast, 2011), 220.

[3] Jean Luc Marion, *In Excess: Studies of Saturated Phenomena*, trans.Ionuț Biliuță (Sibiu: Deisis, 2003), 28.

[4] Marion, *In Excess*, 36.

itself phenomenally, as long as it is manifested in a concrete manner in the human existence. The method of reduction takes us out of the pure abstraction, separated from the concrete existence, makes us return to the things themselves, to the living mundane existence.

## 2. The phenomenological turn in Jean Luc Marion

Phenomenology marks an important change in European philosophy that has a long-standing metaphysical tradition, in that it invites us to begin any philosophical reflection from the things themselves, from the phenomenon, from what is shown to us "from the whole area of what is being given intuitively."[5]

Phenomenology changes the orientation of philosophy by abandoning the idea of transcendence. In metaphysics, the concept of transcendence can be identified with the history of the idea of the being. In metaphysics, it is common to talk about the transcendence of the being as the foundation of the world. Ștefan Vianu, a Romanian philosopher, points out to us that this concept hides a bifurcation, a gap between the idea of God and that of being. This gap was tackled by Nietzsche by means of the phrase "death of God." However, we can ask ourselves who or what died. Jean Luc Marion asserts that, "through this statement, Nietzsche understood something different from challenging (the existence) of God."[6] He saw the concept as void, not being placed in the hypostasis of a person, the proximity of the idol that contrasts sharply with the Incarnation of the Logos that descends into the immanence of the world, takes on human nature, heals it, restores it, and removes its boundaries.

Metaphysics is concerned with the being that operates as foundation, therefore, it goes beyond God or treats Him as foundation, the cause of the world that acquires the function of foundation without exceeding the framework of conceptualization. In this regard, Marion discusses the ontotheological constitution of

---

[5] Husserl, *Ideas*, 91.

[6] Jean Luc Marion, *The Idol and Distance*, trans. Tinca Prunea Bretonnet and Daniela Pălășan (Bucharest: Humaniatas, 2007), 26.

the world as the Supreme Being. Even if we talk about "God," we are actually in front of the metaphysical foundation, of the Supreme Being who is the cause of the world, but who remains at the level of concept; He is the philosophers' "God," He has nothing to do with the God of Christian revelation. Human beings cannot pray to and bring sacrifices to this Supreme Being, seen as *causa sui*; they cannot ask for His help; they cannot be His source of meanings; they cannot say anything to Him about their own fears and pain.

Heidegger, who has never mistaken the idea of Being for that of God, utilizing the distinction between philosophy and theology, brings, however, through the reduction of philosophy to the finitude of human existence, the risk of the "ontologist" idolatry.[7] Heidegger employs this reduction to human finitude and judges everything in the horizon of being as if the inconsistency of being as being may be enough to get the human being out of the paradigm of being-toward-death. The transcendence of *Dasein* and of the other have the same inconsistency, because they end with death, as the human being cannot find an escape other than in the transcendence of the God-centered Human. Stăniloae speaks of the fact that the person is the true depth of being,[8] but he/she needs to be a person having conquered the limit of death and to be capable of continuing the experience of transcendence into eternity. Phenomenally speaking, we need the Embodied Logos which is, at the same time, a historical being and the Son of God. In the person of the Logos, human finitude has no margins, as it exceeds temporality, acquires the character of God by participation, gains strength over death, and lives in the horizon of resurrection.

Marion argues that, in the medieval period, Thomas Aquinas caused a gap in Western theology, substituting *esse* for the name of goodness, through a forced or reverse interpretation of St. Dionysius the Areopagite. Theologically speaking, this name "*I am who I am*" (Exodus 3:14) is related to the Old Testament revelation

---

[7] J.L. Marion, *God without Being*, trans. Thomas A. Carlson, (Chicago and London: University of Chicago Press, 1991), 41.
[8] Dumitru Stăniloae, *Christian Love*, (Galați: Porto-Franco, 1993), 51.

that was not accomplished yet. The emphasis is placed on self-existence, in a continuous present or outside time. To this name, the New Testament revelation is added, according to which *"God is love"* (1 John 4:8 and 4:16). In this context, Marion believes that the primacy given to *esse*, "to be," through Western metaphysics, could create the fertile ground for the above-mentioned bifurcation between God and being.

In chapter IV from *On the Divine Names*, Ps.-Dionysius the Areopagite points out to us that he gave priority to the perfect revelation of the New Testament and shows to us what God is like from the point of view of being. Thus, he states,

> "Therefore, we should move forward with the word *to the* goodness itself, which theologians ascribe par excellence to the divinity that is above divinity and distinguish *it from everything, as they consider it, calling* goodness *the divine existence itself* (*the* divine origin), *which, through* the very fact that it *is the* good, as *the* good *from the point of view of the being* (*through the* being), extends kindness *to all the things that are*."[9]

Further on, Ps.-Dionysius uses the comparison with the sun that spreads its rays unconditionally over the whole world so that we can understand that, from the point of view of being, God is kindness; He is relation. Love that comes from God could not really exist without the Trinity of Persons. Father Stăniloae confirms what Marion said with respect to the most proper name which seems most fitting to the divine subsistence. Renewing the assertion of the Areopagite, where he says that God is "goodness" or "super-goodness," Stăniloae then adds that God goes beyond Himself through His providences in respect of everything. Concerning these providences, he explains to us that they are

---

[9] Dioysius the Areopagite, *The Complete Works and the Scholia of St. Maximus the Confessor*, trans. Dumitru Stăniloae, (Eucharest: Paideia, 1996), 145.

willed acts.[10] God's willed acts are not an emanation of His being, but His works extended from His entire being, from His deep love for human beings. The human being participates in God's life, receiving as a gift the character of God or the resemblance to God.

Marion is radical in his statements precisely because of what metaphysics operated with regard to *ousia* since he states that we have to free God from *esse*. From the theological point of view, I think we can stick with the line followed by Ps.-Dionysius, indicating only that the Christian revelation appeared and perfected the understanding of this divine name: "I am who I am," and he discovered to us that he is One in being and in Trinity, that, from the point of view of being, He is goodness and that, by His very nature, He extends His goodness to all things that exist. The existential way of being is devotion, love, abandoning Oneself, and leaving everything for the things that truly exist. We can conclude that Thomas either did not properly understand Dionysius or his fascination with metaphysics led to his giving priority to the term *esse*, deprived of the content of the Christian revelation of the God of love.

## 3. Revelation or the Incarnation as a saturated phenomenon

Any phenomenon is given to an ego, constitutes itself within a horizon, and meets certain conditions for constitution. The self or the consciousness receives the donor intuitions under the form of experiences. What is not attempted in this way, does not have access to phenomenality. The horizon in which a phenomenon occurs can vary: objectivity (Husserl), being (Heidegger), ethics (Levinas), or the fleshly body (Merleau-Ponty).[11] The following question is raised: what horizon could a revelation tolerate? Marion answers this question by bringing the following argument: "*If the revelation admits a horizon, then it recognizes* a priori, *therefore, it surrenders possibility, it surrenders itself.*"[12] On the other hand, the

---

[10] Stăniloae, *Christian love*, 64.

[11] Jean Luc Marion, *The Visible and the Revealed: Theology, Metaphisics, and Phenomenology*, trans. Maria Cornelia Ică, Jr. (Sibiu: Deisis, 2007), 33.

[12] Marion, *The Visible and the Revealed*, 34.

exclusion of any horizon would make the phenomenal manifestation of revelation impossible. Consequently, Marion states that *"revelation is only staged in a horizon by saturating it."*[13] Revelation disturbs the limits of the phenomenological horizon. The horizon becomes a condition of possibility for the paradoxical manifestation of revelation, but the latter does not accept the *a priori* character of the horizon. The regime of revelation interferes between intuition and intention and produces a real imbalance in favor of the former.

Marion resorts to four exemplary types of phenomenon in order better to approach the meaning of the saturated phenomenon: the event, the picture (the idol), the body, and the icon. All the four phenomena are saturated phenomena that avoid objectification.

The event differs from the objective phenomena by the fact that it is not a serial product *"predictable due to its causes and therefore, reproducible through the repetition of those causes."*[14] It has a sort of uniqueness of its own appearance that *"attests an unpredictable origin."*[15] The event surprises us through its appearance, as a staging, while the intuition is exceeded because it goes beyond what the intention pointed to or anticipated. Marion says that the title of event is attributed to collective phenomena when they meet three conditions: they don't repeat identically; they may not be attributed to a unique cause; and they cannot be predicted.[16]

Through event, phenomenology succeeded to overcome the caesura *"that metaphysics did not cease to dig between the world of objects pretended to be formed, producible and repeatable ... and the one of revealing the Revelation."*[17] Phenomenology opened the field of phenomenality, surrounding the poor and common law phenomena with saturated phenomena, which may take the form of miracles, too. This is the merit of Marion and of French phenomenology for having opened the discussion, not without

---

[13] Ibid., 35.
[14] Marion, *In Excess*, 42.
[15] Ibid.
[16] Ibid., 48.
[17] Ibid., 66.

certain tensions, regarding the inclusion of Christian Revelation with all its implications among phenomena.

The picture or the idol is the second saturated phenomenon approached by Marion, who says that *"it decomposes the object in order to reduce it to the visible therein, to the pure visible that is free of remains."*[18] The image brings everything to visibility, it does not let facets go unnoticed anymore, and that is why *"it reduces what is being given to what is shown according to the idol's regime."*[19] There is a metamorphosis of the image in the idol because it quits the reality it narrates, with its multiple facets, catching only what is shown in that painting. It is the proposal of a world strictly reduced to its possibilities to manifest itself. The image enters the idol's regime as *"it redirects what is being given/donated to surface without withdrawing, without void, depth."*[20] Marion will introduce a distinction between face and façade, showing that while before alterity I may find a counter-intentionality that concerns me, addresses me, interpellates me, in a façade it will never happen even if it represented the image of a human being. Continuing Levinas' thinking, Marion says that the other is not a simple controllable thing. Moreover, Marion says that *"reducing the Other to a strict visibility entails building an idol."*[21] The face my sight encounters represents an infinite experience. This face transforms me in the witness of the discovery of the self, not through a self-formation but rather through a formation due to the other's hospitality, which is a gift for me.[22]

The body represents the third saturated phenomenon. We feel and perceive the world through it. Due to the fact that it feels through the body, the ego then transposes in *cogitatio* the manner it perceived the world. Through the body, we have access to the surrounding world as *"any phenomenalization of the world for me*

---

[18] Ibid., 77.
[19] Ibid., 83.
[20] Ibid., 90.
[21] Brian Robinette, "A Gift to Theology? Jean-Luc Marion's *Saturated Phenomenon* in Christological Perspective," *Heythrop Journal* (2007), 91.
[22] Robinette, "A Gift to Theology?," 91.

*passes through my body.*"²³ I perceive even the other's face in the intentional look of my ego. The body, since the moment "*the ego is embodied, finds itself fixed in itself as to its ground, as to its phenomenological earth.*"²⁴ We cannot disregard our own body in an act of pure contemplation or cogitation; I cannot distance myself from the body because I am the body.

For example, the passage of time marks my body, leaves traces, writes history with every wrinkle on my face. The body ensures the phenomenality of human existence; it causes the appearance, and the soul manifests itself through it. Due to corporeality, phenomenology acquires "bones and flesh" with every phenomenon.

The icon represents the fourth saturated phenomenon which, unlike the picture or the idol, does not fix us on the given surface of the painting, but watches us through an opening outside time. The face watching us contains an excess of intuition which takes it out of the horizon of objectivity. The face from every icon interpellates us, addresses us with a call, invites us to a sort of being it is a look that removes borders. The icon is the look that addresses me and involves an unlimited hermeneutics, because it is an eternal transcendence, an immortal body. The icon is the opposite of the idol, because it takes me out of the closed frame of the painting towards the infinite fields of eternity. Here, my face takes the form of God's face, originating from the human being to look for resemblance, just due to the eternalized sight which interpellates me, which addresses me, which takes me out of the drunkenness of senses. For "*in the Icon of Christ, the "image of the invisible God," visibility and invisibility meet hypostatically, yet are not confused.*"²⁵ Transcendence and immanence are encountered in the visibility of the Embodiment phenomenon, with a greater emphasis on visibility, i.e. on what is hypostasized. But what is hypostasized is the divine spirit. It finds the true depth in the person. This fact is happening because only the being that hypostasizes himself/herself has a concrete, personal existence.

---

²³ Marion, *In Excess*, 106.
²⁴ Ibid., 109.
²⁵ Robinette, "A Gift to Theology?," 93.

The person is a face, and the face makes the invisibility of the being to be visible. Only the paradox may express this relation between being and person. The person unveils the being, and the being veils the person in the mystery of an identity opened to an inexhaustible hermeneutics.

Starting from these four exemplary phenomena in which the excessive intuition avoids the transformation into object, we can direct our attention to the Incarnation of the Word in the world, a phenomenon which interacts with the four hypostases or exemplary saturated phenomena which we took into consideration until now. The Incarnation is a historical event which marked out humanity as we talk about our era and before our era or before Christ and after Christ. Historians of the time preserved information on the historical person of the Messiah, but most of the information originates from Christ's apprentices who witnessed His death, Resurrection and Ascension. A unique, unrepeatable event which has a past through all the prophecies that prepared Him, a present through all the preaching, signs, and miracles of Jesus, and a future through the fact that Jesus becomes the eschatological human. He showed us what all of us are called to become.

In relation to the idol or the picture that catches and exhausts within the frames of the visible, the incarnated Logos went through the three temptations, while refusing the idolatrous dimension of Its presence in the world. The devil asked Jesus to worship him in order to offer him the world. Jesus refused, saying that it is written to: *"Worship and serve God only"* (Mt 4:10). The devil sought to reduce him to the visible in exhausting him, in a definitive embodiment, but Jesus rejected this type of phenomenalization.

Assuming the body, phenomenality from the Logos is just the full assumption of our humanity by the Son of God. From now on, His body becomes the door of eternity as He passed through the gates of death, He defeated Hell, He returned from the dead and He ascended to Heaven with this body. His body is the eschatological model. The body of Jesus who ascended to Heaven is seated at the right hand of God and, through Him, our humanity is assumed, resumed, and has the horizon of deification opened to it. Through Jesus' body, his disciples were able to see, on Mount Tabor, the glory of His deification: "*and His face shined like the sun, and His clothes whitened like the light*" (Mt 17:2).

The Incarnation of Christ becomes the main theme of iconography in the entire world. St. John of Damascus theologically grounds the art of the icon, saying that "through the fact that God showed Himself as a body, lived among people, they make the icon God's visible image. I do not pray to the matter, but I pray to the Creator of the matter, Who became matter for me and Who accepted to live in the matter and achieved my redemption through the matter."[26] The icon appears after the event of the Incarnation, and after Ascension, it becomes the sign of eternity through which we communicate with Him, the One who is the image of God's glory.

## 4. Christological ontology and phenomenology

At the beginning of this presentation, I mentioned the bifurcation appearing in occidental metaphysics between the concept of being and the idea of God. I noted that *philosophia generalis*, namely ontology, seeks in *ousia* a foundation of the world, a *causa sui*, and from Marion's argumentation, I noted that this concept has no content, that it is a simple idol as it does not allow the divine to manifest itself. That is why, from a theological point of view, only a Christological ontology can take us out of the philosophical difficulty of an idolatrous standpoint.

How is this Christological ontology possible? It is concentrated on Christ's name in Daniel's prophecy: "*behold, one like the son of man came with the clouds of heaven, and came to the Ancient of days ... There was given him dominion, and glory, and a kingdom, that all the peoples, nations, and languages should serve him*" (Daniel 7:13–14). This name of Son of Man is also very frequently present in the writings

---

[26] John of Damascus, *The Three Treaties against Iconoclasts*, trans. Dumitru Fecioru (Bucharest: Biblical and Mission Institute of the Romanian Orthodox Church, 1998), 49.

of the New Testament (cf. Mt 16:13; Mk 9:12; Lk. 21:27; Jn 3:13) and in many other places.

The possibility of the Christological ontology resides in this name as we deal with a man who came, through the phenomenality of His Incarnation, among us, the human beings, and this Man or the Son of Man is not a simple man, but a God-embodying Human. Christ is born from the being of the Father, the world is brought to existence *ex nihilo* and receives a being that is different from God's being. In His divine Person, the Son of Man takes on the human nature through which He connects with the world. The Romanian theologian Dumitru Stăniloae says that *"being exists in reality only in the person."*[27] Through these words, the Christological ontology meets phenomenology as the divine person was embodied and became one of us.

The relation of the Son of Man to us, the human beings, is deeper due to the fact that the human being is created in God's own image (Gen 1:26-27). This image is Christ Himself. Therefore, from an ontological point of view, the human being is oriented towards *"the image of the unseen God"* (Col 1:15). Human beings may find their own accomplishment as long as they seek to resemble this image. But what is this resemblance? Christ offered the human beings the possibility of deification, namely the unification with God, but without being a unification of the being, but a participative one, through which they get access to the source of all kindness and love. Father Stăniloae says that *"love is related to God from the point of view of being,"*[28] as it is a Trinity of Persons. We have access to God's love through the Son of Man. Through Him, man's soul is also raised to a special dignity as his body is seen as a temple of the Holy Spirit and totally recovered at the universal resurrection. Body phenomenality disappears for a while, but it is not totally annihilated, surviving the tempory disappearance through the Holy Spirit.

The Resurrected Jesus also opens the Eucharistic dimension of His body and ensures us that this is how we can have life in

---

[27] Stăniloae, *Christian love*, 12.
[28] Ibid., 60.

ourselves. From an eschatological point of view, He tells us: *"Whoever eats my flesh and drinks my blood has eternal life, and I will raise them up at the last day"* (Jn 6:54).

From a phenomenological point of view, what is being given to us through the Incarnation is the transcendence to immanence. He is the God-Man; we look at His body and we see through it, the Changing Face of Jesus from Tabor, the divine nature; we feed on His body and acquire deification. We are witnesses to a phenomenon flooding our intuition, and language is too poor to describe the abundance of the significance of the excess of life given to us. It is like watching an icon and seizing that the face watching us makes our existence unlimited.

Phenomenology may remain in dialogue with the Christological ontology as it favors the Incarnated Person as a saturated phenomenon. From a theological point of view, we do not have access to the being of God, and that is why our approach to Him is made through the Person of the Son and of the Holy Spirit, Persons who came in direct contact with us, the human beings, manifesting themselves in phenomenality through Incarnation and Descent. The hermeneutics of the revelation entails *"reading the intention of the invisible in the visible."*[29] Our intention to decipher and understand encounters a counter-intentionality which precedes us, which interpellates us, which addresses us through revelation. We love God because He was the first Who loved us and in Him we find the spring of love.

## 5. The erotic reduction—toward the self through the (O)ther

Man's continuous search to establish himself into being seems to be doomed to failure. *Cogito ergo sum* places him in a form of certainty, but a poor one. The depth of ourself is not revealed at all to ourselves in a full manner. We understand that we have in front of us one of the great illusions of the human condition, namely each of us must persevere in his/her being through him/herself, starting from him/herself, and revolving around him/herself, even

---

[29] Jean-Luc Marion, *God without Being*, trans. Thomas Carlson, (Chicago: The University of Chicago Press, 1991), 21.

if the otherness enters the question somewhere in the background. According to Marion's view, the Cartesian *Ego* will suffer a real reversal of paradigm through the erotic reduction. Eros is approached in an Areopagitic manner and is synonymous with agape, Christian love.

Marion talks about the subject's four *aporias*: two of them are related to the transcendental *Ego* and the other two to the empirical *self*. The first *aporia* refers to the fact that the transcendental *Ego* cannot achieve any individuation, it has no peculiarity, it is empty. We are talking about universality without peculiarity. The second *aporia* is that of solipsism. The third *aporia* concerns the fact that intuition precedes the intellect, the focus moves from "I think" to "I am moved" by the moment that is constantly renewed. The fourth *aporia* constitutes a duplication of the subject between the transcendental *Ego* and the empirical self. The subject that is defined by "I think" avoids the status of giver.[30]

"I think" remains in the sphere of the abstract without the possibility of being phenomenalized in a donated, given thing. Being reduced to an "I think," "the subject" focalizes on the object whose introducer it is. As soon as it wants to represent itself for itself, it has only its poorest phenomenality the one of the object. This "I think" is ordered in such a manner in the form of the object that it (itself) may not appear otherwise for itself than in an objective manner.[31]

Heidegger noticed how deficient this "I think" is and suggested *Dasein*, because the "subject" in this new horizon does not propose as scope the objectivization of the object any longer, because the ultimate instrument of work intentionality *"has no longer as task the establishment of objects, but opening a world."*[32] Despite all Heidegger's efforts to take away the subject of the Cartesian paradoxes, it continues to remain tributary to the solipsism and objectivity of *Dasein*. As long as this point of departure shall gravitate around the

---

[30] Jean-Luc Marion, *Being Given: Toward a Phenomenology of Givenness*, trans. Maria Cornelia and Ioan I. Ică, Jr. (Sibiu: Deisis, 2003), 392–396.
[31] Ibid., 398.
[32] Ibid., 399.

*The Incarnation as a saturated phenomenon*

Ego, around the subject, around *Dasein*, the paradoxes shall remain active.

In order to overcome these paradoxes of the subject, Marion proposes a radical overturn of reporting the ego to its own ipseity. He suggests alterity as point of departure of any understanding of the self, a "to somebody." He proposes the overcoming of the spontaneity of "I think" with the receptiveness of "I am affected."[33] Being receptive towards the other's interpellation entails availability, an orientation towards the other as point of departure. My ipseity is projected outside it in order to know itself, not in the pantheism of the world, but in the infinity of understanding that the other's face and body opens.

The Cartesian cogitation proved its limits in respect of knowing the subject, as it has shown us that while it acquires confidence, it acquires the aspect of the object. The control over the object creates a false confidence, as paradoxically, when we acquired it, it is no longer of interest to us. An exhaustion in knowing the ipseity appears.

J.L. Marion places the Cartesian certainty before vanity so that he comes to disqualify it. In his opinion, the only certainty that really interests me is the one concerning my ipseity, the certainty about myself which is not to be confused with the products of technique, with the objects of sciences, the propositions of logic and the truths of philosophy. With regard to all these things, Marion uses methodical questions. In this case, he is asking himself: what is it good for? Before this question, the certainty of the world may crumble. The fact of producing my own certainty for myself drives me crazy before vanity.[34] In all these circumstances, Marion introduces the erotic reduction using the question, "does anyone love me?" in order to resist vanity. The world of things crumbles, it has no consistency, it does not offer me an answer to an endless search.

---

[33] Ibid., 405.

[34] Jean-Luc Marion, *The Erotic Phenomenon*, trans. Maria-Cornelia Ică, Jr. (Sibiu: Deisis, 2004), 43–44.

Therefore, the subject needs another subject to confirm him in being, in order to place him into dialogue, to open to him the horizon of love according to his expectations. The subject's waiting for and openness to love gives primacy not to the subject of "to be or not to be," but to the question: does anybody love me? Does anybody somewhere love me?[35] The question sets the idea for me to depend neither on what I can master, nor to challenge another one. Loving another one becomes a kind of epicenter of my ipseity. I depend on another one, not on myself in order to enhance my self-knowledge and to enrich myself in my own being. The endless love of the other is the one that opens to me the infinite horizon of spiritual wealth. However, there is a limit to this acknowledgment in love brought by death. The endless love of the other clashes with the being-toward-death, "*I cannot ask the other to love me as I cannot promise myself to love myself ... as I was able, in my unquestionable finitude, to assure myself ad infinitum.*"[36] For this reason, the subject seeks to assure itself in an infinite love. This love can come to us only through Him who in His being is love, God who is the Trinity of Persons, who sent His Son to come, through the Incarnation, closest to us human beings.

Incarnation as a saturated phenomenon is what brings to us the assurance of the endless love of God's Word. We could conclude that love itself is a saturated phenomenon because it brings an over-abundant life, meaning, and joy, so that intuition is flooded and reason cannot contain the overflow that enlightens it.

---

[35] Ibid., 72.
[36] Ibid., 102.

# Bibliography

Heidegger, Martin. *Being and Time*. Translated by Gabriel Liiceanu and Cătălin Cioabă. Bucharest: Humanitas, 2006.

Husserl, Edmund. *Ideas pertaining to a pure phenomenology and to a phenomenological philosophy. First Book: General Introduction to a pure phenomenology*. Translated by Christian Ferencz-Flatz. Bucharest: Humanitas, 2011.

John of Damascus, *The three treaties against iconoclasts*, Translation, notes, introduction Dumitru Fecioru. Bucharest: Biblical and Mission Institute of the Romanian Orthodox Church, 1998

Marion, Jean-Luc. *Being Given: Toward a Phenomenology of Givenness*. Translated by Maria Cornelia și Ioan I. Ică jr. Sibiu: Deisis, 2003.

———. *God without Being*, Translated by Thomas Carlson. Chicago: The University of Chicago Press, 1991.

———. *The Erotic Phenomenon*. Translated by Maria-Cornelia Ică jr. Sibiu: Deisis, 2004.

———. *The Idol and Distance*, Translated from French by Tinca Prunea Bretonnet and Daniela Pălășan. Bucharest: Humanitas, 2007.

———. *The Visible and the Revealed. Theology, Metaphisics and Phenomenology*, Translated by Maria Cornelia Ică jr. Sibiu: Deisis, 2007.

———. *In Excess: Studies of saturated phenomena*. Translated by Ionuț Biliuță. Sibiu: Deisis, 2003.

Ps.-Dionysius the Areopagite, *The Complete Works and the Scholia of St. Maximus the Confessor*, Translation, introduction and notes by Fr. Dumitru Stăniloae. Bucharest: Paideia, 1996.

Robinette, Brian "A gift to Theology? Jean-Luc Marion's *saturated phenomenon* in Christological perspective," Heythrop Journal, XLVIII, (2007): 86–108.

Stăniloae, Dumitru. *Christian love,* afterword by Sandu Frunză. Galați: Porto-Franco, 1993.

Chapter 10

# Potency of God: hypostaticity and living being in Gregory Palamas

## Raffaele Guerra

### I. κόσμος and ὑπερκόσμος

Some witnesses[1] say that around 1313 the Logothete Theodore Metochites, after a speech by Gregory Palamas on Aristotelian logic, said: "Aristotle himself, if he was present to listen to him, in my opinion would praise him greatly."[2] The deep knowledge of the Aristotelian philosophy by Gregory Palamas is in line with the dominant trends of the Byzantine philosophical culture between the 13th and the 14th century and it is demonstrated by the philosophical background of his theological doctrine. That is greatly evident in the *One Hundred and Fifty Chapters*, written between 1349 and 1350.

In chapter 24, Gregory Palamas faces the primary issue of theological anthropology, i.e. the creation of the human being. The anthropogenesis is set as terminal seal[3] of the subsequent creation of beings (ὄντα) by God, in an order that does not signify just a chronological dimension, but also an ontological hierarchy of the

---

[1] Philotheos Kokkinos, "Λόγος ἐγκωμιαστικὸς εἰς τὸν ἐν ἁγίοις πατέρα ἡμῶν Γρηγόριον Ἀρχιεπίσκοπον Θεσσαλονίκης τὸν Παλαμᾶν," in PG 151, 551- 654, also in Gregorio Palamas, *Atto e luce divina* , ed. Ettore Perrella (Milano: Bompiani, 2003), 1363. The same episode is also present in: Phakrasis Protospator, "Ἐπιστόμος κατὰ τὸ δυνατὸν διήγησις...," in Gregorio Palamas, *Dal sovraessenziale all'essenza*, ed. Ettore Perrella (Milano : Bompiani, 2005), 884, the episode is reported in chapter 14, 939.

[2] " ... καὶ Ἀριστοτέλης αὐτὸς εἴ γε περιὼν παρῆν ἐπήνεσεν ἄν ... ," in Phakrasis Protospator, "Ἐπιστόμος κατὰ τὸ δυνατὸν διήγησις...," 940.

[3] "... καὶ μετὰ πάντα ὁ ἄνθρωπος ...," in Gregorio Palamas, *Che cos'è l'ortodossia*, ed. Ettore Perrella (Milano: Bompiani 2006), 26.

creation. Palamas' exegesis is in accord with the precedent Patristic tradition he refers to: the human centrality in the cosmos is widely maintained by the Fathers of the Church, both in the East and the West: from Irenaeus of Lyon to the Cappadocian Fathers such as Gregory of Nyssa, from Athanasius of Alexandria to Maximus the Confessor, from Pseudo-Macarius to John of Damascus' great theological synthesis.[4] We have to nevertheless underline a peculiarity in Palamas' terminology: the conceptual binomial generally indicated with the terms *visible* and *invisible*, institutionalized in the Church's vocabulary since the first article of faith of the Nicene-Constantinopolitan Symbol,[5] and present in various Patristic texts (to cite just some of them, the chapter 22 of the homily XV of the pseudo-Macarius[6] and John of Damascus' *Expositio fidei*[7]), this binomial of visible/invisible is conceptualized by Palamas with a vocabulary of pseudo-Dionysian inspiration: κόσμος and ὑπερκόσμος.

We have to comprehend these two concepts as two great scopes that structure the episteme of the Palamite work. Beginning from the third chapter, in fact, Gregory Palamas introduces a description of the universe structurally based on the distinction between the heavenly and the earthly plane. The primary source of this binomial is in the Holy Scripture, and precisely in the opening of *Genesis*: "Ἐν ἀρχῇ ἐποίησεν ὁ Θεὸς τὸν οὐρανὸν καὶ τὴν γῆν."[8] What happens in the *Chapters* is that the biblical culture and the pseudo-Dionysian terminology meet the Aristotelian-Ptolemaic cosmology, which was fully assimilated into the Byzantine culture of that time.

---

[4] See: Irenaeus of Lyon, (*Adversus haereses, Epeidixis*), Athanasius of Alexandria (*De Incarnatione contra Arianos*), Gregory of Nyssa (*Oratio catechetica magna*, V: 4), pseudo-Macarius (Homily XV, 22 in: PG 34, 589 D), Maximus the Confessor (*Qaestiones ad Thalassum*), John of Damascus (*Expositio fidei*, 25 [II, 11], 71).

[5] "Πιστεύομεν εἰς ἕνα Θεόν, Πατέρα, παντοκράτορα, ποιητὴν οὐρανοῦ καὶ γῆς ὁρατῶν τε πάντων καὶ ἀοράτων"; for a critical edition of the text of the Symbol: Giuseppe Dossetti, *Il Simbolo di Nicea e di Costantinopoli* (Roma: Herder, 1967). See also: Adolf Martin Ritter, *Das Konzil von Konstantinopel und sein Symbol* (Göttingen: Forschungen zur Kirchen- und Dogmengeschichte, 1965).

[6] Pseudo-Macarius, *Homily XV*, in PG 34, 589 D.

[7] John of Damascus, *Expositio* Fidei 20 (II 6), 50 e 25 (II 11), 71.

[8] Gn 1 : 1: "In the beginning God created the heaven and the earth" (KJV).

It is in chapter 24 that Gregory Palamas uses the binomial κόσμος / ὑπερκόσμος in the context of the ontology of creation, starting from which he ascends to the hyper-ontological speech and to the apophatical one. In other words, if the binomial κόσμος/ ὑπερκόσμος is an epistemic principle of Palamas' reflection and it structures the same human knowledge, it is because this binomial is concretely incarnated in creation. As an application of that in the field of theological anthropology, starting from chapter 24, we can observe that the genesis of Adam includes an ontological difference inside of the human being, a specific difference ascribable to the great binomial of κόσμος/ ὑπερκόσμος. The body is in fact mold with matter and pertains to the sensitive cosmos ("κατ' αἴσθησιν κόσμον"), the soul is instead created at the image of God ("κατ' εἰκόνα Θεοῦ") and comes from God himself, from the hyper-cosmic realities ("ἐκ τῶν ὑπερκοσμίων"). In fact, at the very beginning of the *Chapters*, Gregory Palamas introduces human soul as "... μόνη λογικὴ ψυχή ... , οὐκ οὐράνιος ἀλλ'ὑπερουράνιος, οὐ τόπῳ ἀλλὰ τῇ ἑαυτῆς φύσει, ἅτε νοερὰ ὑπάρχουσα οὐσία,"[9] thus highlighting its hypercosmic nature.

## II. The concept of hypostasis

The concept of hypostasis lead us directly to the relationship between oneness and plurality in Palamas' doctrine. It is an issue of great logical and theological importance, also because it is one of the most important issues of Platonism that structured the Byzantine reception of Aristotle through Porphyry's *Isagoge*. The importance of this issue for Palamism is due to the fact that it constitutes a supporting logical structure for the doctrine at every level: it is for one soul/ plural potencies, as such as for other important doctrinal variations on this logical theme: one divine nature face to three divine hypostases in the Holy Trinity, one human nature/ many human hypostases, and finally the unique

---

[9] "... the only rational soul ..., which is not celestial but supercelestial, not because of its location but by its own nature, inasmuch as it is an intelligent substance," in Palamas, *Che cos'è l'ortodossia*, 8–10; for the English translation see: Saint Gregory Palamas, *The One Hundred and Fifty Chapters*, trans. Robert Edward Sinkewicz (Toronto: Pontifical Institute of Medieval Studies, 1988), 89.

activity of God experienced by human hypostases in differentiated ways.

If we want to outline an archeology of this logical structure in Gregory Palamas, we have to consider two levels of doctrinal elaboration turning back in history: the theology of the Cappadocian Fathers in the 4th century and Porphyry's *Isagoge*.

In a recent essay on the relationship between the Cappadocian ontology and the pseudo-Dionysian *corpus*, Mainoldi[10] argued on the "ontological revolution" of the Cappadocian Fathers that took place in the domain of Triadology and was institutionalized by the Church in the Symbol of Constantinople of 381. The first point of this revolution is characterized, according to Mainoldi, as the Cappadocian difference between essence and activity (ἐνέργεια) in God, retaken in the pseudo-Dionysian theology and reaffirmed by Gregory Palamas. Furthermore, what is important for the issue of oneness and plurality, is the second point of this "Cappadocian ontological revolution": the definitive distinction between the unique οὐσία and the three ὑποστάσεις in God, such as in texts like the *Oratio* 20 by Gregory of Natiantius[11] and in Gregory of Nyssa's *Oratio Catechetica Magna*, III.[12]

The second step, as we have seen, is in the history of philosophy and it concerns Porphyry's *Isagoge*, probably the most important logical work for the history of Trinitarian theology. The importance of this text concerns both the East and the West.[13] Without entering in an in-depth analysis of Porphyry's logic, it is worth to indicate the logical principle that is at work in Palamas' doctrine when arguing on the theme of oneness and plurality. In

---

[10] Ernesto Sergio Mainoldi, "La ricezione della rivoluzione ontologica dei Padri cappadoci: la triadologia dello pseudo-Dionigi Areopagita e i suoi obiettivi," in *Trinità in relazione. Percorsi di ontologia trinitaria dai Padri della Chiesa all'Idealismo tedesco*, ed. Claudio Moreschini (Panzano in Chianti: Feeria, 2015), 167–78.

[11] Gregory of Natiantius, *Oratio XX*, in: PG 35, 1072; cf. Mainoldi, "La ricezione della rivoluzione ontologica," 169–72.

[12] Gregory of Nyssa, *Oratio Catechetica* Magna, in: PG 45, 17 C 13—21 A 12.

[13] Cf. Boethius, *In Isagogen Porphyrii Commenta*, ed. Georg Scheps and Samuel Brandt (Berlin—Leipzig, 1906); Boethius, *The Theological Tractates*, ed. Hugh Fraser Stewart, Edward Kennard Rand, and S. Jim Tester (Cambridge M.A.: Harvard University Press, 1973).

Porphyry's tree, the *species specialissima* (human being) is a part of the general species (animal) and inside of each species every hypostasis shares, in his singular peculiarity, the same *specialissima* and general nature of all the hypostasis. We find at work this Porphyryan logical principle in Gregory Palamas, united with the fundamental anthropological principle of all the Greek reception of Aristotle's *De Anima*, according to which the intellect (νοῦς) is the *proprium* of each singular human hypostasis. That constitutes an unavoidable cultural coordinate of the history of philosophy that goes also for Palamas and that is possible to note most of all in Themistius' commentary on the *De Anima*.[14]

The theology of the Cappadocian fathers as well as Porphyry's *Isagoge* is not only the source of Palamas' way to understand the relationship between oneness and plurality, but also of Palamas' concept of hypostasis. To take just an example from the Cappadocian theology, in Gregory of Nyssa the hypostasis is that concept which, through singular characteristics, presents in a particular reality what is common and general to all the singularities that share the same nature:[15] "πράγματός τινος περιγραφή."[16]

In chapter 46 of the *Second Demonstrative Speech*,[17] Gregory Palamas defines the economical content of the concept of hypostaticity. In this case, Palamas recalls Basil of Caesarea's *Contra Eunomium* 5 and says that the hypostasis of the Son-Logos, as the hypostasis that governs the creation, is the very Hypostaticity, namely the principle (ἀρχή) of each created hypostaticity. As such,

---

[14] "Ἡμεῖς οὖν ὁ ποιητικὸς νοῦς παρὰ μόνου τοίνυν τοῦ ποιητικοῦ τὸ ἐμοὶ εἶναι ... ἄλλο ἄν εἴη καὶ τὸ ἐγὼ καὶ τὸ ἐμοὶ εἶναι, καὶ ἐγὼ μὲν ὁ συγκείμενος νοῦς ἐκ τοῦ δυνάμει καὶ τοῦ ἐνεργείᾳ," in "Themistii in libros De Anima paraphrasis," in *Commentaria in Aristotelem graeca*, ed. Ricardus Heinze (Berlin: Academia Litterarum Regia Borussica, 1899), vol. V. Cf. also: Octave Hamelin, *La théorie de l'intellect d'après Aristote et ses commentateurs* (Paris, 1953); Edomond Barbotin, *La théorie aristotélicienne de l'intellect d'après Théophraste* (Louvain-Paris, 1954); Omer Balleriaux, "D'Aristote à Themistius. Contributions à une histoire de la noétique après Aristote" (PhD diss., University of Liège, 1943).

[15] Gregory of Nyssa, *Ad Petrum: De differentia usiae et hypostaseos*, 3: 10–12.

[16] Ibid.

[17] Gregorio Palamas, *Atto e luce divina*, 201.

the hypostasis of the Son sends on the creation the hypostasis of the Holy Spirit, because the Spirit let himself be experienced according to the hypostatical determinations of the created beings, the creation of which has been chaired by the same hypostasis of the Son.

Finally, to understand the logical aspect of Palamas' concept of hypostaticity, it is worth considering *Tr.* 2, 1: 22. In this passage, the concept of hypostasis is not literary present, but it constitutes the horizon of the speech behind the lines.

"Ἐν οἷς γὰρ ἔχει τὸ εἶναι, ἀπ' αὐτῆς ἂν ἐκεῖνα κληθεῖεν, ὥσπερ καὶ ἄθρωποι πάντες ἡμεῖς ἀπὸ τοῦ καθόλου εἴδους ἀκούομεν ἐν ἡμῖν ἔχοντος τὸ εἶναι. Εἰ τοίνυν μὴ ἐν ἐκείνοις ἡ αὐτοσοφία σοι αὕτη, ποῦ σχήσει τὸ εἶναι;"[18]

Gregory Palamas is now refusing Barlaam's anhypostatical concept of αὐτοσοφία, which he considers a platonistic eidetic concept. As it can be noticed, Palamas' line is that of a radical realism of the universals, so that the ontological reality is always given as hypostatic reality. The central expression "ἐν ἡμῖν ἔχοντος τὸ εἶναι" properly means that the universal εἶναι should not be understood in an eidetic and impersonal way, but rather that it is given only in hypostasis. In Palamas' doctrine, as well as in the Byzantine theology, in fact, εἶναι and ὕπαρξις are distinguishable from a logical point of view, but not in reality, where, as we said, εἶναι is given as ὑπόστασις, i.e. as τρόπος ὑπάρξεως.

## III. Human being as hypostatical microcosm

### III.1. *The Scriptural background*

As we have already said, the primary source of Palamas' doctrine is the Holy Scripture. So, we can say that the ontological difference inherent to the human being is firstly formulated on the exegetical level and its root is in Gen 2:7:

---

[18] Gregorio Palamas, *Atto e luce divina*, 512–513.

"καὶ ἔπλασεν ὁ θεὸς τὸν ἄνθρωπον χοῦν ἀπὸ τῆς γῆς καὶ ἐνεφύσησεν εἰς τὸ πρόσωπον αὐτοῦ πνοὴν ζωῆς καὶ ἐγένετο ὁ ἄνθρωπος εἰς ψυχὴν ζῶσαν."[19]

This first part of the creation of the human being provides for a plasmation in the terrain, which becomes the elementary ontological symbol of the body. Traces of the ontological value of the terrestrial matter emerge in the whole Scripture, but to limit ourselves only to the Adamitic part of Genesis, we could equally cite 3:19: "ὅτι γῆ εἶ καὶ εἰς γῆν ἀπελεύσῃ".[20]

At the same time, Scripture argues on the breath of God as a soul-giving activity and on the soul as a life-giving principle. In fact, we find evidence of the role of human soul in enlivening the body in many biblical passages. To add a further example, we could cite Gen 6: 3:

" ... καὶ εἶπεν κύριος ὁ θεός οὐ μὴ καταμείνῃ τὸ πνεῦμά μου ἐν τοῖς ἀνθρώποις τούτοις εἰς τὸν αἰῶνα διὰ τὸ εἶναι αὐτοὺς σάρκας ἔσονται δὲ αἱ ἡμέραι αὐτῶν ἑκατὸν εἴκοσι ἔτη."[21]

According to the Biblical anthropology, if the soul is the principle of life in man, nevertheless it is not the source of life, which is instead God through his Spirit. In fact, the Scripture says that God "breathed into his nostrils the breath (nešamah, πνοή) of life; and became a living soul (nèphèš, ψυχή)." The enlivening breath is then provided to man for the time of his mortal life:

---

[19] "And the Lord God formed man *of* the dust of the ground, and breathed into his nostrils the breath of life; and man became a living soul" (KJV).

[20] "... for dust thou *art*, and unto dust shalt thou return" (KJV). On the spiritual breath and the soul as a life-giving principle in the human being, see also: Gen 6 : 17, Gen 41 : 8, Gen 45 : 27, 1 Sam 1 : 15, 2 Sam 1: 9, 1 Kings 21 : 5, Ac 20: 10. On the vivifying principle as gift of God : Gen. 6 : 3, Num. 16 : 22, Jb 27 : 3, Ps 103 : 29, Qo 12 : 7.

[21] Gn 6: 3: "And the LORD said, My spirit shall not always strive with man, for that he also *is* flesh: yet his days shall be an hundred and twenty years" (KJV).

" ... ἀποστρέψαντος δέ σου τὸ πρόσωπον ταραχθήσονται ἀντανελεῖς τὸ πνεῦμα αὐτῶν καὶ ἐκλείψουσιν καὶ εἰς τὸν χοῦν αὐτῶν ἐπιστρέψουσιν ... "[22]

It is very important to note that the soul (enlivening principle of the body) and God's Spirit (as the source of the enlivening principle) are two distinct realities. In fact, this conceptual difference permits in the New Testament to talk of "ψυχικοί, πνεῦμα μὴ ἔχοντες" (psychics without spirit)[23] and of soul regressing from spiritual to terrestrial state.[24]

*III.2. The Patristic background*

The principles of Biblical anthropology come to Gregory Palamas also through the Fathers of the Church. One of his sources is John of Damascus, who generally expresses faith conceptions commonly accepted in the Greek East.[25] On the "double creation"[26] the Damascene mentions in turn the *Oratio 28* of Gregory from

---

[22] Ps 103: 29ss: "Thou hidest thy face, they are troubled: thou takest away their breath, they die, and return to their dust" (KJV, Ps 104: 29).

[23] Jd 1: 19: "These be they who separate themselves, sensual, having not the Spirit" (KJV).

[24] I Co 2: 14 and 15: 44, Jm 3: 15.

[25] For a general profile of John of Damascus see: Robert Volk and Andrew Louth, "Jean Damascène," in *La théologie byzantine et sa tradition* T. I/2, ed. Carmelo-Giuseppe Conticello (Turhout :Brepols, 2015). A profile of John Damascene as expressing common faith conceptions of his age already emerged in: Georgy Vasilevic Florovskij, *Vizantijckie Otcy V—VIII stolet* [*The Fathers of the Byzantine centuries V—VIII*] (Paris, 1933), 228-31. An interesting proposal for renewal in the studies on John of Damascus, in line with the historiographical commonplace about the non-originality of John Damascene, is in John A. Demetracopoulos, "In Search of the Pagan and Christian Sources of John of Damascus' theodicy: Ammonius, the Son of Hermeia, Stephanus and John Chrysostom on God's Foreknowledge and Predestination and Man 's Freewill," in *Byzantine Theology and Its Philosophical Background*, ed. Antonio Rigo (Turnhout: Brepols, 2011), 50–86.

[26] Cf. Ernesto Sergio Mainoldi, "Metabolé e matánoia. Il ruolo dell'antropologia biblico-patristica nelle stazioni del pensiero teologico medievale a fronte del problema cosmologico," in *Cosmogonie e cosmologie nel Medioevo : atti del Convegno della Società italiana per lo studio del pensiero medievale (S.I.S.P.M.) : Catania, 22-24 settembre 2006*, ed. Concetto Martello, Chiara Militello, and Andrea Vella (Louvain La Neuve: F.I.D.E.M., 2008), 215–52.

Natiantius[27] and identifies the rational and spiritual soul, infused into the body throughout the divine breath, with the image of God inscribed in the human being, as it is clearly expressed in the *Expositio fidei*.[28]

In the *Philokalia*,[29] a great source for the study of Patristic and Byzantine theological anthropology, it is possible to note how the thought of the Fathers is based on a hylomorphic standpoint rooted in the Scripture and in the identification of the κατ'εἰκόνα with the noetic and rational part of the human being. To cite some references, we can think of chapter 89 of Diadochus of Photiki's century *On Spiritual Knowledge and Discrimination*,[30] of chapter 25 of Maximus the Confessor's third century on love and most of all of Gregory of Sinai's texts on *Commandments and Doctrine*, in which both the noetic and the bodily elements of the human being are considered κατ' εἰκόνα Θεοῦ.[31]

Moreover, Palamas is also the heir of a Byzantine theological tradition which tooks many concepts from Aristotle, such as is the case with Niketa Stethatos.[32] Always in the *Philokalia*, in his chapters *On Spiritual Knowledge*, Stethatos not only argues on the hypercosmic nature of human noetic soul but, most of all through his concept of consciousness (συνείδησις), he also presents a comprehension of the human being deeply rooted in Trinitarian theology.[33] Human nature is made in the image of the Holy Trinity, it has therefore also a triadic structure: intellect (νοῦς), reason (λόγος) and spirit (πνεῦμα) .[34] The triadic soul is therefore the

---

[27] Gregory of Natiantius, *Oratio XXVIII*, in: PG 36, 321 B-D.

[28] About the anthropology of John Damascene, see: *Expositio fidei*, 26 (II 12) 75–80.

[29] For an edition of the Greek original text by Nikodimos the Agiorite and Makarios of Corinth, Φιλοκαλία τῶν νηπτικῶν (Athens: Astir-Papadimitriou, 1982); for the English edition: *The Philokalia*, ed. and trans. Gerald Eustace Palmer, Philip Sherrard, and Kallistos Ware (London: Faber and Faber Limited, 1998).

[30] Palmer, Sherrard, Ware, *The Philokalia*, vol. 1, 89.

[31] Cf. St. Gregory of Sinai, *On Commandments and Doctrines*, in Ibid., ch. 31, vol. 4, 218; ch. 46, 221; ch. 80, 227; ch. 82, 228.

[32] Cf. Niketa Stethatos, *De Anima* 22. For the edition of Stethatos' treatise *On the Soul*, see: Nicétas Stéthatos, *Opuscules et letters*, ed. J. Darrouzès, (Paris: Cerf, 1961).

[33] See: Niketa Stethatos, *On Spiritual Knowledge*, in: *The Philokalia*, vol. 4, 139–42.

[34] Niketa Stethatos, *On Spiritual Knowledge*, PG 150, 1148 C 13–15.

image of God inscribed in the human being and it constitutes its hyper-ontological unavoidable fundament, the irrepressible center of its hypostaticity.

### III.3. Gregory Palamas and the Aristotelian background

Palamas, reiterating the Patristic criticism towards the dualistic Platonic anthropology, turns to Aristotle's *De Anima* precisely because the Stagirite guarantees philosophical instruments that can be integrated in an anthropology based on the Biblical hylomorfism. This integration happens even on a general epistemological level, such as the hylomorfic principle of *De An.* I, 1 403b 2–3: "... ὁ μὲν γὰρ λόγος ὅδε τοῦ πράγματος, ἀνάγκη δ' εἶναι τοῦτον ἐν ὕλῃ τοιᾳδί, εἰ ἔσται."[35]

We can take the following as the general definition of the soul in the *Chapters*: "Ἡ γοῦν ψυχὴ ἐντελέχεια σώματός ἐστιν ὀργανικοῦ, δυνάμει ζωὴν ἔχοντος."[36] As we can see, this definition of the soul corresponds precisely to the Aristotelian one in *De An.* II, 1 412b 5–6; and more precisely, in relation to the Palamite definition of soul, we can consider *De An.* II, 1 412a 19–21 and 22–28: "... ἡ ψυχή ἐστιν ἐντελέχεια ἡ πρώτη σώματος φυσικοῦ δυνάμει ζωὴν ἔχοντος."[37]

Firstly, the difference that can be immediately noticed between the *Chapters* and the Aristotelian text is that Gregory Palamas omits "πρώτη" after "ἐντελέχεια"; this is the classical definition that occurs in the Eastern Fathers[38] such as in Byzantine philosophical

---

[35] "For the notion is the form of the thing, but this notion, if it is to be, must be realized in matter of a particular kind" (for the Greek text in critical edition with English translation, see: Aristotle, *De Anima*, ed. Robert Drew Hicks (Cambridge: C.U.P., 1907), 9.

[36] "The soul then is the actuality of a body possessed of organs and having the potentiality of life" (Saint Gregory Palamas, *The One Hundred and Fifty Chapters*, 87).

[37] "... soul is the first actuality of a natural body having in it the capacity of life" (Aristotle, *De Anima*, 51). On the Aristotelian definition of soul as a principle of life: *De An.* II, 1 412a 11–22; II, 4 415b 12–14.

[38] Robert E. Sinkewicz (87, note 10) mentions: Ippolitus, *Philosophumena* 7.19; Simplicius, *In Aristotelis De Coelo Commentaria* 2.1; John Philoponus, *De opificio mundi* 6.23; Nikiforos Gregoras, *Solutiones quaestionum* 6.1.4.

works. Sinkewicz[39] rightly relates the absence of the word "πρώτη" with the controversy of Anna Komnena on the Aristotelian definition of the soul as "ἐντελέχεια ἡ πρώτη," as George Tornikes illustrates in his oration for her funeral. According to the Empress, the Aristotelian definition could convey an idea of inseparability of soul and body, thus the corruptibility of the former, and because of that she advances the proposal of a "διπλῆ ἐντελέχεια" of the soul.[40]

Secondly, we can focus on the concept of potency (δύναμις) in Palamas' definition of the soul. If we have a look to chapters 31 and 32, we can notice that the concept of potency introduces a difference between "ἀλόγα ζώα" (irrational animals) and "ἄνθρωπος" (man) in as much as they have different ontologies. In fact, Gregory Palamas' text shares with the Aristotelian psychology the idea of a first ontological plan that can be considered universal for all the living beings: the vegetative dimension.[41] The soul gives itself firstly in the physiological activities of a body. Two textual evidences can be considered on the theme of the first , vegetative animation of the living being. The first is in chapter 3, which is dedicated to the rebuttal of the Platonic doctrine of the *anima mundi*.[42] Immediately after having formulated the definition of the soul, Palamas writes that the sky (in which the *anima mundi* would reside) cannot be animated because it has not the potency of life: a

---

[39] Cf. Saint Gregory Palamas, *The One Hundred and Fifty Chapters*, 87, note 10.

[40] According to Darrouzès' reconstruction, the question of the "double entelechy" recalls a question discussed by Photius (IX c.) on the duality of soul, which provoked some reproach by Constantine the Philosopher (cf. Stéthatos, *Opuscules et letters*, 289, note 78). Anyway, the problem of the immortality of soul in the reception of Aristotle by the ellenophone Christian culture has remote roots: Nemesius (IV c.) argues that for Aristotle, soul is immortal (PG 40 572 B), while for Michael Psellos (XI c.) the Aristotelian position is more nuanced (PG 122 1041-1044). Cf. Georges Tornikès, "Λόγος ἐπὶ τῷ θανάτῳ τῆς πορφυρογεννήτου κυρᾶς Ἄννης τῆς καισαρίσσης (*Discours sur la mort de la porphyrogénète kyra Anne la kaisarissa*)," in Georges et Démétrios Tornikès, *Lettre et discours*, ed. Jean Darrouzès (Paris: CNRS, 1970), 220-323.

[41] See the definition of ψυχή as substance of a physical body having life in potency, in: *De An.* II, 1 412a, 20-21.

[42] On the desacralization of creation through the rebuttal of the doctrine of the *anima mundi* in the Greek Fathers, cf. Mainoldi, *Metabolé e matánoia*.

body with organs.⁴³ To say that the sky cannot be animated, Gregory Palamas uses the expression: "οὐδὲ δύναται ζῆν,"⁴⁴ thus denying to the sky the δύναμις of the organic life. Secondly, recognizing, as Aristotle does, a physiological soul to non-human living beings (like, among others, in chapter 31), Palamas draws a distinction between the immortal soul of human beings and the mortal soul of all other animated beings, and in this way the concept of potency delineates a specific difference between irrational beings and humans.

As it has been already shown, in chapter 31 he argues on the soul of living irrational beings: "ψυχή, ζωή ἐστι τοῦ κατ'αὐτὴν ἐμψύχου σώματος ..."⁴⁵ and the same definition is repeated in chapter 32 concerning human beings. However, he adds in the latter: "... ἀλλ' οὐ μόνον ἐνέργειαν, ἀλλὰ καὶ οὐσίαν ἔχει τὴν ζωήν."⁴⁶ We can therefore notice a decisive difference between living irrational (ἄλογος) beings and human beings, who only have a rational soul,⁴⁷ but starting from a common vegetative plan of life. In the Palamite view, the organic nature of the living being constitutes its rootedness in the cosmos and provides the foundation of the physical unity of all the living beings in a unique ontological entity.

The ontological difference between body and soul, however, stands out in a specific way the human being from the rest of the living beings. In fact, non-human living beings belong in ontological terms only to the cosmic dimension, that is, as Palamas writes, they possess life not as οὐσία, but only as activity (ἐνέργεια) and relation⁴⁸ (πρὸς ἕτερον) with the body: in them, life manifests itself only through the vegetative and sensitive faculties. According to the same definition of Palamas, being life an actuality

---

⁴³ "ὁ δὲ οὐρανὸς, μηδὲν ὀργανικὸν μέλος ἢ μέρος ἔχων οὐδὲ δύναται ζῆν": Gregorio Palamas, *Che cos'è l'ortodossia*, 6.

⁴⁴ Ibid.

⁴⁵ Ibid., 34: "The soul ... constitutes the life for the body it animates ..." (Saint Gregory Palamas, *The One Hundred and Fifty Chapters*, 115).

⁴⁶ Ibid., "... the soul possesses life not only as an activity but also essentially ..." (Saint Gregory Palamas, *The One Hundred and Fifty Chapters*, 115–117).

⁴⁷ Gregorio Palamas, *Che cos'è l'ortodossia*, 34.

⁴⁸ Gregory Palamas, *Capita CL*, in PG 150, 1141, A 8–9.

of the soul understood as a life giving principle, the soul of irrational beings will dissolve with their body. The specific division of the living beings in rational and irrational ones, typical of Palamas' anthropocentrism, agrees ultimately with one of the cornerstones of the Aristotelian psychology: the differentiation of living beings according to the type of soul of each species.[49]

The body is thus the cosmic part of the human being and constitutes the ontological plane shared with the living irrational beings. The human soul, however, functions as a principle of ontological difference not only realizing the specific human difference in every hypostasis, but consequently also in the entire created cosmos in relation to the other living species and not-living beings.

The "breath of life" in man, about which Scripture speaks,[50] is comprehended in Palamas as reason (λόγος) and intellect (νοῦς). We can consider in this regard the opening words of chapter 33: "Ἡ λογικὴ καὶ νοερὰ ψυχὴ οὐσίαν μὲν ἔχει τὴν ζωήν, ἀλλὰ δεκτικὴν τῶν ἐναντίων, κακίας δηλονότι καὶ ἀγαθότητος."[51] In passages like this, it is clear that Gregory Palamas draws the Aristotelian philosophy far beyond the psychological doctrine: for he employs its entire categorical apparatus. The human soul, having divine origin, possesses life as activity and relation in the body as well as οὐσία, although it can accept the good and the evil as qualities. This is in line with the Aristotelian principle according to which qualities admit opposites in *Cat.* 8 10b 12, while οὐσίες do not.

From a theological point of view it is relevant that Palamas identifies the logical and intellectual soul with the image of God (εἰκόνα του Θεοῦ) inscribed in the creation of man, according to

---

[49] See: *De Anima*, II, 2 414a 20ss.

[50] It is a fundamental element of the biblical vision that occurs in many passages of the Holy Scripture, beyond Genesis. Cf. note 14; also: Jb 34: 14–15, Qo 12: 7, Ps 89: 3, 103: 29–30.

[51] Gregorio Palamas, *Che cos'è l'ortodossia*, 34: "The rational and intellectual soul possesses life essentially but is susceptible of opposites, namely, good and evil" (Saint Gregory Palamas, *The One Hundred and Fifty Chapters*, 117).

Gen 1: 26-27. It is, ultimately, a Patristic concept that was one of the fundamental pillars of all Byzantine iconological anthropology.

Finally, we can say that Gregory Palamas shares the Aristotelian conception of hypostasis as the activity (ἐνέργεια) of a οὐσία and thinks human being in the Aristotelian terms of totality of matter (body) and form (soul), although the philosophical structure of his speech does not prevent a peculiar theological development rooted in its biblical presuppositions. On several occasions in the *Chapters* Gregory Palamas reiterates the strong union and contiguity of soul and body, so that only a great violence, external or internal to the human hypostasis, could separate them.[52] Again that corresponds with the tenets of Aristotelian psychology, according to which in animal living beings the affections of the soul (τὰ πάθη τῆς ψυχῆς) are inseparable (ἀχώριστα) from physical matter (τῆς φυσικῆς ὕλης).[53] Moreover, the compound of matter and form is what distinguishes in Palamas the human being from the angelic one, who possesses intellect and reason, but who is only spirit (πνεῦμα) unable to give life because he was not given a "body from the earth".[54]

For human being is an ontological compound, in each hypostasis the creationist chronology of the *Genesis* and its inherent ontological hierarchy finds a hypostatic recapitulation: all the ante-human creation is in the human being and each human being is a hypostatical microcosm.

## IV. Hypostaticity and ἐνέργεια

In the argumentation on the uniqueness of the divine activity (ἐνέργεια), in the work Ἡ θεία ἕνωσις καὶ διάκρισις,[55] the benchmark of Gregory Palamas is the theology of the divine names of pseudo-Dionysius the Areopagite, supported with references to Maximus

---

[52] Gregory Palamas, *Capita* CL, in PG 150, 1148 A 11-15.

[53] *De An.* I, 1 403 b.

[54] "ἐκ γῆς σῶμα": Gregory Palamas, *Capita* CL, in PG 150, 1148 A 1-2.

[55] Cf. Gregorio Palamas, *Atto e luce divina*, 960.

the Confessor and Gregory of Nyssa.[56] Still following the pseudo-Dionysian theology, in chapter 91, Gregory Palamas reiterates that the divine energy, despite its unity, assumes different shapes in revelation, according to the peculiarity of the single created being, which had been willed by God himself. In this case it is possible to note how much the logic of plurality and oneness, that we have sketched above, has a structural importance.

In chapter 91 Gregory Palamas states that speaking about the divine activities that preside over creation and revelation means also speaking on the divine prescience, that is on the pre-eternal wisdom which actualizes itself as activity which substantiates, vivificates and makes wise, in agreement with the ontological assumptions created by God.[57] In the case of the human beings, they experience divine illumination according to their hypostatic determinations. For this reason, the uncreated activity is revealed as plural while being a single divine entity.[58] In support to his argumentation, Gregory Palamas also cites chapter 44: 3 of John Chrysostom's commentary on the Psalms,[59] and of the same Father, he also quotes some passages from the commentary on the Gospel of John.[60]

To focus on the problem of oneness and plurality in God in relation to creation, we can consider chapters 82–88.[61] In chapter 82, Palamas indicates with the concepts of ἀγαθότης, σοφία, δύναμις, θειότης, μεγαλειότης what of God is known / knowable (γνωστόν). These divine attributes are what Gregory Palamas considers, on the basis of his Patristic sources, "τὰ πάντα περὶ τὴν οὐσίαν,"[62] implying a gnoseological difference between the attributes and the essence in God: the former are what is known

---

[56] On the issue of the unity of divine energy in relation to the tris-hypostatical unity, see chapter 21 of the work: Ἡ θεία ἕνωσις καὶ διάκρισις and chapter 112 of the Chapters (Gregorio Palamas, Che cos'è l'ortodossia, 122).
[57] Gregorio Palamas, Che cos'è l'ortodossia, 104.
[58] Cf. chapter 69, in: Ibid., 78.
[59] Chapter 74, in: Ibid. 84.
[60] Chapter 110, in: Ibid. 120.
[61] Ibid. 94–101.
[62] Ibid., 94–95.

while the second remains inscrutable. Towards the end of chapter 82, these attributes are conceptualized with a technical term of Palamas' theology: "τοῦ Θεοῦ ἐνέργεια." Although the ἐνέργεια is distinct from the οὐσία ("οὐσία οὐκ ἔστιν"[63]), it is uncreated too, for it is proper to the divine nature. So the uncreated activity of God is what of God is revealed to the creatures, or, in other words, is God from the point of view of his creatures. It can therefore be said that the philosophical problem of oneness and plurality in God is resolved by Palamas in a theological theory of gnoseology and aesthetics that has its conceptual center in the hypostasis as the fundamental structure of creation. At the end of chapter 82, we see how the concept of ἐνέργεια introduces the problem of oneness and plurality in God, as the divine activity is understood as the plural revelation of the unique divine essence. In chapters 83, 84, 85 and 88 the argument about the relationship between oneness and plurality is supported by quotations from Basil of Caesarea,[64] Gregory of Nyssa,[65] pseudo-Dionysius the Areopagite[66] and Maximus the Confessor, the main sources of Palamas' doctrine. In Chapter 87, another interesting concept can be found; Gregory Palamas, in fact, uses the term "παράδειγμα" to indicate the divine attributes already conceptualized with the term "ἐνέργεια." The same divine attributes are then called with two different terms, which introduce therefore a relevant conceptual difference. Ἐνέργεια is in fact a performative concept, indicating the activities of creation, revelation and sanctification of God towards creatures; παράδειγμα is instead a static concept, indicating rather an ontological fundament or, better in the case of Palamas, the hyperontological fundament of the created hypostatic realities. In any case, we are dealing with two relational concepts that indicate God in relation to the creatures.

In many passages of his writings, Gregory Palamas understands the hypostaticity of the creatures as the very image of the God who is in three hypostasis, basing the argumentation on Gen. 1:26. As an

---

[63] Ibid.
[64] Ibid.
[65] Ibid., 96–97.
[66] Ibid.

example, at the end of chapter 11 of the letter to Daniel Metropolitan of Eno,[67] Palamas considers hypostaticity as an intrinsic and structural feature of creation, and the same divine activity (ἐνέργεια) possesses a kind of adaptability to the hypostaticity of the creatures.

In the *Triads*, Gregory Palamas enriches the discourse on the παραδείγματα with more concepts that broaden the perspective. In the first *Triad*, he writes of the "λόγοι κατ'εἰκόνα θεοῦ," indicating the reasons present in the human intellect. In the expression we mentioned above, κατ'εἰκόνα refers to the λόγοι ἐν τῷ δημιουργικῷ νῷ, ontological fundaments of the whole creation in the uncreated wisdom:

*Οὐ μὴν ἀλλ'ἐπεί, ... τῶν ἐν τῷ δημιουργικῷ νῷ λόγων αἱ εἰκόνες ἐν ἡμῖν εἰσι, τί τὸ ταύτας τὴν ἀρχὴν, ἀχρειῶσαν τὰς εἰκόνας; Οὐχ ἡ ἁμαρτία καὶ ἡ τοῦ πρακτέου εἴτε ἄγνοια εἴτε περιφρόνησις;*[68]

In *Tr.* 1, 1: 3 the terminology is much more clarified in the perspective of the fundamental ontological difference between created and uncreated, so that on the plan of the uncreated we have the λόγοι ἐν τῷ δημιουργικῷ νῷ, hyper-ontological fundaments of their εἰκόνες in the human intellect. It can be observed that the concept of the λόγοι κατ'εἰκόνα θεοῦ constitutes, in the final analysis, a sophiological understanding of a concept always recurring in Patristic anthropology,[69] that is the κατ'εἰκόνα θεοῦ of the *Genesis* (Gn 1: 26), the name of the divine ontological footprint in the human being, understood by Palamas in the intellectualistic perspective of a noetic fundament at God's image. This leads to an understanding of the ancestral sin as noetic

---

[67] Ibid., 736-737.
[68] *Tr.* 1, 1: 3, in: Gregorio Palamas, *Atto e luce divina*, 276-278.
[69] Cf. Gregorio Palamas, *Che cos'è l'ortodossia?*, 40-43. It can be also taken as an example Gregory of Nyssa's position on the theme of the "double creation"in: *De opificio homini*, 3, or the position of the same Father on the κατ'εἰκόνα θεοῦ in the *Oratio cathechetica magna* V: 4 and 5. See also John of Damascus' position in the anthropological domain in: *De fide orthodoxa* 26 (II 12) 76. See also: E. S. Mainoldi, "Metabolè e metanoia."

and gnoseological. Even if Palamas adopts the speculation of the Greek Fathers on the κατ'εἰκόνα Θεοῦ in the anthropological domain (as shown by the continuous quotes), this sophiological anthropology has perhaps the main reference in the *Ambigua* of Maximus the Confessor, where the λόγοι are understood as the pre-eternal intentions that preside in the divine intellect over creation. It is a concept far from Platonism in Maximus the Confessor, at least for what concerns its theological content, and despite the same formal aspects of the concept, which seem to lead to neo-Platonism. In fact, Maximus uses this concept to argue against the Platonic and Origenistic assertions on the pre-existence of souls, talking not about a pre-existence, but rather about a pre-eternal rootedness in God of the whole creation.[70] When the noetic λόγοι in the human being are introduced in the Hesychastic ascetic practice,[71] we have that state that Gregory Palamas, in *Tr.* 1, 1: 2, calls συμμορφότης Θεῷ, compliance to God, elsewhere indicated with the more known expression: ὁμοίωσις τῷ Θεῷ.

All created hypostases who participate of the uncreated activities of God realize the ἕνωσις τῷ Θεῷ.[72] The union occurs in fact because the hypostatical principle of the human being, his hypostaticity, is a δύναμις τοῦ Θεοῦ, a potency of (being) God which is inscribed in the human being as its hyper-ontological fundament and which is actuated by the power of God's illumination, that is of God's activity. For this reason, the potency of God as divinization of the human being and as divine activity which possesses hypostatical adaptation constitutes the ontological fundament of the human hypostaticity, and its very perfection in God.

---

[70] Cf. Maximus the Confessor, *Amb.* 7, PG 91: 1080B; Policarp Sherwood, *The Earlier "Ambigua" of Saint Maximus the Confessor and his refutation of Origenism* (Roma: Herder, 1955), 177–180; Irenée Henri Dalmais, "La théorie des *logoi* chez S. Maxime le Confesseur," *Revue des sciences philosophiques et théologiques* 36 (1952): 248–249.

[71] Cf. *Tr.* 1, 1: 3, in Gregorio Palamas, *Atto e luce divina*, 278.

[72] Chapter 92, in Ibid. 104–106.

## Bibliography

Aristotle. *De Anima*. Edited and translated by Robert Drew Hicks. Cambridge: C.U.P, 1907.

Barbotin, Edmond. *La théorie aristotélicienne de l'intellect d'après Théophraste*. Louvain-Paris: Vrin, 1954.

Berti, Enrico. *Aristotele dalla dialettica alla filosofia prima*. Padova: Cedam 1975.

Bradshaw, David. *Aristotle East and West*. Cambridge: C.U.P., 2004.

Kern, Cyprien. "Les éléments de la théologie de Grégoire Palamas." *Irénikon* 20 (1974): 164-93.

Lossky, Vladimir. "La notion des "analogies" chez Dénys le Pseudo-Aréopagite." *Archives d'histoire doctrinale et littéraire du Moyen Âge* 5 (1930): 279-309.

Mainoldi, Ernesto Sergio. "La ricezione della rivoluzione ontologica dei Padri cappadoci: la triadologia dello pseudo-Dionigi Areopagita e i suoi obiettivi." In *Trinità in relazione. Percorsi di ontologia trinitaria dai Padri della Chiesa all'Idealismo tedesco*, edited by Claudio Moreschini. Panzano in Chianti: Feeria, 2015. 167-78.

———. "Metabolé e matánoia. Il ruolo dell'antropologia biblico-patristica nelle stazioni del pensiero teologico medievale a fronte del problema cosmologico." In *Cosmogonie e cosmologie nel Medioevo : atti del Convegno della Società italiana per lo studio del pensiero medievale (S.I.S.P.M.) : Catania, 22-24 settembre 2006*, edited by Concetto Martello, Chiara Militello, and Andrea Vella, 215-52. Louvain La Neuve: F.I.D.E.M., 2008.

Nikodimos the Agiorite, and Makarios of Corinth. Φιλοκαλία τῶν νηπτικῶν. Athens: Astir-Papadimitriou, 1982.

———. *The Philokalia*. Edited and translated by Gerald Eustace Howell Palmer, Philip Sherrard, Kallistos Ware. London: Faber and Faber Limited, 1998.

Palamas, Gregory. *Atto e luce divina*. Edited by Ettore Perrella. Milano: Bompiani, 2003.

———. *Dal sovraessenziale all'essenza*. Edited by Ettore Perrella. Milano: Bompiani, 2005.

———. *The One Hundred and Fifty Chapters*. Edited and translated by Robert Edward Sikewicz. Toronto: Pontifical Institute for Medieval Studies, 1988.

Renczes, Philipp Gabriel. *Agir de Dieu et liberté de l'homme. Recherches sur l'anthropologie théologique de saint Maxime le Confesseur*. Paris : Cerf, 2003.

Ritter, Adolf Martin. *Das Konzil von Konstantinopel und sein Symbol*. Göttingen: Forschungen zur Kirchen- und Dogmengeschichte, 1965.

Scazzoso, Pietro. "Lo pseudo-Dionigi nell'interpretazione di Gregorio Palamas." *Neoscolastica*, 59.6 (1986): 671–99.

Tornikès, Georges et Démétrios. *Lettre et discours*. Edited and translated by Jean Darrouzès. Paris: CNRS, 1970.

Volk, Robert, and Louth, Andrew. "Jean Damascène." In *La théologie byzantine et sa tradition* T. I/1, edited by Carmelo Giuseppe Conticello. Turhout :Brepols, 2015.

# Index

## A

*alienation*, 70, 71, 77, 92, 101, 112
apophaticism, 16, 63, 64
Aristotle, 15, 16, 67, 91, 103, 132, 142, 161, 192, 201, 202, 203, 204, 205, 206, 207, 208, 211, 212, 213, 214, 216, 217, 220, 221, 241, 243, 245, 249, 250, 251, 252, 259
Aristotelian, 12, 49, 191, 192, 200, 202, 203, 213, 217, 220, 241, 242, 250, 251, 253, 254
asceticism, 11, 140, 141, 143, 144, 145, 146, 149, 150, 157, 159

## B

Byzantium, 78, 93, 102, 113, 119, 123

## C

cause, 31, 43, 44, 65, 66, 71, 73, 126, 144, 152, 191, 203, 204, 205, 206, 208, 209, 211, 212, 213, 214, 215, 216, 218, 224, 225, 229
Christianity, 9, 11, 17, 61, 67, 78, 81, 88, 91, 94, 95, 96, 97, 98, 100, 101, 102, 105, 113, 118, 123, 127, 129, 132, 136, 137, 139, 146, 160, 165, 169, 170, 172, 176, 180, 181, 182, 187, 216
church, 9, 11, 12, 18, 23, 24, 35, 38, 39, 61, 62, 63, 64, 67, 76, 77, 78, 82, 83, 85, 91, 92, 95, 101, 104, 105, 107, 112, 113, 114, 115, 118, 121, 124, 129, 131, 132, 140, 141, 142, 144, 145, 146, 149, 160, 161, 168, 169, 170, 171, 172, 177, 178, 179, 182, 183, 186, 187, 188, 189, 193, 194, 195, 196, 197, 208, 214, 216, 218, 219, 220, 233, 239, 242, 244, 248
civilization, 62, 94, 95, 97, 98, 99, 100, 102, 103, 105, 106, 118, 180
communion, 19, 22, 23, 24, 31, 47, 48, 50, 71, 72, 73, 76, 77, 78, 83, 85, 89, 90, 96, 103, 105, 120, 167
community, 69, 87, 91, 179, 188
communo-centric, 67
consciousness, 10, 17, 18, 19, 26, 27, 28, 29, 30, 31, 33, 35, 65, 125, 172, 181, 223, 228, 249
cultural, 19, 25, 26, 28, 32, 33, 34, 35, 68, 98, 100, 111, 114, 115, 118, 119, 120, 121, 122, 124, 127, 128, 129, 130, 131, 132, 133, 134, 135, 136, 137, 177, 179, 181, 245

## D

death, 11, 12, 39, 48, 51, 52, 54, 56, 141, 142, 144, 147, 148, 153, 154, 157, 159, 176, 194, 197, 211, 218, 225, 226, 232, 238
*Demiurge*, 17
democracy, 11, 74, 93, 103

## E

ecclesial event, 77, 78, 89, 101, 104
epistemology, 11, 18, 64, 93, 95, 97, 98, 211
eschatology, 12, 35, 56, 57, 165, 181, 183
Eschaton, 12, 111, 169, 172, 176, 179, 184, 191, 192, 194, 196, 197, 198, 199, 200, 208, 215, 217, 218, 219
ethics, 9, 114, 142, 159, 179, 228

Europe, 61, 94, 96, 98, 99, 100, 101, 102, 103, 104, 105, 107, 108, 110, 111, 112
European, 11, 13, 93, 97, 98, 99, 100, 101, 102, 104, 106, 107, 225
evil, 12, 24, 47, 84, 144, 175, 196, 197, 202, 218, 253
existence, 11, 41, 43, 45, 52, 53, 66, 68, 69, 71, 72, 73, 75, 76, 77, 78, 83, 84, 85, 87, 89, 90, 93, 99, 103, 105, 115, 118, 119, 122, 124, 125, 126, 128, 132, 133, 134, 135, 137, 142, 143, 144, 149, 172, 175, 176, 180, 181, 182, 185, 210, 225, 226, 227, 231, 234, 235, 258
experience, 15, 18, 19, 26, 27, 28, 29, 30, 35, 58, 64, 65, 87, 109, 111, 116, 127, 140, 142, 146, 147, 153, 158, 167, 168, 169, 170, 175, 176, 177, 179, 181, 182, 196, 226, 230, 255

## F

*freedom*, 70, 83, 85, 91, 136, 140, 147, 160, 163

## G

gender, 10, 39, 41, 50, 52, 53, 55, 56, 57, 58
God, 9, 12, 17, 20, 21, 22, 23, 24, 25, 30, 31, 32, 34, 36, 37, 42, 43, 44, 45, 46, 47, 48, 54, 55, 57, 63, 64, 65, 66, 69, 72, 73, 76, 77, 78, 79, 80, 81, 82, 83, 84, 85, 86, 88, 89, 90, 91, 101, 136, 142, 143, 146, 148, 149, 157, 158, 161, 166, 167, 168, 169, 170, 171, 172, 173, 174, 175, 176, 177, 179, 180, 181, 182, 183, 184, 186, 193, 194, 195, 196, 197, 198, 200, 208, 209, 210, 211, 212, 214, 215, 216, 217, 218, 219, 225, 226, 227, 228, 231, 232, 233, 234, 235, 238, 239, 241, 242, 243, 244, 247, 248, 249, 250, 253, 255, 256, 257, 258
Graeco-Roman, 93, 99, 100, 105, 106
Greek philosophy, 17, 97
Gutiérrez, Gustavo, 165, 166, 167, 172, 173, 175, 177, 181

## H

Hegel, G.W.F., 10, 17, 18, 19, 26, 27, 28, 29, 30, 33, 34, 36, 37, 38, 120, 125, 130, 138
Heidegger, Martin, 223, 226, 228, 236, 239
history, 9, 10, 11, 12, 17, 18, 19, 26, 28, 30, 31, 32, 33, 35, 62, 79, 80, 81, 85, 89, 93, 95, 97, 106, 107, 109, 111, 121, 122, 123, 124, 125, 128, 133, 136, 139, 141, 149, 150, 156, 157, 159, 165, 166, 167, 168, 169, 171, 172, 173, 174, 175, 176, 177, 178, 180, 181, 182, 183, 184, 185, 191, 192, 193, 195, 196, 197, 198, 200, 208, 217, 218, 225, 231, 244
historical, 10, 11, 15, 30, 31, 32, 33, 34, 36, 42, 48, 49, 50, 53, 55, 57, 58, 64, 66, 77, 89, 94, 96, 97, 98, 100, 102, 104, 105, 106, 107, 109, 113, 115, 118, 119, 121, 122, 133, 134, 159, 166, 167, 168, 169, 170, 171, 173, 174, 175, 176, 177, 178, 179, 180, 181, 182, 184, 192, 196, 197, 200, 218, 219, 226, 232
hylomorphism, 12, 191, 201, 206, 208, 213, 216, 217

## J

Jesus Christ, 12, 18, 20, 21, 22, 23, 31, 39, 40, 41, 43, 44, 45, 47, 48, 50, 52, 53, 54, 55, 56, 57, 77, 79, 81, 82, 83, 85, 104, 111, 141, 142, 143, 144, 145, 146,

Index    263

147, 148, 149, 157, 160, 161,
166, 170, 173, 174, 175, 176,
177, 178, 181, 182, 184, 185,
186, 187, 189, 191, 192, 193,
194, 195, 196, 197, 198, 199,
200, 208, 209, 210, 211, 212,
214, 215, 216, 217, 218, 219,
221, 226, 231, 232, 233, 234,
235, 238, 245, 246, 248

## K

knowledge, 29, 64, 209, 249

## L

Late Antiquity, 39, 41
logoi, 10, 17, 18, 19, 20, 21, 22,
23, 24, 25, 26, 29, 30, 31, 32,
34, 36, 41, 42, 43, 44, 45, 46,
48, 258
logos, 10, 20, 21, 22, 23, 24, 25,
28, 29, 31, 32, 33, 40, 41, 42,
43, 45, 46, 47, 48, 50, 51, 52,
53, 54, 55, 56, 57, 58, 71, 107,
149
Logos, 10, 12, 17, 18, 19, 20, 21,
22, 23, 25, 31, 40, 43, 44, 45,
46, 54, 149, 167, 168, 169, 174,
175, 176, 177, 180, 181, 225,
226, 232, 245

## M

Marion, Jean-Luc, 12, 15, 224,
225, 226, 227, 228, 229, 230,
231, 233, 235, 236, 237, 239
Maximus the Confessor, 9, 10,
16, 17, 18, 19, 20, 21, 22, 24,
32, 33, 37, 38, 39, 40, 41, 48,
50, 52, 55, 57, 58, 59, 104, 105,
107, 112, 147, 161, 167, 227,
239, 242, 249, 255, 256, 258
Metaphysics, 143, 144, 161, 162,
203, 206, 208, 214, 220, 221,
225
Middle Ages, 39, 94, 98, 100
mode, 10, 21, 39, 40, 41, 42, 45,
47, 48, 50, 51, 53, 54, 55, 57,
58, 66, 69, 96, 99, 101, 103,
107, 108, 109, 110, 111, 122,
125, 130
tropos, 10, 32, 40, 41, 45, 47, 48,
49, 50, 53, 54, 56, 57, 58
multiculturalism, 11, 113, 114,
129, 131, 134, 137

## N

nationalism, 109, 125
nature, 9, 10, 11, 17, 18, 20, 21,
23, 24, 27, 29, 40, 41, 43, 44,
45, 46, 47, 48, 49, 50, 52, 53,
57, 58, 66, 72, 76, 84, 93, 97,
103, 110, 126, 130, 136, 143,
144, 147, 149, 153, 156, 167,
168, 169, 171, 174, 176, 180,
192, 198, 201, 205, 206, 207,
210, 211, 212, 214, 215, 218,
225, 228, 234, 235, 243, 245,
249, 252, 256

## O

O'Donovan, Oliver, 10, 11, 61, 62,
78, 79, 80, 81, 82, 83, 84, 85,
86, 87, 88, 89, 90, 91, 92
ontology, 9, 10, 11, 12, 13, 17, 18,
19, 20, 22, 25, 27, 35, 37, 39,
48, 57, 58, 63, 64, 77, 93, 95,
97, 98, 106, 108, 116, 139, 141,
165, 167, 168, 169, 175, 211,
223, 233, 234, 235, 243, 244
ontological, 10, 11, 12, 17, 18, 19,
22, 25, 27, 31, 35, 36, 37,
42, 45, 46, 56, 58, 63, 66,
73, 93, 97, 104, 105, 107,
108, 114, 121, 141, 157,
159, 168, 170, 171, 176,
182, 210, 234, 241, 243,
244, 246, 247, 250, 251,
252, 253, 254, 255, 256,
257, 258
Orthodox, 9, 11, 12, 16, 22, 38,
54, 61, 62, 65, 66, 67, 75, 76,
77, 78, 79, 83, 90, 91, 92, 95,
96, 97, 101, 111, 112, 113, 115,
118, 120, 121, 122, 123, 124,

125, 126, 127, 129, 131, 132, 134, 135, 136, 137, 139, 140, 142, 145, 146, 157, 159, 160, 161, 162, 165, 饼168, 173, 176, 178, 183, 184, 185, 187, 188, 189, 192, 233, 239

## P

Palamas, Gregory, 12, 15, 181, 187, 241, 242, 243, 244, 245, 246, 248, 249, 250, 251, 252, 253, 254, 255, 256, 257, 258, 259, 260
person, 44, 46, 61, 62, 63, 64, 65, 91, 92, 99, 108, 112, 234, 235
personhood, 11, 48, 65, 66, 69, 71, 73, 74, 77, 84, 89, 93
phenomenology, 15, 18, 19, 26, 28, 29, 30, 33, 35, 37, 38, 120, 125, 138, 223, 224, 225, 228, 229, 231, 233, 234, 235, 236, 239
phenomenological, 12, 18, 19, 27, 29, 35, 143, 225, 229, 231, 235, 239
philosophy, 9, 10, 17, 18, 23, 26, 28, 34, 36, 41, 48, 50, 57, 59, 61, 62, 97, 179, 225, 226, 237, 239, 241, 244, 253
pluralism, 114, 115, 118, 121, 130, 131, 134, 136, 137, 191, 201, 203, 206, 208
political theology, 9, 11, 13, 62, 67, 79, 83, 84, 85, 89
politics, 9, 11, 12, 32, 33, 61, 62, 63, 67, 68, 71, 72, 73, 74, 76, 77, 79, 81, 82, 83, 84, 85, 86, 89, 90, 93, 96, 97, 99, 106, 112, 124, 154, 161, 163, 179
post-modern, 10, 41, 49, 57, 120
presence, 12, 25, 80, 104, 118, 136, 168, 173, 174, 176, 177, 182, 185, 197, 217, 232

## R

relational, 11, 22, 31, 64, 65, 87, 93, 99, 101, 126, 128, 131, 169, 256
religion, 10, 16, 26, 27, 28, 30, 37, 62, 77, 92, 97, 101, 102, 103, 104, 112, 113, 119, 121, 128, 132, 133, 139, 156, 158, 160, 162, 169, 170, 171, 172, 177, 178, 181, 182, 184, 186, 188, 189
religionization, 101, 105
Roman empire, 94, 96, 97, 98, 99, 100, 101, 102, 104, 105, 106, 109, 139, 168, 178

## S

salvation, 12, 44, 80, 81, 89, 105, 124, 141, 143, 144, 147, 148, 149, 172, 173, 175, 176, 177, 181, 182
saturated phenomenon, 12, 223, 224, 228, 229, 230, 231, 235, 238, 239
secularism, 113, 121, 165
sexual, 34, 50, 51, 52, 53, 55, 146, 215
social, 9, 11, 25, 26, 28, 29, 32, 33, 34, 35, 49, 69, 73, 77, 82, 86, 87, 93, 97, 106, 113, 114, 115, 116, 117, 118, 119, 120, 121, 123, 124, 125, 127, 128, 129, 131, 133, 134, 135, 136, 139, 140, 145, 152, 156, 159, 160, 167, 170, 171, 172, 173, 177, 181, 182, 184, 185
Spirit, 28, 29, 36, 37, 41, 43, 44, 45, 85, 104, 120, 125, 138, 139, 140, 141, 144, 145, 160, 163, 168, 209, 210, 217, 234, 235, 246, 247, 248
symphonia, 11, 113, 114, 115, 118, 119, 120, 121, 127, 128, 129, 130, 133, 134, 135, 136

# Index

## T

Taylor, Charles, 36, 114, 116, 117, 118, 119, 120, 123, 130, 131, 132, 138, 203, 220, 221
telos, 18, 20, 25, 31, 72, 77, 89, 90, 136, 205
theology, 9, 10, 12, 13, 15, 16, 17, 18, 23, 32, 36, 40, 43, 54, 61, 62, 67, 70, 71, 78, 79, 80, 82, 83, 84, 85, 86, 89, 90, 93, 95, 97, 105, 107, 111, 113, 139, 165, 167, 168, 170, 171, 173, 174, 177, 179, 181, 183, 216, 223, 226, 244, 245, 246, 249, 254, 256
theology of liberation, 12, 165, 167, 170, 171, 172, 173, 175, 177, 178, 180, 181, 182, 183, 184, 185, 186, 187
time, 19, 20, 21, 22, 25, 27, 30, 31, 32, 34, 35, 40, 42, 46, 78, 87, 100, 102, 104, 117, 123, 124, 132, 150, 152, 154, 155, 160, 166, 167, 168, 171, 174, 176, 177, 178, 180, 181, 183, 185, 193, 195, 198, 199, 207, 211, 226, 227, 231, 232, 242, 247
tradition, 11, 12, 41, 80, 82, 95, 103, 113, 115, 121, 122, 124, 128, 130, 132, 133, 134, 136, 137, 169, 183, 185, 225, 242, 248, 249, 260

transcendence, 51, 52, 56, 58, 101, 118, 119, 120, 123, 126, 134, 144, 173, 176, 225, 226, 231, 235
truth, 27, 28, 45, 64, 71, 76, 79, 83, 97, 98, 99, 121, 168, 169, 171, 178, 180, 183, 210, 224

## V

virtue, 21, 24, 32, 134, 148, 203, 204, 212, 213

## W

Western, 61, 62, 67, 69, 70, 71, 72, 73, 74, 75, 78, 81, 83, 88, 90, 94, 95, 96, 98, 104, 106, 107, 111, 149, 162, 183, 226

## Y

Yannaras, Christos, 9, 10, 11, 22, 38, 61, 62, 63, 64, 65, 66, 67, 68, 69, 70, 71, 72, 73, 74, 75, 76, 77, 78, 79, 81, 83, 84, 85, 86, 87, 88, 89, 90, 91, 92, 93, 95, 96, 97, 98, 99, 100, 101, 102, 103, 104, 105, 106, 107, 108, 109, 110, 111, 112, 141, 147, 163, 165, 166, 168, 170, 189